YOUR BOAT & THE LAW

MARTIN J. NORRIS

*understanding boating laws
and regulations*

*The Lawyers Co-operative Publishing Company
Rochester, New York
1965*

The U. S. Coast Guard pamphlet entitled "Recreational
Boating Guide" (CG–340) from which some of the illus-
trations in this book are taken, is for sale by the
Superintendent of Documents, U. S. Government Printing
Office, Washington 25, D. C.

To my wife Helen

. . . . who charted the course.

*

Foreword

For the owners and operators of pleasure boats I have presented in clear and nontechnical language the maritime law as it applies to boatsmen. At the same time I have tried to avoid oversimplification, which inevitably tends to leave more problems unanswered than solved. The highlights of American admiralty law appear here. I am confident that the scope of the coverage will also be helpful to lawyers who are not maritime law experts.

The operation of a pleasure boat carries with it more responsibility than is encompassed by the mere act of starting the motor or of grasping the tiller. The boatsman's rights, duties, and remedies may be wholly different from anything encountered ashore. He will find laws that have been shaped by early sea codes, by the dictates of foreign commerce, and by international law. These laws have been in existence for centuries and during that time it was scarcely thought that one day they would be applied to the cabin cruiser or the outboard motorboat. Yet the owner of a fourteen-foot outboard motorboat is, in most respects, precisely in the same legal position with regard to responsibility and liability as is the owner of the largest passenger vessel afloat.

To know the rights conferred and the duties imposed by the maritime law is to know how to avoid the many pitfalls and troubles which can beset the average boatsman. As charts and aids to navigation are used by the pilot to avoid dangers, so can the knowledge gained from this book be used for the welfare and peace of mind of recreational boatsmen.

*

References to Legal Decisions in this Volume

The written opinions or decisions of the courts are maintained in volumes of law reports. These books can be found in the law libraries of bar associations, law schools, the courts, many of the lawyers' offices and in certain public libraries in the larger cities.

To conserve space the form of the citations has been abbreviated. The meaning need not be a mystery to the layman. For example, the citation: Kermarac v Compagnie Generale Transatlantique, 358 US 625, 3 L ed 2d 550, 79 S Ct 406, 1959 AMC 597, 1959 means that the plaintiff or the person appealing is Kermarac. The suit is against (v) Compagnie Generale Transatlantique, the defendant. The decision will be found in volume 358 of the United States Reports starting on page 625. The same decision will also be found in volume 3 of the Lawyers Edition, 2d series on page 550; in volume 79 of the Supreme Court Reports on page 406; and in the 1959 edition of American Maritime Cases on page 597. The figure 1959 indicates that the United States Supreme Court decided this case in 1959.

Likewise, the citation of Rothman v U-Steer It, Inc., 247 F2d 803, CA5th, 1957 will be found in volume 247 of the Federal Reporter System, page 803. The case was decided by the United States Court of Appeals for the 5th circuit in 1957.

Similarly, King v Testerman, 214 F Supp 335, DC Tenn 1963 indicates that it will be discovered in volume 214 of the Federal Supplement on page 335 and the case was decided by the United States District Court of Tennessee in 1963.

A citation such as Lockhart v Martin, 1962 AMC 1076, 1959 Cal App 2d 760, 324 P2d 340, D Ct of App Cal 1958, shows that it is a case which has been decided in a state court. It is Lockhart versus Martin and in addition to being recorded in American Maritime Cases it will be also found in two other volumes, the California Appeals, second series and Pacific reports, second series. The appeal was decided by the District Court of Appeals, California in 1958.

Table of Contents

1

purchasing your boat

Investigate Before Buying

Each year since 1950 literally hundreds of thousands of people have become new owners of recreational boats. Increased leisure time and enlightened appreciation of boating as a sport have been impelling factors. Such a boom in boating naturally means an active market in boats, both new and old. The buyers may have included a few experienced boatsmen, but by and large most of the potential skippers are beginners in the business of buying a boat.

Such a neophyte in the ranks of first-time boat buyers was my friend and neighbor. He had set out to acquire an outboard motorboat, preferably one under 16 feet and obtainable at a moderate price. His first inquiries among his boat-owning friends were fruitless. He next scanned the "boats for sale" ads and visited local boatyards and marinas. Finally one advertisement caught his eye. The description of an outboard being offered appeared to be just what he had been seeking. A prompt phone call assured him that the craft was still available.

The seller was an 18-year-old youth who was eager to part with his 14-foot outboard in order to buy a more elaborate craft. A quick inspection and appraisal convinced my friend that this was the boat for which he had been looking. The price was agreed upon. A deposit was given by the buyer and the deal was made. A few days later the balance was paid and the buyer carted his boat home.

Weeks later I asked my neighbor what assurance he had that the seller held good title to the boat, or that it was free from liens. He ruefully expressed ignorance of such things. Indicating, however, that he was not an entirely naive individual he cautiously remarked, "If it had been a $5,000 boat, I would have gotten a lawyer."

It would be more than embarrassing to find that you have bought a stolen boat. That has happened quite frequently. Of course, a stolen boat does not belong to you if you are unfortunate enough to be the innocent purchaser; for it is an elementary rule in law that a thief cannot convey title to stolen property. First cousin to the thief is the confidence man who gives the impression that he is the owner of the boat riding at her moorings. The gullible buyer who accepts his bland assumption of ownership as being tantamount to good title soon experiences a shocked awakening when the real owner appears.

It should be a cardinal and unvarying rule never to buy a boat without adequate investigation. If an investigation is not feasible before paying your deposit, it certainly should be made before finally closing the deal and accepting delivery of the property. Here are some steps you can take in the course of your investigation:

2

(1) Ask to see the state boat registration card or a certificate of number. If nothing more, it will show that the seller has some connection with the boat, that is, unless the certificate was stolen along with the boat. Remember that in virtually all of the states a certificate of number is merely indicative of registration and does not necessarily represent title ownership.

(2) The seller should have a bill of sale from the person from whom he purchased the boat. Ask him for it. You might ask the seller for his auto registration or operator's certificate. If he has one you can compare the signature, address, and physical description listed in the certificate with the seller and with the prior bill of sale.

(3) Inquire whether the seller has insurance on the boat. If he has, then ask to see the policy. It isn't likely that anyone other than the owner would be in possession of the policy.

(4) A boat repairman or supplier could have a lien in rem—that is, a lien against the boat itself—for unpaid necessaries. The necessaries may be repairs and supplies or services consistent with the normal use and operation of the boat. Inquiry concerning unpaid bills for repairs, supplies, or services can be made at the repair yards or suppliers with which the boat seller does business.

(5) A search should be made at the office of the county clerk of the county where the seller lives or where the boat is usually maintained. Any record of a chattel mortgage, conditional bill of sale, or lien, will be found in that office.

Most boat dealers are reputable businessmen and an investigation of the type outlined above is perhaps unnecessary. Certainly it is not indicated when you are dealing with a boat manufacturer or a new-boat dealer.

Get It In Writing

Now to return to my friend and neighbor and his purchase of the 14-foot outboard boat. While he had failed to make any prior investigation, he nevertheless had the good sense to obtain something in writing as evidence of the transaction. It was a receipt for a $30 deposit on a boat and motor. The balance to be paid was specified. Then followed the name of the person paying the deposit and the signature of the person receiving it.

When the balance was paid and the property changed hands, what purported to be a bill of sale was given by the seller. Although it was crudely drawn it contained most of the essential facts. Since the seller was under the age of 21, my friend wisely insisted that the boy's father approve the transaction by signing the contract. Actually the sale should have been made by the parent and, for added caution, the documents should have been signed by both father and son.

The important thing to bear in mind is to have the transaction evidenced in writing. There is good precedent for this edict. Most states of the United States have adopted in one form or another the English statute of frauds. The English law provided that the sale of personal property of a value more than £10 (or $50)* was not enforceable by the courts unless the buyer received all or a portion of the goods; or made

---

* Under the American Uniform Commercial Code and the statute of frauds in effect in most of the states, the minimum amount is fixed at $500.

a part payment; or unless a "writing" of the transaction was made and signed by the party "charged." The party "charged" could be either the buyer or seller.

To avoid the possibility of a reluctant buyer or seller changing his mind about the sale after the parties have agreed upon it, a memorandum of the deal should be made when a deposit is given. A simple memorandum might read as follows:

"September 23, 1963

On this date I, John Smith, have agreed to sell to James Brown my Imperial runabout, 16 feet in length, with 18 H.P. Champion motor, official number CT 8080BF. Terms: $400 cash. Deposit of $50, the receipt of which is hereby acknowledged. Balance of $350 to be paid upon delivery on or about October 1, 1963.

(s) John Smith, Seller

(s) James Brown, Buyer"

Bill of Sale

A bill of sale is a written document by which one person transfers his title or right to, or interest in, personal property, to another. There is no standard form of bill of sale. It can vary greatly depending upon the skill and imagination of the drafter and the property or business that is the subject of the sale. A bill of sale can be prepared in the simplest and most informal language or, if drawn by a lawyer, in the nomenclature of the legal scrivener. Printed forms which are on sale at stationery stores may be used.

The salient facts which should appear in a bill of sale are: the date, the names of the parties, the stating of the passing of consideration, a description of

5

the property involved, the fact that the property has been sold, and the signature of the seller.

Here is a sample of a formal BILL OF SALE:

BILL OF SALE

KNOW ALL MEN BY THESE PRESENTS, that I, John Smith, residing at 80 Lovett Lane, Town of Westport, County of Fairfax, State of Connecticut, party of the first part, for and in consideration of the sum of one dollar in lawful money of the United States and other valuable consideration to me in hand paid, at or before the ensealing and delivery of these presents, by James Brown, party of the second part, the receipt whereof is hereby acknowledged, have bargained and sold, and by these presents do grant and convey unto the said party of the second part, his executors, administrators, and assigns, Imperial 16′ runabout boat, mfrs. number G 5482, official number CT 8080 BF, with 18 H.P. Champion outboard motor, serial number 862144, and the contents of said boat now found therein. To have and to hold the same unto the said party of the second part, his executors, administrators and assigns, forever. And I do, for myself, my heirs, distributees, executors and administrators, covenant and agree to and with the said party of the second part, to warrant and defend the sale of the said boat and outboard motor hereby sold unto the said party of the second part, his executors, administrators and assigns, against all and every person and persons whomsoever, and do warrant that the said boat and motor are free and clear of all liens and encumbrances and further that the within-described boat and motor are being sold on an "as is, where is" basis.

6

IN WITNESS WHEREOF, I have hereunto set my hand and seal this 2d day of October, one thousand nine hundred and sixty-three.

John Smith [Seal]

Sworn to before me this
2d day of October, 1963.
    Peter Prunty
      Notary Public.

Please keep in mind that this is a sample form. It does not have to be followed slavishly. You may wish to delete some of the language or add clauses. Do not, however, omit any of the *essential requirements* of a valid bill of sale.

The buyer might also request of the seller that he furnish an affidavit to be attached to the bill of sale reciting that the seller is the sole owner of the described property and has the absolute right to sell it; that no petition in bankruptcy has been filed by or against the seller; that the seller has no creditors except those listed in the affidavit; that the affidavit is made for the purpose of inducing the purchaser to purchase the boat and motor knowing that the purchaser will rely thereon and pay good and valuable consideration therefor; and that the seller agrees to indemnify the purchaser for any loss to the purchaser occasioned by a breach of any condition contained in the affidavit.

A prospective purchaser of a boat agreed to make an even exchange of his used boat for one which was of comparable value. A paper headed "order" recited these facts. It was held that such a document was not a bill of sale which would transfer title and in fact was nothing more than an order to purchase a new boat. Such a document could not be used to defeat the

7

claim of a creditor who sought to attach the used boat. [The Amable, 32 F Supp 451, 1940 AMC 709, DC NY 1940.]

Warranties

Fortunately for the unwary buyer, the law gives certain protections of which he may not have knowledge. These are known as warranties. They are of two types—the "express" warranty and the "implied" warranty.

An express warranty is a promise or statement made by the seller relating to the boat, which is intended or has the tendency to induce the purchaser to buy the boat. The buyer must rely upon the promise or statement in making the purchase if he is to hold the seller to the warranty. A statement that a boat can make 30 miles per hour would be an express warranty. However, an expression merely of the seller's opinion will not be considered as a warranty. Such words as "she's a beauty," or "the best buy on the Eastern Shores," or "you'll enjoy using this boat," are regarded as representations and not warranties. The law recognizes certain exuberances on the part of the seller which are called "salesman's puff" or "seller's talk," which a buyer is expected to recognize as such. These are not to be relied upon.

An implied warranty is one which the law imposes upon every seller of personal property. First, and perhaps most importantly, the seller impliedly warrants that he has good title and the right to sell the property. Being implied, such a warranty spontaneously goes with the sale. But if the contract specifically states, or where circumstances are made known to the buyer, that the seller does not claim title in himself, or that he is selling only such right or title as he

8

or another person may have, then no implied warranty can be inferred. [Uniform Commercial Code—Sales, § 2–312a.]

Another implied warranty is one of quiet possession. The seller is presumed to warrant that at the time of the sale no legal claims exist which will interfere with the purchaser's possession and use of the boat.

A third implied warranty is that the boat is free from any lien or encumbrance of which the buyer at the time of contracting has no knowledge. [Uniform Commercial Code—Sales, § 2–312b.]

There is an implied warranty that the boat is "merchantable." This is an implied warranty which a boat manufacturer or boat dealer gives to you upon the sale of the craft. [Uniform Commercial Code—Sales, § 2–314.] The warranty is that the boat is of average quality and that it is resalable.

There is also an implied warranty of fitness for a particular purpose. When the purchaser makes known to the seller, either specifically or by implication, the particular purpose for which the boat is required, and the purchaser relies upon the seller's skill or judgment, a warranty is implied that the boat will be reasonably fit for such purpose.

Finally, there is an implied warranty of quality. If, however, the boat is sold "as is" or "with all faults" or where the buyer has inspected the boat or has refused to inspect it, then the warranty is not made effective by implication. [Uniform Commercial Code—Sales, § 2–316.] The well-known legal phrase caveat emptor, meaning "let the buyer beware," is indicative of the fact that the purchaser has some responsibilities in completing the deal and cannot shift it all on to the seller. The trend of the law today, however, decidedly places a greater burden upon the seller.

The law treats a warranty in an entirely different sense when it is employed in the sale of goods than when it is used in connection with insurance. When goods are sold a warranty places an obligation upon the seller. The seller's breach of the warranty enables the buyer to recover a judgment for damages from the seller.

In the law of insurance a warranty made by the insured goes to the very essence of the contract. So that if you, the insured, warrant that your boat will be used only for recreation and not for commercial purposes, a breach of this warranty does not result in damages but relieves the insurance company from any duty to pay under the policy. [Smith and Roberson: Business Law, p. 414, 1962.]

The Buyer's Remedies

Suppose you find that your recently purchased boat has certain latent defects which were not apparent upon inspection and which you have now learned the seller knew about at the time of the sale. What can you do about it? Well, the first and perhaps the soundest advice I can give you is this: get a lawyer!

But aside from this there are several courses of action which you can take. They are:

1. Return the boat and demand the return of your money. If it is not forthcoming within a reasonable time then bring suit for the return of your money and in addition the necessary costs and disbursements.

2. Return the boat and demand that you be supplied with one that meets your requirements. If the seller will not accept the boat, or if he does and neither fulfils your requirements nor returns your money, then bring suit for damages.

10

3. If title has not been taken on the boat, then refuse to take title, and sue for your damages.

4. Sell the boat after your demands for relief have been denied by the seller and sue for the difference between what you have received at the sale and what the boat cost you.

5. If you have sold the boat and purchased another of comparable value, you can sue for damages, which would be the difference in the amount which you received on the sale and the amount which you had to pay for the comparable boat.

Conditional Bills of Sale

You are negotiating for the purchase of a boat. The seller tells you that he had previously bought the boat under a "conditional sales contract" or that he had obtained a "conditional bill of sale." (You may have learned of this either by examining the document which the proposed seller had received when *he* bought the boat or by a search in the county clerk's office.) What to do?

Knowledge by the buyer of the existence of a conditional bill of sale should act as a red danger signal. The reason for this lies in the essential difference between a bill of sale and a conditional bill of sale. A bill of sale passes title for the personal property conveyed. In the case of a conditional bill of sale title never leaves the seller. The seller retains the title to the personal property until the purchase price is paid. [Jackson v Parks, 49 Ga App 29, 174 SE 203, 1934.] Therefore, one who has a boat in his possession by reason of a conditional bill of sale and who has not paid the balance due on the purchase price has no title which he can pass on to a buyer.

11

Since the purported seller does not have good title, you can back out of the deal. If, however, you still want to purchase the boat then you can do either one of two things. Have the possessor of the boat pay the balance owed. He should then get a "satisfaction piece" which is a document attesting to the fact that the terms of the conditional sales contract have been satisfied. Or, together with the possessor of the boat, pay the balance owed on the conditional sales contract and obtain the "satisfaction piece" from the conditional sales contract vendor and a bill of sale from the possessor and seller.

A conditional sales contract must be filed in the county where the vendee (the original purchaser) resides, or where the boat will be maintained. When it is filed properly in the office of the county clerk it acts as notice to the world and to any potential purchaser in good faith that the title remains in the vendor (the original seller). If the conditional bill of sale has not been filed in the county clerk's office and an innocent purchaser buys the boat in good faith without knowledge of an outstanding conditional sales contract, the buyer will be recognized as the title owner. In some states the filing of a conditional bill of sale is made in a town or city office. Be sure to learn where the filing takes place in your particular state.

2

registration
and numbering

The Need for State Regulation

Now that you have purchased your boat the next step which will concern you undoubtedly will be the registration of the craft. Registration and regulation of recreational boats is now required in 45 states of the United States and in the Virgin Islands.

State regulation of boating, in its present form, was introduced by the passage of the Federal Boating Act of 1958. Regulation by the various states reflects, in a large measure, the minimum equipment requirements advocated in the past by Congress and the elimination of some of the glaring misdeeds of recreational boat operators. These improper practices include the following:

(1) excessive speed;

(2) overloading of boats;

(3) operating a boat while under the influence of intoxicating liquor, drugs, etc.;

(4) wrongful water-skiing practices;

(5) "buzzing" other boats and bathers;

(6) riding the gunwales;

(7) ignoring a warning issued by the Coast Guard and deliberately proceeding into dangerous waters;

(8) failing to take reasonable precautions during the approach of bad weather; and

(9) standing up in a boat.

The period immediately following World War II saw a phenomenal rise in the popularity of recreational boating. It has been estimated that in 1947 there were 2,500,000 pleasure boats in operation. Today, an educated guess places the figure at well over 7,000,000, a three-fold rise.

Several reasons have been advanced for the manifest popularity of boating. The shorter workweek with its consequent additional leisure time for all income groups has undoubtedly been an important factor. The crowding of the nation's highways has been suggested as another reason for millions of our citizens turning to the waterways. With increased popularity and use of pleasure boats, particularly in the outboard class, have come mechanical improvements in the form of reliable motors, increased engine efficiency, and more imaginative use of materials in boat hulls. The large man-made lakes created by flood-control and irrigation projects in various parts of the United States have made available vast areas of water for recreational boating in regions where this sport has not previously existed. Finally, mass-produced lightweight craft plus efficient compact outboard motors have made the use of the auto trailers in connection with boats feasible. The auto trailer has contributed to portage mobility and has enabled the boatowner to enjoy his sport in areas previously inaccessible to him. [House Report No. 378, 85th Congress, April 18,

1957, entitled "Study of Recreational Boating Safety."]

The tremendous popularity of boating brought with it new problems in the field of accident prevention and safety education. The inevitable foolhardy boat operator whose concept of self-attraction consisted in "tearing" up and down a lake at breakneck speed, "buzzing" bathers, fishermen, and other boat operators alike, became an increasing menace. Then too, the appalling ignorance of new boatowners with respect to simple regard for elementary rules of safe operation and equipment made necessary more effective supervision by an authoritative governmental body. The very efficient Coast Guard, with its manifold responsibilities and duties to shipping, just did not have the manpower to regulate over 7,000,000 recreational boats. Furthermore, the Coast Guard's authority was limited to the deep sea and the navigable waters of the United States. Boating on the inland nonnavigable lakes and rivers was outside the Coast Guard's province. The answer lay in giving this function to the state authorities, and Congress did just that by enacting the Federal Boating Act of 1958. [Public Law 85–911, 85th Congress, HR 11078, September 2, 1958.]

Numbering of Boats

The Federal Boating Act of 1958 set up the machinery for state regulation and numbering of recreational boats. The state system had to be approved by the Secretary of the Treasury, the agency within which the Coast Guard operates in peacetime.

The act called for the numbering of all boats propelled by machinery of more than 10 horsepower. Specifically exempt from the numbering requirement were:

(1) Foreign vessels temporarily using the navigable waters of the United States, its territories, and the District of Columbia;

(2) Public vessels of the United States;

(3) State and municipally owned vessels;

(4) Ships' lifeboats; and

(5) Those vessels or that class of vessels which may, from time to time, be declared exempt by the Secretary of the Treasury.

While the act calls for the numbering of all machine-propelled boats of *more* than 10 horsepower, it apparently has been interpreted by some states as mandatory only with respect to boats of more than that power, and permissive with regard to boats of less power. The majority of the states regulate all boats irrespective of the amount of horsepower. In some states regulation begins with boats of more than 5 horsepower; in another, it is over 6 horsepower; and in still another the starting point is 7½ horsepower. A listing of the states and the numbering requirement by vessel horsepower will be found further on in this chapter.

Reciprocity

A keystone objective of the Federal Boating Act of 1958 is to secure the co-ordination and co-operation of the states in the interest of uniformity of boating laws. A section of the act [§ 3(7)] provides that each state is to recognize the validity of a number awarded to a boat by another state for a period of at least 90 days. This recognition is known as reciprocity. A boatowner from, let us say Illinois, can take his boat into the waters of Ohio and for a consecutive period of 90 days operate his boat in Ohio without the necessity of obtaining an Ohio certificate of number. If he remains in the other state for more than 90 days he must (if

16

the law of the visited state so provides, and it usually does) register his boat. Should he become a permanent resident of the other state a new number will be issued to him.

One state, Florida, undoubtedly having the long-staying winter visitor in mind, designates him as a "sojourner." A sojourner can stay on in Florida for an indefinite time without the necessity of procuring a Florida certificate of number. His number and the certificate issued by his home state will receive full recognition by the Florida boating authorities. If the sojourner becomes a permanent resident of Florida, then a Florida filing and a new certificate of number will be issued to him.

Certificate of Number

The owner of a boat which is required to be numbered by the laws of the state in which the boat is principally used must apply for a number to the boating authorities of that state and pay the necessary fee. He will then be assigned a number and given a certificate of number.

The certificate of number should be of pocket size, and it is required to be available at all times for inspection on the boat for which it has been issued whenever that boat is in use.

The certificate of number is valid, according to the Federal Boating Act of 1958, "for a period not exceeding 3 years, unless cancelled or surrendered, and may be renewed for additional periods." In most states the 3-year period prevails. However, in other states the life of the certificate is shorter. These states are as follows: *One year*—Alabama, Arkansas, Kentucky, Nebraska, North Carolina, Oklahoma, Oregon, South Dakota, Utah, Vermont, West Virginia, and Wyoming. *Two Years*—Florida, Iowa, Minnesota, and Mississippi.

17

Affixing the Number

The number awarded to the boat operator must appear on both sides of the bow of the boat. It may be either painted on or attached. The numbers must be of plain block design and not less than 3 inches high. They must be of a solid color to contrast with the boat's background, as for example, dark numbers on a light-colored hull and light numbers on a dark-colored hull. The number is to be read from left to right and should be placed in such position as to provide maximum visibility.

The number issued by each of the states is divided into parts. The first part consists of the state designator. For instance, California bears the designation of CF; Connecticut is Ct; New York is NY, and so forth. The second part consists of the number, with a maximum of 4 digits. The third part consists of letters which furnish individual vessel identification. Each part of the number must be separated by a hyphen or an equivalent space. An identifying number which would appear on a California boat would be as follows: CF 421 AF

The District Commander of the Third Coast Guard District issued an announcement in 1963 setting out the correct and incorrect way of showing the identifying numbers. Here it is:

CORRECT	WRONG
NY 7 AZ	NY7AZ
	(NO SPACE BETWEEN LETTERS AND NUMERALS)
NY 789 AZ	NY 789 AZ
	(DIFFERENT SIZE LETTERS)
NY-2345-AZ	NY-2345-AZ
	(IMPROPER LETTERS AND NUMERALS)

18

After the Federal Boating Act was passed in 1958, the Commandant of the Coast Guard, under delegation from the Secretary of the Treasury, issued a regulation that the letters and numbers should be "in block characters of good proportion." Because of a misunderstanding regarding this regulation, the Commandant, in 1961, issued a further regulation in which he declared that "the phrase 'block characters of good proportion' shall mean that the numbers and letters are vertical (not slanted)." A manufacturer who had in stock a large supply of slanting letters and numbers brought suit to set aside the regulation, claiming that it had not been established after public notice and hearing.

In holding against the manufacturer's contention the court stated that the regulation of 1961 was of a clarifying type and therefore did not require the giving of notice and the holding of a public hearing. Furthermore, the court held, the regulation was neither arbitrary nor capricious. The manufacturer's action to set aside the regulation was defeated. [Garelick Mfg. Co. v. Dillon, 114 App DC 218, 313 F2d 899, 1963 AMC 711, 1963.]

The edict with respect to vertical letters is obviously designed for the purpose of boating uniformity and to enable an observer to have a greater degree of clarity in reading the identifying marking.

It had been found that vessels of an unconventional design cannot have their numbers placed on either side of the bow and still have them readily apparent or legible. When the number was placed on the obscured underside of a flared bow the angle was such that the number could not be seen readily from another vessel or from ashore. In such instances the

Coast Guard, where it has jurisdiction, has permitted the number to be firmly attached on the forward half of this type of boat by use of a bracket or fixture. There is no change of the rules with respect to legibility, size, and style of numerals and letters, and contrast with the background. [46 Code of Federal Regulations, § 171.05–6b.]

Fees

"The States may charge fees in connection with the renewals thereof." This succinct statement appears in the Federal Boating Act of 1958. [§ 3c(10).] Thus, the amount of the fee to be charged for the issuance of the certificate of number is left to the individual states. As can be expected perhaps, the fees vary considerably.

Some states, by law, earmark the moneys received as fees for boating purposes. The laws of Arizona, for example, require that the money thus obtained be used for improvement of the waterways, lakes, ramps, piers, mooring areas, etc. In New York the revenue received from boating fees is used for educational purposes, particularly for the giving of safety courses for young boat operators.

In most states the fee is the same for all boats irrespective of size. By and large it can be said that they are nominal. For example, in Arizona, California, Michigan, Montana, North Dakota, Rhode Island, and Wisconsin the fee is $3 for 3 years. In Idaho it is $2 for 3 years and in Mississippi $1.25 for 2 years.

In other states the size of the fee varies according to the size of the boat. Inequality is displayed when a 45-footer requires a fee of $4 for one year in Wyoming and $25 for one year in Vermont.

20

Coast Guard Boarding and Inspection

Under section 8(c) of the Federal Boating Act of 1958, Coast Guard commissioned, warrant, and petty officers have the right to board any vessel required to be numbered. They may do so for the purpose of addressing inquiries to the people on board, to require appropriate proof of identification, and to examine the certificate of number and inspect the boat for compliance with the safety equipment requirements as set forth in the Motorboat Act of 1940. If a certificate of number is not produced the boarding party can demand that the owner of the boat give appropriate proof of identification.

The Coast Guard authority extends to boats on the high seas and the navigable waters of the United States. It does not have authority in the nonnavigable waters, such as a river or lake lying entirely within the borders of a state and unconnected with another state or with navigable waters. (The matter of navigable waters is explained fully in the chapter on "Limitation of Liability.") State and local law enforcement officers, under the boating laws of the individual states, are also given boarding rights regarding boats on the waters of those particular states.

Under the Motorboat Act of 1940 [46 United States Code §§ 526n and 526o], the Coast Guard has the authority to cause arrest and to impose and assess a penalty for violations of this act. Usually a warning notice is given to the boat operator calling for the correction of the violation, such as improper or insufficient life preservers, absence of a flame arrestor, etc. The Coast Guard District Commander of the district in which the violation took place is authorized to determine whether or not to prosecute the offender or to mitigate or to remit the penalty. [46 Code of Federal Regulations, 2.50–20.]

When the boat operator has cleared the violation by compliance, he will be notified by the Coast Guard that the case is closed. If the penalty is assessed it must be paid within 30 days.

The offender is given the right to appeal to the Commandant from the actions of the Coast Guard District Commander if the amount of the penalty assessed exceeds $50. The decision of the Coast Guard District Commander in cases where the penalty is $50 or less is final.

If the penalty is not paid within 30 days from the date of the notice, or if an appeal has not been taken, court action by the United States attorney to collect the penalty will generally follow. [United States v Hall, 1963 AMC 725, DC Fla 1962.]

The Coast Guard's policy is to secure the public's compliance with the boating laws by the educational process rather than by reliance on monetary penalties. Prompt correction of a numbering violation can mean the remission of the penalty. Failure to have the required equipment may result in a minimum penalty of $10 for a first offense and $20 for a second offense. In the case of a reckless or negligent operation the minimum penalty for a first offense is generally $25. If the circumstances indicate aggravating factors the assessed penalty may be higher.

Refusing to allow a Coast Guard boarding officer to inspect your boat while it is in navigable waters can result in the imposition of a penalty. A boat owner was in his craft called the Ride-Ann-Hour-Too (the owner's name was Ridenour) when he was hailed by a Coast Guard petty officer. A Coast Guard patrol boat crew was inspecting pleasure boats on the San

Joaquin River in Hog Island Cut, California. The petty officer requested permission (merely a ceremonial act) for a routine boarding and inspection of the Ride-Ann-Hour-Too. The boat owner refused to allow the boarding and inspection. The Coast Guard assessed a civil penalty of $100, which was not paid. The Government then brought an action in the Federal District Court for a judgment in the amount of the assessed penalty.

As to the right and discretion of the Coast Guard officer in seeking to inspect the boat, the court said:

"Safety on navigable waters requires the final determination in this regard to be the responsibility of Coast Guard personnel. The chaotic results of allowing each small boat operator to determine whether or not boarding should be allowed are so apparent so as to require no prolonged comment. It seems sufficient to recognize the fact that small-boat, pleasure-boat operators are unlicensed and frequently inexperienced, as well as irresponsible. Coast Guard facilities are the only means by which the unfortunate results of this situation can be controlled to any extent. Action by Coast Guard personnel will not be held to be arbitrary or capricious in the absence of convincing evidence. No such evidence has been presented in this case."

A judgment of $100 plus costs in the amount of $79.08 was given in favor of the government. [United States v M/B Ride-Ann-Hour-Too, 1963 AMC 997, DC Cal 1962.]

Safety Rules

The motorboating safety requirements enforced by the Coast Guard are set out in the Motorboat Act of 1940. [Act of April 25, 1940; 46 United States Code §§ 526 et seq.] They relate to the use of lights,

23

whistles, bells, life preservers, etc. The equipment requirements have been discussed in detail in this book in the chapter entitled "Boat Safety and Accident Prevention." Every state, in differing degrees, has incorporated these requirements in its boating laws. Adherence to the minimum safety requirements of the Coast Guard should make your boat equipment and safety practices acceptable in each of the states.

The Federal Boating Act of 1958 includes a prohibition against the operation of a motorboat in reckless or negligent manner. The act also provides for the giving of assistance in the event of a boating accident and the manner of reporting the casualty. The ban on reckless and negligent boat operation and the requirement calling for the rendering of assistance and the reporting of accidents have been incorporated in the boating laws of all the states.

Coast Guard Registration

A few of the states and possessions do not have boating laws and regulations. They are: Alaska, District of Columbia, Guam, Hawaii, New Hampshire, Tennessee, and Washington. In those areas recreational small boats are numbered by the United States Coast Guard. Boats which are used on the navigable waters of the United States and on the high seas must be registered and numbered. Boats which are used only on the inland nonnavigable waters of those particular areas are not required to be numbered. Some owners voluntarily seek Coast Guard registration and numbering.

Before January 31, 1964 the Post Office Department assisted the Coast Guard by distributing the application forms and by accepting the completed application

24

for a number and the prescribed fee. After this date the Post Office ceased accepting applications and fees, but it continues to make the forms available to owners in those states where the Coast Guard is issuing numbers.

The completed application for a number should be sent to the Commandant (FA–1), United States Coast Guard, Washington 25, D.C. The required fee can be in the form of a personal check or money order made payable to the United States Coast Guard.

Within 90 days of the expiration date of the certificate of number the renewal application can be sent to the Coast Guard at the address shown in the preceding paragraph. The application for a duplicate certificate of number is made in a similar manner as the application for the original number.

In addition to the Post Office stations the required United States Coast Guard boating forms can be obtained at the Coast Guard district offices; all marine inspection offices; and at all Coast Guard units in those states where the Coast Guard is numbering boats.

Highlights of State Boating Laws

The highlights of the boating laws of the various states of the United States (including the Virgin Islands) are set forth in the pages which follow. Obviously, space prohibits the printing of the complete laws of each state, for the boating laws of many of them are quite lengthy.

Following the analysis of the principal boating laws of the respective states appear the name and address of the governing body of each state. The reader who desires to obtain further information or the complete laws may do so by writing the appropriate authority.

ALABAMA

Fees:

Certificates and licenses are valid for 1 year. Class 1, less than 16 feet, $2. Class 2, over 16 feet and less than 26 feet, $3. Class 3, over 26 feet and less than 40 feet, $6. Class 4, 40 feet or over, $12. Class 5, dealer's or manufacturer's temporary license, $10 for the first license purchased, and $1 for each additional license. Upon change of ownership, new owner must file a new application with fee of $1. Lost certificate replacable by payment of 50 cents.

Safety Rules:

A diver's flag must be displayed on the surface of any water where skindivers are operating.

Operating boats or manipulating water skis, aquaplanes, or similar devices in a reckless or negligent manner or while under the influence of any narcotic, drug, barbiturate, or marijuana, is subject to a fine of not more than $500 and/or imprisonment of not more than 6 months for each violation. Conviction of a second offense, suspension of owner's certificate of registration up to one year; third offense, revocation.

Water-skiing and aquaplaning prohibited between the hours from one hour after sunset to one hour before sunrise. Towing boats require, in addition to the operator, a person to observe persons being towed. A wide-angle rearview mirror permitted in place of an observer.

Within 10 days after an accident a detailed written report must be filed by the boat operator with the

26

Division of Water Safety, Department of Conservation, Administrative Building, Montgomery, Alabama.

Children under 12 years of age cannot operate boat unless accompanied by a qualified older person.

> State of Alabama
> Department of Conservation
> Montgomery 4, Alabama

ARIZONA

Fees:

Owners of numbered boats from out of state should record the number prior to operating the boat beyond the 90-day reciprocity period. Certificates of number expire on July 1, 1962, and every 3 years thereafter. The fee for all boats is $3. Ninety percent of the tax received on the sale of motor fuel used in propelling watercraft goes into a state lake-improvement fund for the maintenance of public launching ramps, public piers, marinas, marking buoys, public toilets and sanitation facilities, public tables and facilities, etc.

Safety Rules:

Boats are not to be loaded with passengers or cargo beyond safe carrying capacity.

Persons operating a boat while under the influence of intoxicating liquor, narcotics, or habit-forming drugs are subject to fine and imprisonment.

Boats towing people must be occupied by at least two persons; one to operate the boat and the other to observe the towed person. Night skiing is prohibited.

Boats must carry a Coast Guard approved lifejacket, buoy, or buoyant cushion in serviceable condition for each person on board. Children under 8 years of age must wear a life preserver at all times while on board.

27

Dumping of refuse or debris on the shoreline or waterways is prohibited.

Operators of powered boats must yield the right of way to any craft not under power. Boats leaving the shoreline area must yield the right of way. Normal traffic moves counterclockwise.

> State of Arizona
> Motor Vehicle Division
> Boat Number Section
> 1739 West Jackson Street
> Phoenix, Arizona

ARKANSAS

Fees:

Certificates of number issued to all boats cost $2. Certificates are valid from July 1 to June 30 of the following year. Annual renewal, $1. Numbers must be displayed on both sides of the bow of the boat. Upon the sale of a boat, the new owner files an application and fee of $1 with the county clerk. A new number is issued and the old number is canceled. Out-of-state numbered boats have reciprocity for 90 days.

Safety Rules:

Required equipment—a life preserver, buoyant vest, ring buoy, or buoyant cushion of a type approved by the Coast Guard for each person on board or a ski belt in good serviceable condition for each person. For night operation, a light sufficient to make the boat's presence known within a reasonable distance. A natural or mechanical ventilation system for enclosed motorboats.

Children under 12 years of age not permitted to own or to have control of a motorboat, except under the direct visible and audible supervision of a parent, guardian, or other person over 17 years old.

A guest does not have a cause of action against the boat owner for injury unless the boat has been operated wilfully and wantonly in disregard of the rights of others. A boat owner is not liable for injury or damage unless the boat has been used with his express or implied consent.

Operating boats or manipulating water skis, aquaplanes, or similar devices in a reckless or negligent manner or while under the influence of any narcotic, drug, barbiturate, or marijuana, is subject to a fine of not more than $500 and/or imprisonment of not more than 6 months for each violation.

Night skiing prohibited except in controlled areas. Towing boat must be equipped with a wide-angle rearview mirror in lieu of a person, other than operator, acting as observer.

Written report of fatal boating accident must be filed within 48 hours of accident; other accidents, within 5 days.

State of Arkansas
Arkansas Game and Fish Commission
Little Rock, Arkansas

CALIFORNIA

Fees:

Certificate fee is $5, valid for 3 years. Renewal fee is $3. Within 30 days after the 90-day reciprocity period, an out-of-state visitor must apply for a certificate, fee $5. Upon change of ownership, an application must be filed by the new owner, fee $3.

Safety Rules:

Every peace officer of the state, city, and county has

the authority to stop and board any vessel subject to the state boating law. Violators of the law can be punished by a fine up to $500 or imprisonment up to 6 months, or both.

A towing boat must have two persons aboard, an operator and one to observe the skier. The observer must be at least 12 years of age. The towing of water-skiers from sunset to sunrise is prohibited. An exception is made in case of differing local laws or where professional exhibitions, regattas, races, or parades are authorized.

In the event of an accident the operator of an involved boat (a) must give assistance to other persons involved; (b) give his name, address, and identification of his boat in writing to any injured person or to the other boat owner; and (c) report the accident to the Division of Small Craft Harbors, Sacramento 14, California, within 5 days. In a death casualty, within 48 hours.

In general, California follows the federal equipment requirements with respect to life preservers, fire extinguishers, lights, sound-producing devices, safety precautions against fire, etc.

> State of California
> Department of Natural Resources
> Division of Small Craft Harbors
> Sacramento 14, California

COLORADO

Fees:

The numbering of boats does not apply to a motorboat of 10 horsepower or less, to boats propelled manually, or to sailboats. The fee for a certificate of number is $5 and it is valid for 3 years and renewable for a further period of 3 years. Transfer of certificate or replacement of a lost certificate requires a fee of $1. Application form and check or money order is sent to: State Park and Recreation Board, 211 State Services Building, Denver 3, Colorado. Check or money order is made payable to State Treasurer.

Safety Rules:

Motorboats operated on the waters of the state park system of more than 10 horsepower are required to have in force, liability insurance in the amount of $25,000 for bodily injury to one person, $100,000 for aggregate bodily injuries, and $1,000 property damage.

Boats towing water-skiers must be occupied by at least one competent person in addition to the operator. Take-off in skiing from established ski beaches or docks provided for this purpose; not permitted from shore. The skier must wear a life preserver or ski belt in good condition.

Operating a motorboat "in a careless or reckless" or "careless and imprudent manner," or "in any manner endangering or placing in peril persons, other water craft or property," or "wanton or wilful disregard of the safety of persons or property," is forbidden and is subject to revocation of certificate and license.

Equipment requirements include: whistles, life preservers, life belt or ring buoy, fire extinguishers, back-fire flame arrestor, efficient natural or mechanical ventilating system, muffler, lights, etc.

No boat should be operated by a person under the influence of intoxicating liquor, narcotics, or habit-forming drugs, or having mental or physical disability.

31

An accident report must be filed within 72 hours after the accident.

> State of Colorado
> Colorado State Park Recreation Board
> 211 State Services Building
> Denver 3, Colorado

CONNECTICUT

Fees:

All vessels propelled by machinery of more than 5 horsepower must be numbered, fee $5. The certificate of number is valid for 3 years. Boats of 5 horsepower or less can be voluntarily numbered. Boat liverymen and marine dealers must obtain a certificate of number, fee $5. Only one boat may be operated under one certificate of number at one time. A boat number is not transferable; it remains on the boat. The purchaser must obtain a new certificate of number. The seller of a numbered boat who buys another boat will be credited with the unexpired portion of his certificate; he must obtain a new certificate of number, fee $1. Duplicate certificate of number, fee $1. Town clerks who issue certificates of number are entitled to assess a fee of 50 cents for each certificate issued. Numbered out-of-state boats have reciprocity for 90 days. If they are kept in Connecticut beyond 90 days, the number must be recorded, fee $2.

Safety Rules:

Skindivers must mark their position with a clearly discernible flag, buoy, or other device.

A boat towing water-skiers must have, in addition to the operator, a responsible person at least 12 years of age assisting the operator and observing the progress of the water-skier. Water-skiing is prohibited from one hour after sunset until sunrise.

An accident report must be filed by the boat operator in cases of death within 48 hours after the accident. In cases of personal injury or property damage in an amount of $100 or more the report must be submitted within 5 days.

Connecticut towns have local ordinances regarding boating.

Speed limits for shore towns: Branford: not more than 4 m.p.h. on the Branford River. Stratford: 4 m.p.h. when passing boats and anchorages. Bridgeport: not more than 5 knots. Darien: 5 m.p.h. north of Nun Buoy #2. Norwalk: 5 m.p.h. in inner harbor. Westport: 5 m.p.h. speed limit in harbors and congested areas. Madison: 6 m.p.h. within 100 yards of shore. Westbrook: 6 m.p.h. or not to cause destructive wake, whichever is less.

River and Lake Towns: Barkhamsted: not more than 6 m.p.h. within 75 feet of shore, dock, etc. Bethlehem: 15 m.p.h. East Hampton: slowest operating speed within 75 feet of shore, dock, pier, float, etc. Granby: 5 m.p.h. in areas under restrictions. Middlebury: (Lake Quassapaug) 10 m.p.h. from first day of fishing season to Tuesday after Labor Day. Rest of the year not more than 25 m.p.h. New Hartford: (West Hill Pond) not more than 6 m.p.h. within 75 feet of shore, dock, etc. Portland: (Great Hill Lake) 12 m.p.h. Salisbury: 35 m.p.h. Not over 6 m.p.h. within 200 feet of any canoe, rowboat, etc. Sharon: 6 m.p.h. Weathersfield: not more than 6 m.p.h. in Weathersfield Cove. Winchester: 6 m.p.h. within 50 feet from shore.

State of Connecticut
Boating Safety Commission
650 Main St.
Hartford, Conn.

33

DELAWARE

Fees:

There is an annual fee of $3 for the certificate of number. When the boat is sold the number may be transferred by the owner, fee $2. Duplicate certificate when original is lost may be obtained for $1. Reciprocity for out-of-state numbered boats up to 90 days.

Safety Rules:

Motorboats are divided into four classes: Class A, less than 16 feet in length. Class 1, 16 feet or over and less than 26 feet in length. Class 2, 26 feet or over and less than 40 feet in length. Class 3, 40 feet or over. The regulations of the U. S. Coast Guard prescribing equipment for the respective classes are applicable to Delaware licensed boats.

Water-skiing is not permitted on (a) Lewes-Rehoboth Canal; (b) channel through Massey's Landing; (c) Fenwick Ditch; (d) Assawoman Canal; and (e) any other public swimming area. The towing boat must be occupied by at least two competent persons unless the boat is equipped with a wide-angle, rearview mirror. No skiing or aquaplaning between one hour after sunset to one hour before sunrise unless at an authorized water-ski tournament, competition, exhibition, or trial, where adequate lighting is provided.

In the event of collision, a boatowner, without serious danger to his own vessel, crew, or passengers, should render assistance. An accident report must be filed if casualty involves death, personal injury, or damage to property in excess of $100.

A boatowner is not civilly liable unless the boat is being used with his express or implied consent. If the boat is operated by a spouse, father, mother,

34

brother, sister, son, daughter, or other member of the owner's family, knowledge and consent is presumed.

> Delaware Commission of Shell Fisheries
> Small Boat Safety Division
> P.O. Box 48, Rehoboth Beach
> Delaware

FLORIDA

Fees:

All pleasure boats propelled by machinery of more than 10 horsepower must have numbered registration certificates. They are obtained from the local county tax collector. Boats less than 16 feet in length, $1.75; 16 feet or over and less than 26 feet in length, $2.75; 26 feet or over and less than 40 feet in length, $5.25; 40 feet and over, $10.25. The certificates of number are good for 2 years, beginning on July 1 of the registration period and ending on June 30 of the second year following. Out-of-state boats are given reciprocity. If the owner of a numbered out-of-state boat intends to use his boat in the state for longer than 90 days he must register the boat and can retain his number. He is considered a "sojourner," intending to stay for an indefinite period of time. If he intends to remain in Florida permanently, the boat must be registered and will receive a Florida number. Transfer of Florida number on change of ownership permitted, fee $1. If old certificate is not available the new owner can register with proof of ownership shown, fee $1.

Safety Rules:

In case of accident the boat operator must give all assistance possible to minimize the danger. If there is death, personal injury, or the damage is in excess of $50, a report must be filed within 10 days with any

35

sheriff, tax collector, or any conservation or game officer.

Reckless operation of a boat occurs when a person willfully or wantonly operates a boat or manipulates water skis, aquaplane, or a similar device with disregard for the safety of persons or property. Penalties: first offense, $25 fine or imprisonment for not more than 30 days, or both; second offense, $50 fine, or not more than $250, or imprisonment for not more than 3 months, or both.

Operation by a person whose normal functions are impaired by liquor or narcotics is prohibited.

United States Coast Guard safety equipment requirements for boats in Classes 1, 2, and 3 are followed.

Boats towing skiers and aquaplaners must have two persons, unless a broad wide-angle rearview mirror is used.

No skiing or aquaplaning from one-half hour after sunset to one-half hour before sunrise.

> State of Florida
> Florida Board of Conservation
> Division of Salt Water Fisheries
> Tallahassie, Florida

GEORGIA

Fees:

All boats propelled by machinery of more than 10 horsepower and all commercial fishing vessels regardless of horsepower must be registered and numbered. Class A, less than 16 feet, $5.25. Class I, 16 feet or over but less than 26 feet in length, $7.75. Class II, 26 feet or over but less than 40 feet in length, $10.25. Class III, 40 feet or over, $15.25. Certificate of number is valid for 3 years. Reciprocity granted to numbered out-of-state boats up to 90 days. The number must be recorded with the Game and Fish Commission before the boat is used. Upon sale of a boat, the new owner must file a new application form and pay the fee; the license number is not transferable.

Safety Rules:

It is unlawful to operate, or for an owner to permit operation of, any watercraft while the operator is under the influence of intoxicants, narcotics, or habit-forming drugs. It is unlawful for any person to be in a watercraft while in an intoxicated condition from the excessive use of wines, beers, liquors, narcotics, drugs, or opiates. The intoxicated condition must be made manifest by boisterousness, or by indecent condition or action, or by vulgar, profane, or unbecoming language, or loud and violent discourse of the person in the intoxicated condition.

Overloading is prohibited. Loading passengers or cargo greater than the maximum recommended or indicated on the watercraft by label or tag of the watercraft is prima facie proof of a violation of the Georgia boating act.

Riding or sitting on either the starboard or port gunwales or on the decking over the bow of the vessel is prohibited unless it is provided with adequate guards, railings, or other facilities to prevent passengers from being lost overboard.

Towing a person on water skis, aquaplane, or similar device is prohibited from the period of one hour after sunset to one hour before sunrise.

> State of Georgia
> Georgia Game & Fish Commission
> Motorboat Registration Unit
> 401 State Capitol
> Atlanta 3, Georgia

IDAHO

Fees:

All motorboats operating on the waters of Idaho must be numbered. The fee is $2. A certificate of number is valid for 3 years. The purchaser of a numbered boat can have the certificate of number transferred to him within 15 days of acquiring it, fee $2. A lost, mutilated, or illegible certificate of number can be replaced, fee $1. Manufacturers and dealers of motorboats may obtain certificates of number for use in the testing or demonstration of boats; fee $3 for each registration.

Safety Rules:

It is forbidden to operate a boat propelled by machinery at a speed of more than 10 m.p.h. when within 50 feet from another craft, or at a speed in excess of 10 m.p.h. at any time unless vision is unobstructed 300 feet ahead. Approach to a dock, pier, or shore of any lake must be at a reduced and safe speed.

Operating any watercraft in a manner that will endanger the life or limb, or damage the property, of any person, is reckless operation punishable by imprisonment of not more than 6 months, or by a fine of not more than $500, or both. Careless or heedless operation is punishable by a fine of not more than $100 or by imprisonment of not more than 30 days, or both.

Boats towing persons on water skis, aquaplanes, etc., must have two occupants unless a wide-angle, rearview mirror is used. Towing skiers is prohibited between the period of one hour after sunset and one hour before sunrise.

Operators of boats of 18 feet or less shall not allow any person to ride or sit on the gunwales or on the decking over the bow, except for mooring or casting off.

Overloading and overpowering a boat is not permitted.

It is unlawful to operate any watercraft while under the influence of intoxicating liquor, narcotic, or habit-forming drugs.

> State of Idaho
> Department of Law Enforcement
> Motor Vehicle Bureau
> Boise, Idaho

ILLINOIS

Fees:

Motorboats must be registered to receive a certificate of number. The fee is $3 and the number awarded is good for 3 years. If the certificate of number is lost, destroyed, or mutilated, it can be replaced upon payment of a fee of $1. Purchaser of a numbered boat can apply for a certificate to be transferred to him, within 15 days of purchase, fee $1. Persons engaged in the boat-renting business or boat dealers or manufacturers may obtain certificates for use in testing or demonstrating the boats upon payment of $3 for each registration. Reciprocity given to out-of-state numbered boats for use in Illinois for a period of up to 90 days; thereafter an Illinois number must be obtained.

Safety Rules:

An accident report must be made by a boat operator involved in an accident resulting in death or injury to a person or property damage in excess of $100.

Operation of motorboat or vessel or manipulation of water skis, aquaplanes, or similar devices while intoxicated or under the influence of narcotics, barbiturates, or marijuana is forbidden.

39

Boats towing water skis, aquaplanes, or similar contrivances must be occupied by at least two competent persons. No water-skiing, aquaplaning, etc., from the period of one-half hour after sunset to one-half hour before sunrise.

Motorboats shall not be equipped with any motor or other propulsion machinery beyond its safe power capacity, taking into consideration the type and construction of such motorboat and other existing operating conditions. No motorboat shall be loaded with passengers or cargo beyond its safe carrying capacity, taking into consideration weather and other existing operating conditions.

Operation of a motorboat in a careless or heedless manner or in such a manner as to endanger the life or limb or property of any persons is forbidden.

> State of Illinois
> Department of Conservation
> Motorboat License Division
> 400 So. Spring St.
> Springfield, Illinois

INDIANA

Fees:

All motorboats having propelling machinery exceeding 6 horsepower must be registered. A certificate of number is valid for 3 years, fee $3. Upon the sale of the boat a new application form and the appropriate fee must be submitted. A new registration certificate will then be awarded. In the event that the certificate is lost or destroyed the certificate will be reissued, fee $1. Manufacturers and dealers can receive a certificate of number, fee $3. Out-of-state numbered boats have reciprocity recognition for 90 days.

Safety Rules:

Every peace officer of Indiana has the authority to enforce the boating laws and can stop and board any motorboat subject to the boating act.

No person may operate any motorboat in a circular course around any other boat where an occupant is engaged in fishing, or around a person engaged in swimming.

Operating or sounding a siren is prohibited except by a duly appointed peace officer.

In towing any one on water skis, watersled, aquaplane, or similar object, the towing boat must have an occupant engaged in giving his entire attention to the operation of the boat.

An operator involved in an accident should stop immediately, return to the scene of the accident, render reasonable assistance, and give his name and address, the name and address of the owner, and exhibit his operator's license. An immediate report must be made to the sheriff of the county in which the accident occurred, or to the state police or to the nearest conservation officer, where there has been loss of life, disappearance of any person, incapacitating injury, or property damage of $50 or more. Within 24 hours a written report of accident must be filed with the department of conservation.

> Indiana Department of Conservation
> 311 West Washington St.
> Indianapolis, Indiana

IOWA

Fees:

All motor-propelled boats must be numbered. The certificate of number is valid for 2 years expiring on

July 3, 1963, and every two years thereafter, fee $4. Upon transfer of ownership the certificate must be surrendered within 5 days and the name and address of the purchaser reported. Within 5 days the purchaser must file a new application form, fee $1. The transfer of the number will then take place. Duplicate registration certificate, fee $1. If the boat is destroyed or abandoned the State Conservation Commission must be notified and the registration certificate returned within 10 days.

Safety Rules:

An operator of a motorboat while engaged in a race must wear a crash helmet and life preserver.

Operation of a vessel or the manipulation of water skis, surfboard, or similar device, while intoxicated or under the influence of any narcotic drug, barbiturate, or marijuana, is prohibited.

Also prohibited is the operation of a vessel or manipulation of water skis, surfboard, or similar device in a careless, reckless, or negligent manner so as to endanger the life, limb, or property of any person.

A boat towing a person on water skis, surfboard, or similar device must have in addition to the boat operator, a responsible person in a position to observe the person towed.

Boats may be inspected at any time by the State Conservation Commission for seaworthiness. No person is permitted to place or allow to remain in waters under the jurisdiction of the commission a boat which has failed to pass inspection.

No person owning or operating a vessel is permitted to have that vessel occupied by more passengers and crew than the registration capacity permits.

42

An accident report must be filed within 48 hours in death cases; within 5 days in other cases.

> State of Iowa
> State Conservation Commission
> East 7th and Court Ave.
> Des Moines 8, Iowa

KANSAS

Fees:

Motorboats or vessels powered by machinery of 10 horsepower or greater require certificates of number, fee $5. The certificate is valid for 3 years. Lost certificates can be replaced, fee $1. Upon the sale of a boat the new owner must apply for a transfer within 15 days. The sale terminates the number and a new application must be filed, fee $5, and thereupon a new number will be issued. Manufacturers and dealers must register boats used for testing and demonstrations only, fee for each vessel, $10, good for 3 years. Reciprocity given to numbered out-of-state boats for 90 days.

Safety Rules:

Operation of motorboats or vessels or manipulation of skis, surfboards, or similar devices in a reckless or negligent manner so as to endanger the life or property of any person is forbidden. Also prohibited is the operation of a boat or skis, etc., while under the influence of any narcotic, barbiturate, or marijuana.

Boats should not be loaded with passengers or cargo beyond their safe carrying capacity, taking into consideration weather and other operating conditions.

No water-skiing or surfboarding between the hours from one hour after sunset to one hour before sunrise.

43

In the event of an accident the boat operator is required to stop and render aid and assistance. If the accident results in death or injury or property damage in excess of $100 a full report must be filed with the commission. If death occurs as a result of an accident the report must be filed within 48 hours after the accident; otherwise the report must be made within 5 days.

Towing boats for skiing must be operated with two persons in the boat, unless a wide-angle rearview mirror is used.

> State of Kansas
> Kansas Forestry, Fish and Game Commission
> Pratt, Kansas

KENTUCKY

Fees:

Every motorboat on the waters of Kentucky must be numbered. A certificate of number is valid for 1 year. Boats up to 16 feet in length, fee $3. Boats 16 feet to 26 feet, fee $5. Boats 26 feet to 40 feet, fee $8. Boats 40 feet and larger, fee $10. Annual registration fee for all inboard motorboats, fee $10. Boats for hire, up to 16 feet, fee $1; 16 feet to 26 feet, fee $2.50; 26 feet to 40 feet, fee $4; 40 feet and larger and inboard motorboats, fee $5. A purchaser of a numbered boat can have a new certificate issued to him, fee $1. A lost certificate may be replaced, fee $1.

Safety Rules:

No vessel may be equipped with any motor or other propulsion machinery beyond its safe power capacity, taking into consideration the type and construction of the vessel and other existing operating conditions.

Vessels are not to be loaded with passengers or cargo beyond their safe carrying capacity, taking into consideration weather and existing operating conditions.

Persons being towed on water skis, surfboards, etc., must wear a ski belt or an approved safety device.

Water-skiing, surfboarding, etc., is prohibited from one hour after sunset until one hour before sunrise.

Boating accidents must be reported. If a death occurs the report must be filed by the boat operator involved within 48 hours of the accident. In case of personal injury or property damage in an amount in excess of $100 the report must be filed within 5 days.

Operating a motorboat or manipulating water skis, surfboards, etc., in a reckless or negligent manner so as to endanger the life or property of any person is forbidden. Water-skiing within 100 feet of regular boat docks, moorage harbors, or swimming areas, or within 2000 feet of a dam or lock is prohibited.

> State of Kentucky
> Department of Public Safety
> Division of Boating
> Frankfort, Kentucky

LOUISIANA

Fees:

Every motorboat of more than 10 horsepower operated on the waters of Louisiana must be numbered. Certificate of number, fee $5. It is valid for 3 years. Upon sale of the boat the new owner must file a new application, fee $1, and a new certificate of number will be issued, valid for the remainder of the 3-year period. Duplicate certificate will be issued if the original has been lost or destroyed, fee $1. Change of address, fee 25 cents. Certificate of number to a boat dealer, which may be transferred from boat to boat, fee $25. Certificate of number to a liveryman renting to individuals for fishing, first 3 boats, fee $5 each; additional boats $3 each.

Safety Rules:

Operating a motorboat or vessel or manipulating water skis, surfboards, or similar devices in a reckless or negligent manner so as to endanger the life or property of any persons is prohibited. Also prohibited is such operation while intoxicated or under the influence of any narcotic drug, barbiturate, or marijuana.

The boat operator must file an accident report within 5 days if the accident has resulted in personal injury causing incapacitation in excess of $100. When there has been loss of life the report must be filed within 48 hours.

Required equipment generally follows the U.S. Coast Guard minimal requirements.

A boat operator is required to render assistance in the event of an accident so far as he can do so without serious danger to his own vessel, crew, and passengers.

> State of Louisiana
> Louisiana Wild Life and Fisheries
>   Commission
> 400 Royal Street
> New Orleans 16, Louisiana

MAINE

Fees:

Every undocumented motorboat on the waters of the state of Maine which is propelled by machinery of more than 10 horsepower must have a certificate of number. The number once awarded remains permanently with the boat until the boat is destroyed, abandoned, or permanently removed from the state. The certificate of number is valid for 3 years following its issuance. The fee for a certificate of number is $5. For motorboats used primarily for commercial fishing on coastal waters, fee $3. Dealers and manufacturers, fee $10. Duplicate certificate of number, fee $1. Certificate of number issued with transfer of ownership, fee $1. The seller of a motorboat pays $1 for a new number; the buyer pays the regular fee for a new certificate. Dealers and manufacturers can temporarily transfer the certificate of number from one boat to another owned by them. A license is required in order to operate a motorboat carrying passengers for hire.

Safety Rules:

It is unlawful to operate any watercraft within 200 feet of the shoreline, or in a water safety zone, except at a reasonable and prudent speed for existing conditions, and also unlawful to operate a motorboat within an area marked for bathing.

It is unlawful for any person to operate watercraft, water skis, surfboard, or similar device recklessly. Also prohibited is the operation of watercraft while intoxicated or under the influence of narcotic drugs, barbiturates or marijuana.

A child under 12 years of age cannot operate a boat propelled by machinery of more than 10 horsepower unless under the immediate supervision of a person located in the motorboat who is at least 16 years of age.

Violation of the boating regulations is a misdemeanor punishable by a fine of not less than $10 nor more than $500, or by imprisonment for not more than 90 days, or by both.

> State of Maine
> Bureau of Watercraft Registration
>   and Safety
> Room 107
> State Office Building
> Augusta, Maine

MARYLAND

Fees:

All vessels equipped with propelling machinery of more than 7½ horsepower and sailboats of 25 feet or more in length must be numbered, fee $6, valid for 3 years. A lost or destroyed certificate can be replaced, fee $1. In the event of a sale of a boat the new owner must make a new application for a transfer of the certificate, fee $2. Upon a sale, if the former owner wishes a certificate for an acquired boat he may file an application for a transfer certificate and a new number, fee $2.

Safety Rules:

In the event of an accident assistance must be rendered if it can be done without serious danger to passengers, guests, crew, the boat operator, or to the boat. A report must be made within 5 days of any accident where personal injury is involved or property damage is in excess of $100. In cases of death or disappearance the report must be made within 48 hours. If a Maryland numbered boat is involved in an accident outside of Maryland waters a report to Annapolis must be made within 30 days where death, disappearance, personal injury, or property damage in excess of $100 is involved.

48

Municipalities or other local authorities cannot establish regulations of a local nature not in conformity with state regulations.

Vessels towing persons on water skis, aquaplanes, or similar devices must have two occupants, an operator at least 12 years of age, and an observer at least 12 years of age. Towing shall not take place between the hours of sunset and sunrise.

Boat equipment is the same as that called for by federal regulations.

A sailboat which has a motor is considered to be a motorboat. Sailboats must carry one lifesaving device of a type approved by Coast Guard for each person aboard.

> State of Maryland
> Department of Tidewater Fisheries
> State Office Building
> Annapolis, Maryland

MASSACHUSETTS

Fees:

Motorboats of 5 horsepower or more must be numbered. Class A, less than 16 feet in length. Class 1, 16 feet or over and less than 26 feet in length. Class 2, 26 feet or over and less than 40 feet in length. Class 3, 40 feet or over. Fee for original certicate of number for boats of all classes is $5. Certificate of number is valid for one year ending on the anniversary of the date of birth of the applicant. If the certificate of number is issued to other than an individual, it expires one year from the date of issuance. Renewal of certificate of number, fee $3. Substitution of a certificate of number for a motorboat previously registered, fee $1.50. Duplication of lost, destroyed, or mutilated certificate, fee $1.

49

Safety Rules:

The operation of a boat while under the influence of intoxicating liquor, narcotic drug, barbiturate, or marijuana, is prohibited.

Motorboats must be equipped with a muffler or underwater exhaust. The use of cutouts is prohibited except for motorboats competing in an approved race.

A report of accident must be filed by the boat operator with the Division of Motorboats, within 48 hours where there is a death involved; otherwise, within 5 days.

The person operating a motorboat towing a person or persons on water skis, surfboard, or other similar device, must be in a position to observe the person or persons being towed. The towing motorboat must be equipped with a ladder, steps, or similar means by which any person being towed could be taken from the water.

Arrests without a warrant can be made by the director of the Division of Motorboats or his authorized agents, by harbormasters and assistant harbormasters, and by police officers specifically assigned to harbor police, harbor patrol, river, lake, or stream patrol, or harbormaster duties. Such officers may, in the performance of their duties, enter upon and pass through or over private lands and property whether or not covered by water.

> Commonwealth of Massachusetts
> Division of Motorboats
> 100 Nashua Street
> Boston, Mass.

MICHIGAN

Fees:

All motorboats require a number. The fee is $3, and the certificate of number is valid for 3 years. A lost, mutilated, or illegible certificate of number may be replaced, fee $1. Certificate of number for manufacturers or dealers using boats for demonstration or testing, fee $5.

Safety Rules:

The owner of a vessel is personally responsible for damage to life or property resulting from a wake or swell created by the negligent operation of the vessel where the vessel is being operated with the owner's consent.

It is unlawful to operate a vessel while under the influence of intoxicating liquor, narcotic drugs, or barbitals. It is also unlawful for the owner knowingly to authorize or permit such operation.

Towing boats of persons on water skis, water sled, aquaplane, etc., must have two persons, one of whom is competent to observe the progress of the person being towed. If a wide-angle rearview mirror of not less than 170 degrees is used, the use of an observer may be dispensed with. Towing prohibited during the period one hour after sunset to one hour prior to sunrise.

A person who operates a vessel at an immoderate rate of speed or in a careless, reckless, or negligent manner, but not wilfully or wantonly, causes the death of another, is guilty of a misdemeanor, punishable by imprisonment for not more than 2 years or by a fine of not more than $2,000, or both.

The operator of a vessel involved in an accident resulting in injury or death to any person, or property damage of $50 or more, must report such accident as soon as possible to the nearest peace officer, state police post, or the sheriff of the county in which the accident occurred.

> State of Michigan
> Michigan State Waterways Commission
> Lansing 18, Michigan

MINNESOTA

Fees:

All watercraft (except a duck boat during the duck-hunting season, sailboat, canoe, rice boat during the harvest season, and seaplane) must be licensed. Watercraft 16 feet in length or under, fee 75 cents. An additional fee of 25 cents for each foot over 16 feet must be paid. Rented boats, fee 75 cents. Dealer's license, $5 regardless of the number of boats owned by the dealer. Duplicate license, fee 75 cents. Upon sale of boat new owner can obtain a duplicate license. Licenses are valid for a period of 2 years. Numbered boats from out of state have reciprocity for 90 days.

Safety Rules:

Boats should not be operated when loaded with passengers or cargo beyond their safe carrying capacity, or when equipped with any motor or other propulsion machinery beyond their safe power capacity.

Persons are not allowed to ride or sit on the port or starboard gunwales or the decking over the bow of any motorboat less than 26 feet in length while underway, unless the boat is provided with adequate guards or railing.

Towing of persons on water skis, aquaplanes, surfboards, saucers, or similar devices not permitted from one and one-half hours after sunset to sunrise of the following day. The towing boat must have an operator and an observer. A curved rearview mirror or commission-approved safety warning device can be used in lieu of the observer.

Operating a boat in a reckless or grossly negligent manner causing personal injury or property damage, fine $100 or imprisonment of not more than 90 days, or both. If death results, fine $1,000 or imprisonment in state penal institution for not more than 5 years, or in a county jail or workhouse for not more than one year, or both fine and imprisonment in the workhouse or county jail.

Operation of a boat by a person under the influence of intoxicating liquor or narcotic or habit-forming drugs is forbidden.

> State of Minnesota
> Department of Conservation
> Boat Water Safety
> Centennial Office Building
> St. Paul 1, Minnesota

MISSISSIPPI

Fees:

A certificate of number must be obtained for boats propelled by machinery of more than 10 horsepower, fee $1.25. It is valid for 2 years from the anniversary of the date of birth of the applicant next succeeding the issuance of the certificate. Renewal of number, fee $1.25, valid for the next 2 years. Reissue of lost or destroyed certificate of number, fee $1.25.

Safety Rules:

Every vessel must comply with all federal regulations applicable to vessels of each particular class. Mississippi requires every vessel to have on board a

Coast Guard approved life preserver for each person aboard the vessel, a paddle, and during the hours of darkness a light sufficient to make the vessel's presence and location known within a reasonable distance.

Boats towing water skis, aquaplanes, or similar devices, must have two persons aboard; the observer must be more than 10 years of age. No limitation with respect to skiing, aquaplaning, etc., during night hours.

When an accident results in death an accident report must be filed by the boat operator within 48 hours. When personal injury or property damage of more than $100 is involved, the report must be filed within 5 days.

Prohibited is operation of a vessel "in a reckless or negligent manner, or at a rate of speed greater than is reasonable and prudent under the then existing circumstances, or when the operator is physically or mentally incapacitated so as to be incapable of operating such vessel safely or while the operator is under the influence of intoxicating liquor or narcotics, or when such vessel is overloaded beyond its reasonable carrying capacity."

> State of Mississippi
> Game and Fish Commission
> Jackson, Miss.

MISSOURI

Fees:

Every motorboat on the waters of the State of Missouri must be numbered. The fee is $5 and the certificate of registration is valid for 3 years. It can be renewed at the end of that period by filing a new application and paying the $5 fee. Dealer's fee, $10. The registration of a boat expires with the transfer of the boat to another individual. When a person purchases a used boat, he may apply for the number already on that boat, avoiding the necessity of placing another number on the boat. The certificate of registration must be with the boat when the boat is in operation.

Safety Rules:

Prohibited is the operation of any motorboat or vessel or the manipulation of water skis, surfboards, etc., while the operator is intoxicated or under the influence of any narcotic drug, barbiturate, or marijuana.

A vessel towing a person or persons on skis, surfboard, or similar device must have two persons in the boat, unless a ski mirror approved by the Missouri Boat Commission is used, in which case the boat operator alone is sufficient. Water-skiing, surfboarding, etc., is prohibited between one hour after sunset and one hour before sunrise.

The minimum required equipment is that required by the U.S. Coast Guard for the various boat classes.

Report of collision or accident in which death is involved must be made within 48 hours. When there is an accident involving personal injury or property damage in excess of $100 a report must be filed within 5 days.

> State of Missouri
> The Boat Commission
> Boat and Motor Registration
> Jefferson City, Missouri

MONTANA

Fees:

All motorboats of more than 10 horsepower must be numbered. Those below 10 horsepower may be numbered if desired, for purposes of identification and protection. Application for certificate of number may be made to a local license agent (anyone who sells hunting and fishing licenses), fee $3. The certificate of number is valid for 3 years. Upon sale of a numbered boat, the new owner must make a new application and pay the $3 fee. Numbered out-of-state boats are allowed reciprocity for 90 days.

Safety Rules:

Water-skiers being pulled by motorboats must wear a life preserver, buoyant vest, or ring buoy. No skiing, surfboarding, etc., between the hours from one hour after sunset to one hour before sunrise. There is no regulation regarding an observer or wide-angle mirror in the towing boat.

It is prohibited to make a reckless approach to, or passage by, a dock, ramp, diving board, or float. Also prohibited is the operation of a boat at a rate of speed greater than will permit an operator, in the exercise of reasonable care, to bring the vessel to a stop within the assured clear distance ahead.

Operating a boat with passengers or cargo beyond its safe carrying capacity taking into consideration weather and other normal operating conditions is disallowed. Neither can a vessel be equipped with a motor or other propulsion machinery beyond its safe power capacity.

The operator must report immediately any accident involving death, personal injury, or property damage in excess of $100.

> State of Montana
> Department of Fish and Game
> Helena, Montana

NEBRASKA

Fees:

All craft powered by any mechanical device, except seaplanes, must be registered. Fees are paid according to the classification of the boat. Class 1, less than 16 feet and powered by motors of 5 horsepower or less, fee $1. Class 2, less than 16 feet in length and powered by motors totaling more than 5 horsepower, fee $3. Class 3, 16 feet or over and less than 26 feet in length, fee $5. Class 4, 26 feet or over and less than 40 feet in length, fee $10. Class 5, 40 feet or over, fee $20. Class 6, dealers and manufacturers of motorboats, for demonstration purposes, fee $3. The certificate of number is valid for one year and expires on December 31 of each calendar year. Renewal applications can be made until April 1 of the following year. Lost certificate can be duplicated, fee $1. The sale of a boat terminates the number; the new owner must file an application and pay the required fee in order to receive a new number.

Safety Rules:

No one under 14 years of age can lawfully operate a motorboat whether accompanied by an adult or not. Children under 12 years of age are not allowed aboard motorboats without wearing a life preserver. It is unlawful to operate any motorboat or vessel or manipulate any water skis, surfboards, or similar devices while intoxicated or under the influence of any narcotic drug, barbiturate, or marijuana.

In case of accident resulting in death, a report must be filed with the Game Commission within 48 hours; where there is personal injury or property damage in excess of $100, within 5 days.

No towing of skiers, aquaplaners, etc., from the period of one hour after sunset to one hour prior to

57

sunrise. Two persons must be in the towing boat unless a wide-angle rearview mirror is used.

> State of Nebraska
> Game, Forestration and Parks Commission
> State House
> Lincoln 9, Nebraska

NEVADA

Fees:

All motorboats operated on the waters of Nevada must be numbered, fee $5. Numbers issued to manufacturers and dealers may be used interchangeably upon motorboats operated by them for demonstration, sale, or exchange, fee $5. Upon sale of a numbered boat the new owner must file a new application, fee $5. The seller can transfer his registration to another motorboat, fee $2. Duplicate of registration certificate, fee $2. Change of address, fee $1. Certificate of number valid for 3 years. Numbered out-of-state boats have reciprocity for 90 days.

Safety Rules:

Operating a motorboat or vessel or manipulating any water skis, surfboard, or similar device while intoxicated or under influence of any narcotic drug, barbiturate, or marijuana is prohibited.

No person may operate any motorboat or vessel, or manipulate any water skis, surfboard, or similar device in a reckless or negligent manner so as to endanger the life or property of any person.

A boat towing a person on water skis, surfboard, etc., must have two people in the boat, one of whom must be in a position to observe the person being towed. If the waters are not congested a suitable rearview mirror may be used by the boat operator. No

58

skiing, surfboarding, etc., permitted between the hours of one hour after sunset to one hour before sunrise.

Every sheriff and other peace officer may stop and board any vessel subject to the boating regulations to enforce such regulations.

No owner or operator shall knowingly permit loading with passengers or cargo beyond the maximum weight capacity, taking into consideration weather and other conditions.

Marine toilets must have affixed a suitable treatment device. Inadequately treated sewage is not permitted to be discharged into the state waters.

> State of Nevada
> Department of Motor Vehicles
> Carson City, Nevada

NEW JERSEY

Fees:

All power vessels of more than 10 horsepower must be registered. Registration is required for power vessels on tidal and nontidal waters, fee $6. The certificate of number is valid for 3 years. The certificate of number is not transferable. Upon the sale of a numbered boat the new owner files a new application and pays the $6 fee. The fee for the issuance of a duplicate certificate of number is $1. An operator's license must be procured to operate a boat on the nontidal waters of New Jersey. Minimum ages for this license are 16 years for inboard motor vessels and 13 years for outboard motorboats.

Safety Rules:

Power boats towing ski or aquaplane riders must keep at least 100 feet from shore, wharf, pier, bridge structure, abutment, or persons in the water. In passing another boat the towing boat must keep at least 100 feet distant from any other craft. The towing boat must have a crew of at least two persons. Towing lines cannot be longer than 75 feet. Water-skiing or aquaplaning permitted only during the hours between sunrise and sunset.

The minimum equipment for motorboats is as called for by U.S. Coast Guard regulations.

Detachable or outboard motors must be equipped with a muffler.

The boat operator is not permitted to allow any person to ride or sit on the forward decks or gunwales of the vessel, or in any other position on the vessel when in motion, so as to obstruct the view of the operator or endanger the life or limb of any person or persons.

Power vessels cannot be operated on Lake Hopatcong in excess of a speed of 15 m.p.h. between the hours of sunset and sunrise.

Operating a power boat while under the influence of intoxicating liquor or narcotic or habit-forming drugs is prohibited.

> State of New Jersey
> Department of Conservation and
>   Economic Development
> Trenton, New Jersey

NEW MEXICO

Fees:

All motorboats of 10 horsepower or more must be numbered. The fee is $5 and the certificate of number is valid for 3 years. Renewal of certificate of number, fee $2. Upon the sale of a numbered boat, the new owner must file an application and pay the $5 fee. Reciprocity to numbered out-of-state boats for 90 days recognized.

Safety Rules:

Boats towing a person on water skis, surfboard, or similar device must have a person in the vessel in addition to the operator, unless there is in the boat a device capable of letting the operator have an unobstructed view of the person or object towed.

Water-skiing, surfboarding, etc., not permitted between the hours from one hour after sunset to one hour before sunrise.

The boat operator involved in any collision, accident, or other casualty which results in death, personal injury, or property damage in excess of $100 must file a report with the State Park Commission. The boat operator involved in the collision, accident, or other casualty has the duty, so far as he can do so without serious danger to his own vessel, crew, and passengers, to render aid and assistance to other persons affected, so far as is practicable.

Operation of a boat or manipulation of water skis, surfboards, etc., in a reckless or negligent manner so as to endanger life or property, as well as such operation or manipulation while intoxicated or under the influence of any narcotic drug, barbiturate, or marijuana, is prohibited.

State of New Mexico
State Park Commission
P.O. Box 958
Santa Fe, New Mexico

NEW YORK

Fees:

All boats of mechanical propulsion must be registered and certificate of number obtained. Certificates are valid for 3 years. Boats under 16 feet in length, fee $3. Boats 16 feet to 26 feet, fee $6. Boats 26 feet or over in length, $10. Income from the boat fees is earmarked for the New York State boating program. The certificate is not transferable. Upon sale or transfer of ownership the Division of Motor Boats must be notified within 15 days. The new owner can register the boat during this period. Numbered out-of-state boats have reciprocity up to 90 days.

Safety Rules:

Children under 10 years of age may not operate a mechanically propelled vessel unless he or she is the holder of a boating safety certificate or unless accompanied by a person over the age of 14.

Internal combustion engines must be effectively muffled. Cutouts prohibited except in authorized regattas.

It is unlawful to flash searchlights into the eyes of the operator of an approaching vessel.

No vessel shall be operated within 100 feet of the shore, dock, pier, raft, float, or anchored boat at a speed exceeding 5 m.p.h.

Accidents resulting in death must be reported within 48 hours to the Division of Motor Boats. Personal injuries or property damage in excess of $25 must be reported within 7 days.

A boat towing a water-skier must have two persons in it, one to operate the boat and the other to observe the progress and safety of the skier. The observer must be 10 or more years of age. Water-skiing is prohibited from one hour after sunset to one hour after sunrise.

It is forbidden to dump or deposit refuse or offensive matter into navigable waters of the state.

Every boat operator has the duty to give assistance to other vessels in distress whenever possible.

> State of New York
> Division of Motor Boats
> Conservation Department
> New York State Campus
> Albany 1, New York

NORTH CAROLINA

Fees:

All boats operated with any motor or other mechanical type of propulsion of over 10 horsepower must be numbered, fee $3. The certificate of number is valid for one year. With change of ownership a new application form with a fee of $1 must be filed with the Wildlife Resources Commission. A lost certificate can be replaced for 50 cents. Numbered out-of-state boats have reciprocity for 90 days.

Safety Rules:

Internal combustion engines used in motorboats must be equipped with mufflers. Cutouts are prohibited except for motorboats competing in an approved regatta or boat race, and in official trials for speed records, not to exceed 48 hours immediately preceding such regatta or race; and not to exceed 48 hours immediately following such regatta or race.

An accident report must be filed within 10 days following a collision, accident, or other casualty resulting in death or injury to a person or damage to property in excess of $100.

Boats towing persons on skis or surfboards must have a person in addition to the operator in a position to observe the person or persons towed, unless the skier wears a life preserver or unless the boat is equipped with a rearview mirror.

Operating any motorboat or vessel or manipulating any water skis, surfboard, or similar device while intoxicated or under the influence of any narcotic drug, barbiturate, or marijuana is forbidden.

It is prohibited to operate any motorboat or vessel or to manipulate any water skis or surfboard in a reckless or negligent manner so as to endanger the life, limb, or property of any person.

> State of North Carolina
> Wildlife Resources Commission
> Raleigh, North Carolina

NORTH DAKOTA

Fees:

Every motorboat propelled by a motor having 10 horsepower or more must be numbered, fee $3. Certificate of number is valid for 3 years. The number is not transferable. The new owner must register and pay the $3 fee. If the certificate of number is lost it can be replaced at the same cost as a new number. Rental boats are in eight classes, depending on carrying capacity, fee for each boat from $1 to $10. Reciprocity recognized for 90 days for numbered out-of-state boats.

Safety Rules:

Operating a boat in such a manner as to molest or

annoy persons lawfully engaged in fishing is prohibited.

Towing persons on skis or surfboards between the hours from one hour after sunset to one hour before sunrise is not permitted. Water-skiers and surfboarders must wear a life preserver of a type approved by the Game and Fish Department. No person shall operate any vessel or manipulate any towrope or other device in a manner that will cause a water-skier to collide with any other object or person.

Forbidden is the operation of any vessel, water skis, or surfboard while the operator is intoxicated or under the influence of any narcotic drug, barbiturate, or marijuana.

Operation of a motor-driven vessel in any water area designated as a swimming or bathing area is not allowed.

No boat may be loaded over capacity. The formula used to determine capacity is: length of boat times width of boat times depth of boat times .6 divided by 12 and multiplied by 150 equals maximum carrying capacity.

If an accident has resulted in death or injury or property damage in excess of $100 an accident report must be filed with the Game and Fish Department.

> State of North Dakota
> Game and Fish Department
> Bismarck, North Dakota

OHIO

Fees:

Every watercraft operating on the waters of Ohio must be numbered. Rowboat, canoe, barge, outboard hull, fee $1. Sailboat, fee $3. Inboard boat including motor under 100 horsepower, fee $7.50. Inboard boat including motor of 100 horsepower or more, $10. In addition, a fee of 25 cents is charged, and retained, by the issuing agent. Outboard motors used on watercraft on the waters of this state must be separately registered, fee 25 cents. Certificate of number is valid for one year. Duplicate certificates of registration, fee 25 cents.

Safety Rules:

No person is permitted to operate any watercraft if that person is so mentally or physically incapacitated that he is unable to operate the watercraft in a safe or competent manner. No person who is under the influence of alcoholic beverages, narcotic drugs, or opiates is permitted to operate or to be in physical control of any watercraft underway.

Towing boat of persons on water skis, surfboards, or similar devices must have an observer in addition to the operator. The boat cannot tow more than two persons simultaneously, except upon special permit issued. Skiing, surfboarding, etc., not permitted between sunset and sunrise. Riders of skis, surfboards, etc., must wear a lifejacket, lifevest, or lifebelt filled with kapok, styrofoam, or cork.

Mooring or anchoring any watercraft in a designated speed zone or water-ski zone is forbidden. No person shall purposely sever the mooring lines, set adrift, injure, or damage in any manner any watercraft which is moored, docked, or buoyed, or tied up on the waters of the state; or purposely alter, injure, damage, or destroy any buoys, markers, aids, or lights necessary for the safe operation of watercraft upon the waters of the state.

Killing a person unintentionally while violating a boating law is manslaughter in the second degree.

State of Ohio
Department of Natural Resources
Division of Watercraft
1800 West Fifth Ave.
Columbus 12, Ohio

OKLAHOMA

Fees:

Vessels with a motor of 11 horsepower or more must be numbered. Class A, boats of 16 feet or less without a motor, fee $1.50. Class B, boats over 16 feet and less than 26 feet without a motor, fee $2.50. Class C, inboards 26 feet or less in length, fee $7. Class D, inboards over 26 feet, fee $10. Outboard motors 11 horsepower through 14 horsepower, fee $1.50. Outboard motors 15 horsepower or more, fee $2.50. Duplicate licenses, $1. Dealers' licenses, $10. The certificate of number is permanent and it is not transferable. The certificate is valid for 1 year. Numbered out-of-state boats are given reciprocity for a 90-day period.

Safety Rules:

Boats are not permitted to be operated when loaded with passengers or cargo beyond safe capacity.

A vessel towing a person on water skis, surfboard, or similar device must have an observer in addition to the vessel operator unless a rearview mirror is used.

It is prohibited to operate a vessel or manipulate water skis, surfboards, or similar devices in a reckless or negligent manner so as to endanger the life or property of any person. Towing persons on water

67

skis, surfboards, etc., is prohibited between the hours from one hour after sundown to one hour before sunrise.

It is also prohibited to operate any vessel or manipulate any water skis, surfboard, or similar device while under the influence of any narcotic drug, barbiturate, or marijuana.

Boat trailers used on highways must be equipped with two red taillights plainly visible at a distance of 500 feet to the rear, and two red reflectors plainly visible at night from all distances from 300 to 30 feet. If the boat or trailer is of such dimensions that it obscures the stoplight on the towing vehicle, then the trailer must be equipped with one red stoplight and a turn indicator.

> State of Oklahoma
> Oklahoma Planning and Resources Board
> Boat and Motor License Division
> 533 State Capitol Building
> Oklahoma City 5, Oklahoma

OREGON

Fees:

All watercraft of more than 3.5 horsepower and sailboats of 12 feet or more in length must be registered. A certificate of number is valid for 1 year. Motorboats less than 12 feet in length, fee $3; renewal fee, $2. Motorboats and sailboats 12 feet in length or more but less than 16 feet, fee $6; renewal fee $4. Motorboats and sailboats 16 feet in length or more but less than 20 feet, fee $8; renewal fee $6. Motorboats and sailboats 20 feet or more in length, fee $8 plus $1 for each foot or part of a foot in excess of 20 feet in length; renewal fee $6 plus $1 for each foot or part of a foot in excess of 20 feet in length. Dealers' certificates are issued, fee for the first number applied for, $10; for each additional number, fee $2; renewal fee for each number is $2. Oregon issues a certificate of title. A certificate of title is prima facie evidence of the ownership of a boat.

Safety Rules:

The operator of a boat must keep a proper lookout at all times.

A boat towing persons on water skis, aquaplanes, surfboards, saucers, or similar devices must have an observer in addition to the operator unless the boat is equipped with a curved, rearview mirror.

No boat shall be operated nor shall water skis, surfboards, etc., be manipulated by a person or persons under the influence of intoxicating liquor or narcotic drugs or barbital or who is a habitual user of narcotic drugs or barbital.

No boat shall be loaded with passengers or cargo beyond its safe carrying capacity, taking into consideration weather and other normal operating conditions.

Riding or sitting on the gunwales or on the decking over the bow while the boat is under way is prohibited unless the motorboat is provided with adequate guards or railing. Standing on the bow for the purpose of mooring or casting off is permitted.

Towing a boat for skiers, surfboarders, etc., is not allowed from one hour after sunset until one hour before sunrise.

> State of Oregon
> State Marine Board
> Salem 10, Oregon

69

PENNSYLVANIA

Fees:

All motorboats regardless of horsepower or size must be registered. Certificate of registration is valid for one year. Boats of less than 16 feet, fee, $4. Over 16 feet, fee, $6. Certificates can also be issued by the county treasurer or other issuing agent, who can charge and retain an additional fee of 25 cents. Dealer's registration bearing the additional mark "X," fee $5 for the initial set and $5 for each additional set. Valid for one year from April 1 of one year to March 31 of the succeeding year.

Safety Rules:

No person shall operate any vessel in a negligent manner so as to endanger any other person, vessel, or property.

No person shall operate a vessel while intoxicated.

Motorboats must limit speed to a slow, minimum-height-swell speed when within 100 feet of the shoreline, piers, floats, docks, swimmers, and anchored or moored boats, except for skiing floats, which should be 100 feet from shore, and except in zoned ski areas.

The boat towing a person on water skis, aquaplane, or similar device must have at least one competent person in a position to observe the progress of the person being towed unless the boat is equipped with a wide-angle rearview mirror. In shipping channels a second person is required. Ski towropes are not to be more than 80 feet in length. No skiing, aquaplaning, etc., between the hours from one hour after sunset to one hour before sunrise.

No person shall dump, deposit, place, throw, spill, or leave refuse, trash, rubbish, debris, filthy or odorif-

70

erous objects or substances, oil, or gasoline on any waterways or the shorelines of any waterways of the Commonwealth of Pennsylvania.

Overloading a boat with passengers or cargo beyond its safe carrying capacity is prohibited, weather and other existing operating conditions taken into consideration.

> Commonwealth of Pennsylvania
> Pennsylvania Fish Commission
> Watercraft Safety Division
> Harrisburg, Pennsylvania

RHODE ISLAND

Fees:

All motorboats of 65 feet or less and propelled by machinery must be numbered, fee $3. On the sale of a boat the seller transfers the certificate of number to the buyer. The buyer must, within 10 days, apply for a new certificate of number; he may continue to operate the boat under the old certificate for 20 days, fee for new certificate $3. Lost or mutilated certificate replaced, **fee** $2. Numbered out-of-state boat must be recorded if remaining in Rhode Island more than 90 days, fee $3. A certificate of number is valid for 3 years.

Safety Rules:

No boat is to be loaded with passengers or cargo beyond its safe carrying capacity, taking into consideration weather and existing operating conditions.

In any boating accident in which there is loss of life a report must be made within 48 hours. Where there is personal injury causing a person to remain incapacitated for a period in excess of 72 hours or where

71

there is property damage in excess of $100, a report must be filed within 5 days after the accident.

Every internal combustion engine used on a motorboat must be equipped with a muffler. Outboard motors must be equipped with underwater exhausts. Cutouts are prohibited except for use in an approved regatta or boat race.

No person is permitted to operate a motorboat or manipulate any water skis, surfboard, or similar device while intoxicated or under the influence of any narcotic drug, barbiturate, or marijuana. A person arrested under these circumstances has the right to be examined at his own expense immediately after his arrest by a physician selected by him. The arresting officer must inform him of this fact.

Operating a boat or manipulating water skis, surfboards, etc., in a reckless or negligent manner is prohibited.

> State of Rhode Island
> Department of Public Works
> Division of Harbors and Rivers
> Boat Regulation Section
> 100 State Office Building
> Providence 3, R.I.

SOUTH CAROLINA

Fees:

A boat having propulsion machinery of 10 horsepower or more must be numbered, fee $5. The certificate of number is valid for 3 years. Numbered out-of-state boats have reciprocity for 90 days; beyond that the boat must be registered, fee $5. The purchaser of a South Carolina numbered boat can have the registration card transferred to him, fee $1. A lost or destroyed registration card can be replaced, fee $1.

Safety Rules:

The exhaust of every internal combustion engine used on a motorboat must be muffled effectively. Cutouts are prohibited except for boats competing in an approved regatta or boat race.

Boats towing persons on water skis, aquaplanes, or similar devices must have two people in the boat, one of whom shall observe the person or persons towed. The boat can dispense with the observer if it is equipped with a wide-angle rearview mirror mounted in such a manner as to permit the operator of the motorboat to observe the progress of the person or persons being towed. No towing or manipulation of water skis, aquaplanes, etc., between the hours from one hour after sunset to one hour before sunrise. Ski belts or life preservers must be worn by skiers, aquaplaners, etc., except performers and persons holding ratings of first class or higher in the American Water Ski Association.

Peace officers of South Carolina have the authority to enforce the state boating laws and can stop and board any boat subject to it.

In accidents resulting in death an accident report must be filed within 48 hours. In accidents resulting in personal injury or property damage in excess of $100 the accident report must be filed within 72 hours.

> State of South Carolina
> South Carolina Wildlife Resources
> Department
> Boating Division
> P.O. Box 360
> Columbia, S.C.

SOUTH DAKOTA

Fees:

All boats regardless of size, shape, or age which are propelled with a motor of more than 6 horsepower must be numbered, fee $2. Certificate of number is valid for 1 year. A lost or destroyed certificate can be replaced, fee $1. Numbered out-of-state boats have reciprocity for 90 days.

Safety Rules:

A boat operator is responsible for any damage or injury caused by the wake or wash of his boat.

Boats towing persons on water skis, aquaplanes, or similar devices must have two competent persons in the boat or be equipped with a 180-degree wide-angle rearview mirror. Towing of water-skiers, aquaplaners, etc., is not permitted from one hour after sunset until one hour before sunrise.

Every law enforcement officer of the state and its subdivisions has authority to stop and board any vessel to inspect the vessel and its equipment for compliance with the boating law and regulations.

Motorboats must stay clear of safety zones exclusively set up for bathing and swimming.

In the event of an accident which results in personal injury or property damage in excess of $100, the boat operator involved must file an accident report within 15 days.

Closed fuel compartments must be ventilated properly and efficiently.

> State of South Dakota
> Department of Game, Fish and Parks
> State Office Building
> Pierre, South Dakota

TEXAS

Fees:

All motorboats of more than 10 horsepower must be numbered. Class A, boats of less than 16 feet in length, fee $1. Class 1, 16 feet but less than 26 feet in length, fee $5. Class 2, 26 feet but less than 40 feet in length, fee $10. Class 3, 40 feet and over, fee $12.50. The certificate of number is valid for 3 years. The purchaser of a numbered boat can have the certificate of number transferred to him, fee $1. Lost, mutilated, or illegible certificate may be replaced, fee $1. Numbered out-of-state boats are given reciprocity for 90 days. Livery boat operators, fee determined by boat class. Dealers' and manufacturers' certificates of number which can be used for each boat shown, demonstrated, or tested, fee $25.

Safety Rules:

All peace officers of the state have the power and authority to enforce the provisions of the boating law by arrest and taking into custody any person who violates any provision. A person shall not be taken into custody unless he first refuses to sign a promise to appear in court within 30 days.

Whenever a boating accident results in loss of life a written report must be filed by the boat operator within 48 hours. Where personal injury or property damage in excess of $100 is involved a report must be filed in 5 days.

No water skiing, aquaplaning, etc., from the period of one hour after sunset to one hour prior to sunrise. All towing boats shall be operated in a careful and prudent manner and at a reasonable distance from persons and property so as not to endanger the life or property of any person.

75

Operating any vessel or manipulating water skis, aquaplanes, etc., while intoxicated or under the influence of intoxicating liquor, narcotic drugs, barbiturates, or marijuana is prohibited. If convicted, such person is subject to fine of not less than $50 or more than $500, or to imprisonment of not more than 6 months, or both.

> State of Texas
> Texas Highway Department
> Motor Vehicle Division
> 40th and Jackson Avenue
> Austin 14, Texas

UTAH

Fees:

All boats propelled by machinery must be numbered. The fee for a certificate of number is $5 and it applies to all motorboats regardless of size. The certificate of number is valid for one year. If the certificate of number is lost, destroyed, or stolen, a duplicate can be issued, fee $1. If a duplicate sticker is issued the fee is $2. Upon the sale of a numbered boat the buyer can file a new application and a new certificate of number will be issued, fee $1. Numbered out-of-state boats have reciprocity for a period of 90 days.

Safety Rules:

Persons under the age of 16 are not permitted to operate a motorboat except when accompanied by a responsible adult experienced in motorboat operation.

Operating a vessel or manipulating water skis, aquaplanes, etc., in a reckless or negligent manner so as to endanger the life, limb, or property of any person is prohibited.

It is forbidden to operate a vessel or manipulate water skis, aquaplanes, etc., while intoxicated or under the influence of any narcotic drug, barbiturate, or marijuana.

The owner of a vessel is liable for injury or damage occasioned by the negligent operation of the vessel by a minor under the age of 18 years who operates it with the express or implied consent of the owner.

An accident report must be filed by the boat operator; where death is involved, within 48 hours, where there is personal injury or property damage in excess of $100, within 5 days.

Towing boat pulling water-skiers, aquaplaners, etc., must have an operator and an observer. If a suitable wide-angle rearview mirror is used the observer can be dispensed with. No skiing or aquaplaning between one hour after sunset and one hour before sunrise. Skiers, aquaplaners, etc., must wear a life preserver, ski belt, ski suit, or other flotation device.

> State of Utah
> State Park & Recreation Commission
> Boating Division
> Room 256–U.P. Annex Building
> 19 West South Temple
> Salt Lake City, Utah

VERMONT

Fees:

All boats with a motor operating on the waters of the state must be numbered. Class A, less than 16 feet in length, fee $2.50. Class 1, 16 feet or over and less than 26 feet in length, fee $5. Class 2, 26 feet or over and less than 40 feet in length, fee $10. Class 3, 40 feet or over, fee $25. Dealers' certificate of number, first number applied for, fee $25; each additional number, fee $5. Upon sale of a boat, the seller may register in his own name another motorboat of the same class, fee $1. Certificate of number is valid for 1 year. Numbered out-of-state boats have reciprocity recognition for 90 days.

Safety Rules:

Towing boats are not permitted to tow a person or persons on water skis or a surfboard unless the person towed wears a life preserver or a lifebelt. It is prohibited to tow a person on water skis, surfboard, etc., within 100 feet of a person swimming, or a canoe, rowboat, or other light craft conveying any person.

In the event of an accident, collision, or other casualty resulting in death, injury, or property damage in excess of $100, an accident report must be made within 36 hours.

Operating a boat while under the influence of intoxicating liquor, narcotic drugs, or barbiturates is not permitted.

Prohibited is the operation of a motorboat within 200 feet of the shores of a bathing beach or other recreational spot, or approach within 100 feet of a person swimming, or a canoe, rowboat, or other light craft conveying any person, except at a speed of 5 m.p.h.

Every internal combustion engine used on any motorboat must be effectively muffled. Cutouts prohibited except for boats competing in a regatta or an approved race.

A boat shall not be loaded with passengers or cargo beyond its safe carrying capacity, taking into consideration weather and other existing operating conditions.

> State of Vermont
> Department of Public Safety
> Marine Division
> Montpelier, Vermont

VIRGINIA

Fees:

All boats on Virginia's waters with propulsion of 10 horsepower or more must be numbered, fee $5. The certificate of number is valid for 3 years. Dealer's certificate of number, fee $15. Manufacturer's certificate of number, fee $25. Upon change of ownership the purchaser must file for a new certificate of number, fee $5. If a certificate has been lost a new one will be issued, fee 50 cents. Additional certificates of number for manufacturer, $8; for dealer, $8. Numbered out-of-state boats recognized and given reciprocity for 90 days.

Safety Rules:

The towing boat pulling water skiers, surfboarders, etc., must have two persons one of whom shall observe the person or persons towed. If the person or persons towed are wearing life preservers the observer can be dispensed with. Skiing, surfboarding, etc., is not permitted between the hours from one hour after sunset to one hour before sunrise. No person shall operate or manipulate any vessel, towrope, or other device by which the direction or location of water skis, a surfboard, or similar device may be affected or controlled, in such a way that would cause the water skis, surfboard, or similar device, or any person thereon to collide with any object or person.

In case of death or damage in excess of $1,500, the accident must be reported immediately. A report of accident must be filed by the boat operator within 72 hours where there has been personal injury or property damage in excess of $100. The boat operator is required to render assistance to other persons affected by the accident as may be practical and necessary in

79

order to save them or minimize any danger resulting from the accident.

Operating a boat or manipulating water skis, surfboards, etc., while intoxicated or under the influence of any narcotic drug, barbiturate, or marijuana is prohibited. Such person may be found guilty of a misdemeanor and punished for such.

Commonwealth of Virginia
Commission of Game and Inland
        Fisheries
Box 1642
Richmond 13, Virginia

VIRGIN ISLANDS

Fees:

All motorboats must be numbered. Class A, less than 16 feet in length, fee $5. Class 1, 16 feet or over but less than 26 feet, fee $15. Class 2, 26 feet or over but less than 40 feet, fee $25. Class 3, 40 feet or more in length, fee $35. Certificate of number valid for 3 years. With change of ownership of a numbered boat the purchaser must make new application and pay the required fee. Numbered out-of-state boats have reciprocity for 90 days.

Safety Rules:

Operation of any vessel or the manipulation of water skis, surfboard or similar device while intoxicated or under the influence of any narcotic drug, barbiturate, or marijuana is prohibited. Operation of such vessel or water skis, surfboards, etc., in a reckless or negligent manner so as to endanger the life or property of of any person is also prohibited.

The owner of a boat livery must keep a record of the name and address of the person or persons hiring a vessel; the identification number of the boat; the departure date and time, and the expected time of return. The record must be kept for at least 6 months.

No water-skiing, surfboarding, etc., between the hours from one hour after sunset to one hour before sunrise. The towing boat must have at least two persons in it of whom at least one shall observe the progress of the person or persons being towed.

In case of collision, accident, or other casualty involving death, personal injury, or property damage in excess of $100, an accident report must be filed. In death cases the report must be filed within 48 hours; in the other instances, within 5 days.

> Department of Commerce
> St. Thomas
> Virgin Islands

WEST VIRGINIA

Fees:

Every boat propelled by machinery must be numbered, fee $5. The certificate of number is valid for 1 year. If a numbered boat has been sold the purchaser must file a new application form and fee of $5; a new certificate of number will be issued. Numbered out-of-state boats have reciprocity for 90 days.

Safety Rules:

It is forbidden to operate a pleasure vessel within 20 feet of the exterior boundary of a water area which is clearly marked by buoys, or some other distinguishing device, as a bathing or swimming area. Also forbidden is the operation of a vessel without permission within 20 feet of a person engaged in fishing, unless unavoidable.

Boats should not be loaded with passengers or cargo beyond safe carrying capacity, taking into consideration weather and other normal operating conditions. Boats should not be equipped with any motor or other propulsion machinery beyond safe power capacity, taking into consideration the type and configuration of the boats and other existing operating conditions.

Operators of boats involved in a collision, accident, or other casualty must file an accident report. In death cases, within 48 hours; personal injury or property damages of more than $100, within 5 days.

Skiers being pulled by motorboats must have on their person a life preserver, buoyant vest, or ring buoy. Water-skiing, surfboarding, etc., forbidden between the hours from one hour after sunset to one hour before sunrise. Two persons must be in the towing boat, one acting as an observer, unless a wide-angle rearview mirror is mounted on the boat.

Operating a boat or manipulating water skis, surfboards, etc., while intoxicated or under the influence of any narcotic drug, barbiturate, or marijuana is forbidden.

> State of West Virginia
> West Virginia Department of
> Natural Resources
> Motorboat License Section
> State Office Building No. 1
> Washington Street East
> Charleston, West Virginia

WISCONSIN

Fees:

All boats propelled by machinery must be numbered, fee $3. Certificate of number is valid for 3 years.

Livery boats, fee $5 plus 50 cents per boat. Lost or destroyed certificate may be duplicated, fee $1. Upon sale of a numbered boat the purchaser pays a fee of $1 if the certificate is issued for the remainder of the numbering period for which the previous certificate was issued. Numbered out-of-state boats have reciprocity for 90 days.

Safety Rules:

No person shall operate a motorboat at a speed greater than is reasonable and prudent under the conditions and having regard for the actual and potential hazards then existing. On Brule River or any of its tributaries in Douglas County, speed limit, 8 m.p.h. Waupaca Chain o' Lakes, located in the towns of Farmington and Dayton in Waupaca County, 15 m.p.h.

It is prohibited to operate a motorboat so as to approach or pass another boat in such a manner as to create a hazardous wake or wash. The operator of a motorboat is liable for any damage caused to another person or to property by the wake or wash, unless the negligence of the other person was the primary cause of the damage.

Operating a boat by going in a circular course repeatedly around another boat or around any person who is swimming, if the circular course is within 200 feet of such boat or swimmer, is prohibited.

Riding or sitting on the gunwales or the decking over the bow while the boat is under way is not permitted, except for the purpose of anchoring, mooring, or casting off.

It is unlawful to operate a boat while under the influence of an intoxicant or a narcotic drug.

No person shall unnecessarily sound a horn, whistle, or other sound-producing device on any boat while at anchor or under way.

83

Overloading a boat with passengers and cargo beyond its safe carrying capacity or equipping its propulsion machinery beyond its safe power capacity is not permitted.

> State of Wisconsin
> Wisconsin Conservation Department
> Box 450
> Madison 1, Wisconsin

WYOMING

Fees:

Every motorboat powered by a motor of more than 5 horsepower must be numbered. Class A, less than 16 feet in length, fee $1.50. Class B, 16 feet or over and less than 26 feet, fee $2. Class C, 26 feet or over and less than 40 feet, fee $3. Class D, 40 feet or over, fee $4. Certificate of number is valid for one year and expires on December 31 each year. The purchaser of a numbered boat can have the certificate of number transferred to him, fee $1. A lost, mutilated, or illegible certificate can be replaced, fee $1. Manufacturers or dealers can receive a certificate of number, fee $3 for each registration. Numbered out-of-state boats have reciprocity for 90 days; those remaining beyond that time must be registered.

Safety Rules:

One operating a watercraft in a careless or heedless manner so as to be grossly indifferent to the person or property of others; or at a rate of speed greater than will permit, in the exercise of reasonable care, the bringing of the watercraft to a stop within the assured clear distance ahead, is guilty of the crime of careless operation and subject to a fine of not more than $100 or imprisonment of not more than 30 days, or both. Reckless operation is punishable by a fine of not more than $500 or imprisonment of not more than 6 months, or both. Operating any watercraft at an immoderate rate of speed or in a careless or negligent manner which causes the death of another is criminal homicide and punishable by imprisonment of not more than 2 years or a fine of not more than $1,000, or both.

Watercraft shall not be equipped with a motor or other propulsion machinery beyond its safe power capacity.

Operating any watercraft while under the influence of intoxicating liquor or narcotic or habit-forming drugs is forbidden.

Operators of boats of 26 feet or less in length shall not allow any persons to sit on gunwales or on the decking over the bow while underway unless the motorboat is provided with adequate guards or railings. Occupying the decking while mooring, allowed.

Two persons must occupy towing boat for water-skiing, aquaplaning, etc., unless the boat is equipped with a wide-angle rearview mirror. No water-skiing, aquaplaning, etc., between the period of one hour after sunset to one hour prior to sunrise.

> State of Wyoming
> Wyoming Game and Fish Commission
> P.O. Box 378
> Cheyenne, Wyoming

NONFEDERAL SYSTEMS

There are a few remaining states which have not come within the regulatory system as set out in the Federal Motorboat Act of 1958. They are as follows:

ALASKA

Alaska does not have a boat numbering system.

85

There is no requirement with respect to reporting an accident on the inland and territorial waters of this state. Accidents on the navigable waters of the United States must be reported, within 48 hours in death cases and within 5 days in cases involving property damage in excess of $100 or incapacitation in excess of 72 hours, to the nearest U. S. Coast Guard marine inspection office.

Boat trailers are licensed, fee $4, expiring on March 1 of each year. Nonresidents can use their licensed trailers without registration for a period of 90 days. Directional signals required on trailers manufactured after January 1, 1958. Speed limit, 50 m.p.h. Dimensional limits of trailer: 60 feet overall length of towing vehicle and trailer; 12½ feet high; 8 feet wide. Trailers of more than 1,500 pounds gross weight require brakes if manufactured after January 1, 1958. Trailers of 3,000 pounds or more gross weight also require brakes if manufactured before January 1, 1958. All trailers require reflector, stoplights, and taillight mounted at extreme rear.

HAWAII

Fees:

All boats except rowboats, nonpowered sailboats, and boats registered by the United States Coast Guard must be registered. The registration fee and the fee for renewal is $2.50. Persons who operate nonregistered boats on the shore waters of Hawaii are subject to a fine of not more than $1,000. Purchased vessels must be re-registered by the new owner.

Reciprocity for 90 days is given to transient boats visiting Hawaii.

Safety Rules:

It is a crime to endanger life, limb, or property of

another by operating a motorboat in a reckless or negligent manner. Conviction of reckless operation is punishable by a fine of not more than $1,000.

Speed limits: 10 knots for sampans, launches, motorboats, and other small craft in Honolulu Harbor inside of Sand Point Light, Kapalama Basin, and Kewalo Basin. 3 m.p.h. in the harbor area and 6 m.p.h. in the channel of Ala Wai boat harbor. 5 m.p.h. within 50 feet of the west shore of Sand Island in Keehi Lagoon, Honolulu Harbor. 5 m.p.h. in any shore waters where a greater speed would endanger swimmers. Regulations pertaining to harbors, and orders of harbor masters, superintendents, and wharfingers and federal rules and regulations to have precedence over this speed limit.

Discharging garbage, refuse, excreta, or other foul or deleterious matter into the Ala Wai canal, Ala Wai boat harbor or channel, or into any harbor or shore waters is prohibited. All vessels maintained as residences must be equipped with a toilet in working condition. All toilets (except on out-of-state boats visiting for a period of not more than 60 days) to be equipped with a sewage ejector chlorinator.

There is no requirement to report an accident on state territorial waters. Accidents on the navigable waters of the United States must be reported, within 48 hours in death cases and within 5 days in cases involving property damage in excess of $100 or incapacitation in excess of 72 hours, to the nearest United States Coast Guard marine inspection office.

> State of Hawaii
> Department of Transportation
> Harbors Division
> P.O. Box 397
> Honolulu 9, Hawaii

NEW HAMPSHIRE

Fees:

On nontidal waters of the state, outboard motors up to and including 5 horsepower, fee $3. From 5.1 horsepower to 13.9 horsepower, fee $4. Outboards of 14 horsepower and over, fee $5. Inboard motorboats of up to and including 18 feet, fee $5. Over 18 feet but not more than 26 feet, fee $8. Over 26 feet, fee $10. All fees are on a one-year basis. The Coast Guard numbers all boats of over 10 horsepower principally used on navigable waters, fee $3 for 3 years.

Safety Rules:

Operating any motorboat or vessel while intoxicated or under the influence of any narcotic drug, barbiturate, or marijuana is prohibited.

The operation of power boats and outboard motors is prohibited on Lucas Pond in the Town of Northwood, Lake Whittemore in the Town of Bennington, and Abbot Forest Pond in the Town of Stoddard. Houseboats are barred on Squam Lake.

Boats capable of a speed of 25 miles per hour or more shall not be operated by any person under 12 years of age.

A towing boat used in water-skiing, aquaplaning, etc., must have a second person as observer who must be at least 12 years of age. Water-skiing, aquaplaning, etc., shall not take place between one-half hour after sunset and one-half hour before sunrise. A state permit is required for placing a water-ski jump on the public waters of the state.

Marine toilets must be equipped with suitable treatment device to disinfect human wastes before discharge into the waters of the state.

Wilful removal, destruction, or injury to any beacon,

floating guide, or other light placed
public waters of the state for navigatio
ing to any vessel, boat, scow, or raft, i

TENNESSEE

Fees:

A boat numbering system does not exist in Tennessee.

Safety Rules:

There is no requirement that accidents be reported when occurring on the nonnavigable waters of the state. Accidents on the navigable waters of the United States must be reported, within 48 hours in death cases and within 5 days in cases involving property damage in excess of $100 or incapacitation in excess of 72 hours, to the nearest United States Coast Guard marine inspection office.

Water-skiing is prohibited during the period from one hour after sunset to one hour before sunrise. A violation is punishable by a fine of not more than $50 plus court costs.

For operating a motorboat with a cutout or an unmuffled exhaust, a fine of not more than $50 plus costs will be imposed.

Operating a motorboat in a reckless or negligent manner is punishable by a fine of not more than $50 plus costs.

Overloading a boat with passengers or cargo beyond its safe carrying capacity, taking into consideration the weather and existing operating conditions, is prohibited, and is punishable by a fine of not more than $50 plus court costs.

Operating a boat or manipulating water skis, a surfboard, or similar device while intoxicated or under the influence of a narcotic drug, barbiturate, or marijuana, is forbidden. A violation is subject to a fine of not more than $50 plus court costs.

WASHINGTON

Fees:

Washington does not regulate recreational boating. Local units of government, especially the county governments, have ordinances pertaining to pleasure boats. Boats used on nonnavigable state territorial waters are not subject to numbering by the state.

Boats of over 10 H.P. operating on the navigable waters of the United States continue to be numbered by the Coast Guard, fee $3, valid for 3 years.

Safety Rules:

There is no requirement to report an accident on state territorial waters. Accidents on the navigable waters of the United States must be reported within 48 hours in death cases and within 5 days in cases involving property damage in excess of $100 or incapacitation in excess of 72 hours, to the nearest United States Coast Guard marine inspection office.

3

boat safety and accident prevention

Introduction

The application of common sense is the most important aspect in operating your boat safely. All of mankind's laws, rules, and regulations come to naught if the use of simple common sense is missing. It is well known that the most frequent causes of boat accidents are carelessness and the failure to use common sense. We are all too prone to think that accidents will happen to the other fellow. Whether it is egotism or our natural optimism, the fact remains that almost everyone feels instinctively that the lessons to be learned in boat safety have particular meaning for the careless and accident-prone individual and, of course, that is the well-known "other guy."

Let me be the first to say that I am no exception. Many years ago, I made my first ocean cruise on a large and beautiful ocean liner. On the first morning after sailing, we passengers had been told that a fire and boat drill would be held on the boat deck. We were all to assemble at our designated stations and were expected to wear the life preservers provided in each cabin. It was not long before the "wise" and experienced passengers sent the word along that only neophytes and dopes would be wearing life preservers. Since I did not wish to be placed in either category, I attended the lifeboat drill sans jacket and sans common sense. With the wisdom of afteryears I've learned to appreciate the fact that the life preserver is the passengers' and the sailors' best friend. Innumerable boating accidents—literally in the thousands—which have resulted in deaths by drowning could have meant lives saved had life preservers been worn. Today I will never board a boat or vessel without ascertaining first the location of life preservers and assuring myself that they are readily at hand in the event of trouble.

Boating is a safe recreational sport so long as the need for safety is constantly kept in mind. There are many hazards faced in land and air transportation. There are hazards of other kinds involved in water transportation. If your auto runs out of gas, the car gradually comes to a halt. You can leave the car and make the necessary arrangements to secure fuel. If you are careless enough to leave the dock or harbor with an insufficient quantity of fuel for the journey ahead of you, the consequence of "running out of gas" can be dire. A fire in an automobile can be a serious affair, but you will usually have ample opportunity to step out of the car into relative safety. A boat fire, on the other hand, is generally extremely dangerous. If at sea it may mean going overboard, and although the absence of a life preserver may not place you in a hopeless situation, your chances of survival would be far greater *with* one. In the course of this chapter there will be many illustrations given of boating accidents, some of which could have been prevented by the simple expedients of ordinary thoughtfulness, precaution, and the use of common or "horse" sense. It may well be that the advice regarding safety precautions will be forgotten; I doubt that you will forget these many tragic accidents.

Motorboat Classes

All motorboats are divided into four classes according to length under the Motorboat Act of 1940. [46 United States Code §§ 526 et seq.]

The word "motorboat" as used in this Act means any vessel 65 feet in length or less which is propelled by machinery. Excepted are tugboats and towboats propelled by steam. A "motorboat" includes any boat temporarily or permanently equipped with a detachable motor or one propelled by steam. Therefore, outboard motors would be included in these classes.

The classes are:

Class A—Any motorboat less than 16 feet in length.

Class 1—Any motorboat 16 feet or over and less than 26 feet in length.

Class 2—Any motorboat 26 feet or over and less than 40 feet in length.

Class 3—Any motorboat 40 feet or over and less than 65 feet in length.

Length is measured from "end to end over the deck excluding sheer." "End to end over the deck" is that measurement taken parallel to the centerline from the foremost part of the vessel to the aftermost part of the vessel. The length is not measured from the outside of the hull plating or planking. Neither are extensions outside of the hull, such as the bowsprit, included.

The requirements with respect to equipment lights are directly related to these classes.

Classes A to 3 of motorboats include the auxiliary sailboat equipped with a motor, provided it is not in commercial service and not more than 65 feet in length.

Recreational sailboats not carrying paying passengers do not come under the regulation of required equipment as do motor-powered boats.

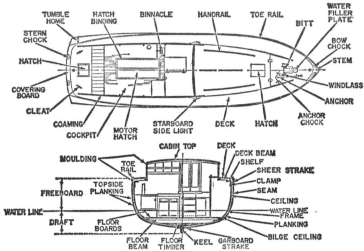

Top View and Cross Section of Typical Wood Inboard

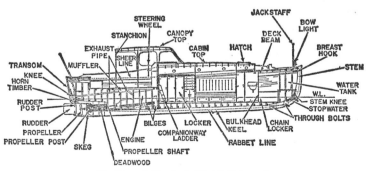

Profile of Typical Wood Inboard

Required Equipment

All motorboats in the classes previously described are required by the Motorboat Act of 1940 [46 United

94

States Code §§ 526 et seq.] to have certain essential equipment installed and present at all times. Because this equipment is required by law, it is sometimes referred to as "legal equipment" and "government equipment."

The equipment is as follows:

Class A: Up to 16 feet

Backfire Flame Arrestor: One approved device on each carburetor of all gasoline engines, except outboard motors.

Lifesaving Devices: One Coast Guard-approved life preserver, buoyant vest, ring buoy, or buoyant cushion for each person on board.

Lights: A combination light in the forepart of the boat, showing red to port and green to starboard from right ahead to two points abaft abeam, visible for one mile. Stern light: A bright white light aft showing all around the horizon, visible for at least 2 miles.

Ventilation: At least two ventilators fitted with cowls or their equivalent, capable of removing gases from the bilge in every engine and fuel tank compartment on boats constructed or decked over after April 25, 1940, using gasoline or other fuel of a flashpoint less than 110° F.

Fire Extinguishers: At least one B–I type Coast Guard-approved, hand-portable fire extinguisher. The fire extinguisher is not required on outboard motorboats of less than 26 feet in length and of open construction. The approved types of fire extinguishers are: carbon dioxide; dry chemical (cartridge-operated or stored pressure); foam. Toxic vaporizing-liquid types of fire extinguishers, such as those containing

95

carbon tetrachloride or chlorobromomethane, have not been acceptable since January 1, 1962, as required approved extinguishers.

Bell: None required; however, the "Rules of the Road" require the sounding of proper signals.

Whistle: None required; however, the "Rules of the Road" require the sounding of proper signals.

Class 1: 16 feet to less than 26 feet

The regulations pertaining to Class 1 motorboats are the same as those in Class A, with the exception of the regulations regarding the whistle. Class 1 motorboats require a hand-, mouth-, or power-operated whistle or horn to be audible at least one-half mile.

Class 2: 26 feet to less than 40 feet

Backfire Flame Arrestor: One approved device on each carburetor of all gasoline engines, except outboard motors.

Lifesaving Devices: One Coast Guard-approved life preserver, buoyant vest, ring buoy, or buoyant cushion for each person on board.

Lights:
Port Side Light: One on port side properly screened to show red from right ahead to two points abaft abeam, and visible at least one mile.

Starboard Side Light: One on starboard side properly screened to show green from right ahead to two points abaft abeam, and visible at least one mile.

Stern Light: One bright white light aft, showing all around the horizon, visible at least 2 miles.

Ventilation: At least two ventilators fitted with

cowls or their equivalent, capable of removing gases from the bilge in every engine and fuel tank compartment on boats constructed or decked over after April 25, 1940, using gasoline or other fuel of a flashpoint less than 110° F.

Fire Extinguishers: At least two B–I Coast Guard-approved, hand-portable fire extinguishers; OR at least one B–II type Coast Guard-approved, hand-portable fire extinguisher. (This is required when there is NO fixed fire-extinguishing system installed in the machinery spaces.) If the boat contains a fixed fire-extinguishing system installed in the machinery spaces, then the equipment required calls for at least one B–I type Coast Guard-approved, hand-portable fire extinguisher.

NOTE: B–I and B–II are symbols used to designate different capacity and contents of fire extinguishers. B–I fire extinguishers contain: foam, 1¼ to 2½ gallons; carbon dioxide, 4 to 15 pounds; dry chemical, 2 to 10 pounds. B–II type fire extinguishers contain: foam, 2¼ gallons; carbon dioxide, 15 pounds; dry chemical, 10 to 20 pounds.

Bell: One which, when struck, produces a clear bell-like tone with full round characteristics.

Whistle: One hand- or power-operated, and audible at least one mile.

Class 3: 40 feet to not more than 65 feet.

Backfire Flame Arrestor: One approved device on each carburetor of all gasoline engines, except outboard motors.

Lifesaving Devices: One Coast Guard-approved lifesaver or ring buoy for each person on board. Buoyant

97

cushions or buoyant vests do not meet the requirements on Class 3 boats.

Lights:

Port Side Light: One on port side properly screened to show red from right ahead to two points abaft abeam, and visible at least one mile.

Starboard Side Light: One on starboard side properly screened to show green from right ahead to two points abaft abeam, and visible at least one mile.

Stern Light: One bright white light aft, showing all around the horizon, visible at least 2 miles.

Ventilation: At least two ventilators fitted with cowls or their equivalent, capable of removing gases from the bilge in every engine and fuel tank compartment on boats constructed or decked over after April 25, 1940, using gasoline or other fuel of a flashpoint less than 110° F.

Fire Extinguishers: At least three B–I type Coast Guard-approved, hand-portable fire extinguishers; OR at least one B–I type PLUS one B–II type Coast Guard-approved hand extinguisher. (This equipment is required when NO fixed fire-extinguishing system is installed in machinery spaces.)

Where a fixed fire-extinguishing system is installed in machinery spaces, the requirements call for at least two B–II type Coast Guard-approved, hand-portable fire extinguishers; OR at least one B–II type Coast Guard-approved, hand-portable fire extinguisher.

Bell: One which, when struck, produces a clear bell-like tone with full round characteristics.

Whistle: One hand- or power-operated, and audible at least one mile.

TABLE I.

MINIMUM EQUIPMENT REQUIRED UNDER FEDERAL LAW

EQUIPMENT	CLASS 4 (Less than 16 feet)	CLASS 1 (16 feet to less than 26 feet)	CLASS 2 (26 feet to less than 40 feet)	CLASS 3 (40 feet to not more than 65 feet)
BACK-FIRE FLAME ARRESTOR	One approved device on each carburetor of all gasoline engines installed after April 25, 1940, except outboard motors.			
VENTILATION	At least two ventilators fitted with cowls or their equivalent for the purpose of properly and efficiently ventilating the bilges of every engine and fuel-tank compartment of boats constructed or decked over after April 25, 1940, using gasoline or other fuel of a flashpoint less than 110° F.			
BELL	None.*	None.*	One, which when struck, produces a clear, bell-like tone of full round characteristics.	
LIFESAVING DEVICES	One approved life preserver, buoyant vest, ring buoy, or buoyant cushion for each person on board.			One approved life preserver or ring buoy for each person on board.
WHISTLE	None.*	One hand, mouth, or power operated, audible at least ½ mile.	One hand or power operated, audible at least 1 mile.	One power operated, audible at least 1 mile.
FIRE EXTINGUISHER—PORTABLE — When NO fixed fire extinguishing system is installed in machinery space(s).	At least One B-I type approved hand portable fire extinguisher. (Not required on outboard motorboat less than 26 feet in length and of open construction.)		At least Two B-I type approved hand portable fire extinguishers; OR At least One B-II type approved hand portable fire extinguisher.	At least Three B-I type approved hand portable fire extinguishers; OR At least One B-I type *Plus* One B-II type approved hand portable fire extinguisher.
When fixed fire extinguishing system is installed in machinery space(s).	None.	None.	At least One B-I type approved hand portable fire extinguisher.	At least Two B-I type approved hand portable fire extinguishers; OR At least One B-II type approved hand portable fire extinguisher.

B-I Type Approved HAND PORTABLE FIRE EXTINGUISHERS contain: Foam, 1¼ up to 2½ gallons; or Carbon Dioxide, 4 up to 15 pounds; or Dry Chemical, 2 up to 10 pounds.
B-II Type Approved HAND PORTABLE FIRE EXTINGUISHERS contain: Foam, 2½ gallons; or Carbon Dioxide, 15 pounds; or Dry Chemical, 10 up to 20 pounds.

*NOTE.—Not required by the Motorboat Act of 1940; however, the "Rules of the Road" require these vessels to sound proper signals.

Outboard Motorboats

With the exception of the requirements for the back-fire flame arrestors and for ventilation, outboard motorboats must meet the same requirements regarding safety equipment that pertain to the general classes of motorboats of identical length. Outboard motorboats of less than 26 feet in length and of open construction,

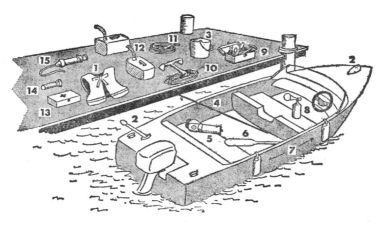

Safety Check List

(Nebraska Game, Forestation and Parks Commission)

1. Approved lifesaving device for each person
2. Proper lighting (if operated at night)
3. Bailing bucket
4. Boat hook
5. Fire extinguisher
6. Paddle or oars
7. Fenders
8. Horn or whistle
9. Tool kit
10. Anchor
11. Line
12. Emergency gasoline supply
13. First-aid kit
14. Flashlight
15. Bilge pump

and not carrying fare-paying passengers, are not required to carry fire extinguishers.

Other Equipment

The items of equipment listed in the preceding section constitute the bare legal minimum requirements. Good safety planning requires the anticipation of difficulties which may be encountered and the means and methods of overcoming them.

Safe boating can be the rule. Whatever mishap occurs can be minimized if the proper equipment is readily at hand. Even a well-built boat may leak a little. Your boat should have a bailing device, either a good hand pump (one capable of throwing 15 or 20 gallons per minute), a motor-driven or electric pump, or a bailing bucket.

Flares in a watertight container to summon help when in distress are a necessity.

A first-aid kit, the 10- to 20-unit type, is a must. A good kit should contain one-inch adhesive bandages; 3" x 3" sterile gauze squares; one-inch and two-inch roller bandages; an ointment for treating burns; aromatic spirits of ammonia; triangular bandages; mild iodine; nonelastic tourniquet; etc. Accompanying the kit should be a first-aid manual.

Other items of equipment are:

One or more flashlights for use after dark. They are invaluable for picking out shore contours, buoys, and boat landings in the dark.

A serviceable bucket for firefighting and for bailing.

Mooring lines for bow and stern. Breast lines for the larger boats.

A good supply of fresh water and emergency rations. (Canned food, pilot biscuits, balanced liquid foods, etc.)

An anchor or anchors, depending upon the size of the boat. The type of bottom in the waters on which you use your boat must be considered in choosing an anchor. It should be one that holds well and can be stored easily. The anchor line should be either good manila or nylon, and should be at least 6 to 8 times as long as the depth of any water in which you will anchor.

The above items are regarded as essential equipment. Other suggested items are: a kit of tools and spare engine parts, spare batteries, light list (a listing of lights to aid you in navigation), fenders, compass, boathook, sounding line, local charts, extra supply of motor oil and grease, heaving line, etc.

Overloading

Never crowd your boat with passengers. Overloading is one of the most serious breaches of boat safety. Your boat is designed to carry a safe load of passengers and gear. In most instances the manufacturer has stamped the load capacity into a plate and affixed it to the boat. Good judgment should be exercised in connection with the look and "feel" of the boat after it has been loaded. If it looks or feels overloaded, then the chances are that it is. Watch the freeboard! (That part of the boat's side which is "free" of the water—in other words, which is not submerged.) The more weight that is added to the boat the deeper she will settle in the water. Allowance should be made for any peculiar design characteristics of the boat; weather conditions; the kind of waters where the boat is expected to go; and any unusual circumstances, as choppy seas, large wake, etc.

The weight of the passengers and gear should be evenly distributed so that the boat may be made trim. When the boat is in motion the passengers should be seated and should avoid walking about. In small boats they should move low, using the gunwales for support, and avoid standing up while the boat is in motion.

In one case two men and their two adult sons departed on a fishing trip in a 14½-foot boat with a 25-horsepower motor. The four weighed over 800 pounds. In addition, the boat was weighted down with the motor, fishing gear and other equipment. The freeboard was about 5 inches. Shortly after setting out, the wind rose and the water became choppy. Although the waves were not high, the water came over the bow. The boat sank and two of the party were drowned. Life preservers were not worn even though they were available.

102

In another case, seven people, together with considerable gear consisting of an extra outboard motor, camp stove, food, camping equipment, guns, etc., crowded into a 14-foot outboard. The boat's freeboard was only 2 inches. Needless to say, sailing in a boat with a freeboard clearance of only 2 inches is reckless and sheer stupidity. Obviously the boat either capsized or was swamped. No one wore life preservers. All were drowned.

A boatowner had recently acquired a 28-foot Baby Gar speedboat, capable of doing 40 miles per hour. He was giving rides to members of the American Legion, who were picnicking. His boat had a rated capacity of 10 persons. He took 18 individuals aboard, several of them children. The seats were filled. Two men were sitting or lying on top of the cab. The owner took the boat across the bar into the open ocean for about one-half mile. On the return, the boat capsized with loss of life. Experts testified that with such overloading affecting the center of gravity, the boat was liable to capsize with the slightest provocation, such as shifting the helm at high speed or by the action of waves in the open sea. The owner was held liable for his negligent operation. [Calanchini v Bliss, 88 F2d 82, 1937 AMC 203, CCA9th 1937.]

Changing your outboard motor for a more powerful one means an increase of weight, with the patent possibility of overloading. The effect of increasing horsepower is illustrated in a recent government publication. The author stated:

"One of the important variables is the size engine a boat carries. The popularity of water skiing has created a demand for more powerful engines than many boats are intended for. If we ignore the question of horsepower and think only of the engine's weight, we

103

find that the combined engine and fuel weight for engines less than 25 hp., runs about 125 pounds. Above that point, although the weight per horsepower declines, the larger engine uses more fuel—we go farther faster—and another fuel tank is acquired, adding another 50 pounds. Get beyond 60 hp., and we need a battery to start the engine, another 65 pounds. By now, all told we are up to 300–400 pounds or more. This weight is well aft in the boat, sort of like having 'Man Mountain' Dean sitting on the transom." ["Safe Loading Of Small Boats" by Cdr. R. I. Price, USCG, Proceedings of the Merchant Marine Council, February 1964.]

Most of the state boating regulations considered in the preceding chapter specifically forbid overloading of recreational boats. It is possible that the boat owner or operator who overloads his craft may find himself prosecuted under the state reckless operation statutes.

Influence of Intoxicants, Drugs, etc.

The late afternoon cocktail, highball, or the drink "on the rocks" can be one of the accepted social rites and a pleasant one too. But if indulged in on boats, it should be reserved for that time when serious navigating has been completed. Certainly, no boat operator in his right mind should ever run his boat when under the influence of intoxicants, narcotics, or habit-forming drugs. Safe boating requires common sense and clear judgment at all times.

The laws of many states forbid the operation of any watercraft when the operator is in such condition. Severe penalties in the form of fines and imprisonment are exacted.

Three sport fishermen had stayed up most of the night in order to make an early start on their fishing

trip. They passed the night in playing cards and drinking. At a marina where the boat was stored, they were warned by the local people that the weather and water conditions were too hazardous for a small boat. Nevertheless, they went out only to return within the hour. They beached their boat and waited for the weather to subside. While doing so they continued their drinking. Although again warned about going out in such weather in a small boat, they persisted in making another try. They were never seen alive again.

Water-Skiing

As a sport, water-skiing is an exhilarating experience. When practiced sensibly and with reasonable forethought, it can be the source of great pleasure. With the co-operation of the boat operator it can also be a safe sport. There are a few simple rules which the boat operator should follow both for his safety and that of the skier.

1. Be certain that the skier is wearing a proper lifesaving device; either a life preserver, a lifejacket, or a lifebelt.

2. The boat should carry two people, the skipper at the helm and an observer facing the skier. The observer is to watch the skier, the towrope, and the wake, and, more importantly, to pass along the skier's signals to the boat operator.

3. The skier should not be towed in narrow or heavily trafficked waters. The boat and the skier when at high speed should be at least 150 feet away from docks, buoys, floats, swimmers, and fishermen. Give all boats a wide berth.

4. When the skier has taken a tumble, circle slowly back and approach him from the lee side. Before

taking him aboard, stop your motor or have it in neutral, so that the propeller is not turning.

5. Be careful not to swamp your boat. The skier should board at the stern or bow, whichever is safer. In smaller boats it is generally safer to take the skier aboard at the stern.

6. Learn the basic water-skiing signals and be certain that the skier knows and understands them too. Don't try to do the skier's thinking for him. Follow his signals and be of help to him.

Negligent or reckless operation of the towing boat will almost certainly bring liability to the boat owner and operator for personal injuries to persons in and on the water, and for damage to boats and other property. Grossly negligent conduct of the towing boat operator may also mean that he will be liable for damages in the event that the skier is injured.

An accident involving two boats, both engaged in towing skiers, took place in August, 1956, off Normandy Beach, Barnegat Bay, New Jersey. A water skier being towed by a boat operated by his brother took a tumble. While in the water he was struck by another boat which was in the act of towing another skier. The injured skier sued the owner of the boat which had struck him. That party in turn brought into the action the brother, claiming that he had handled his boat in a negligent manner. The court ruled that this could be done under a New Jersey law which permits one wrongdoer to collect from the other. [Frueh v Kupper, 1960 AMC 2161, Sup Ct NJ 1959.]

Night skiing can be a dangerous affair. There have been many instances of skiers hitting docks, seawalls, bridge abutments, and floating objects. Skiing in the dark has also resulted in the skiers being run down by their own or by other boats. Many states have outlawed night skiing.

It will undoubtly prove helpful not only to the water-skiing enthusiasts but also to the owners of boats used in connection with this sport, to read the state boating regulations regarding it, contained in the previous chapter.

Recommended Water Skiing Signals

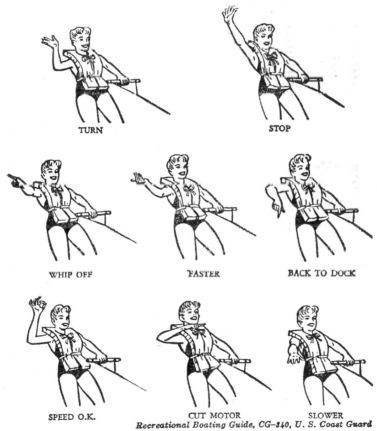

TURN	STOP
WHIP OFF	FASTER	BACK TO DOCK
SPEED O.K.	CUT MOTOR	SLOWER

Recreational Boating Guide, CG–340, U. S. Coast Guard

Man Overboard

The dread cry of "Man overboard!" when shouted

aboard a large vessel on the high seas is usually the signal for instant and determined action. If there is time, a lifering will be flung out in the direction of the victim; alarm whistles will be blown to call the crew topsides and to inform the man overboard that he has been seen; the ship will make a wide turn and a lifeboat will be lowered. In a surprisingly large number of cases the endeavor is successful, even in rough seas, and the victim is snatched from the embracing sea.

When someone falls into the water from a recreational boat it is an equally serious matter. With the application of common sense on the part of the boat operator and the adherence to a few simple rules, loss of life can be kept to a bare minimum.

Should someone fall overboard while your boat is in operation, the most important thing to do is to swing the stern of the boat away from the victim instantly in order to keep the propeller from hitting him. The boat should be steered toward the side from which he fell. Throw out the clutch, putting the engine in neutral, until it is established that he is clear of the propeller.

Throw a lifering to him but avoid hitting him with it, so that he is not rendered unconscious. If a lifering is not handy, then throw any lifesaving device, such as a life preserver or anything buoyant which will help him to stay afloat. Quick action is imperative.

Keep the victim in sight at all times. If you have another person with you, have him act as lookout so that the person overboard is not lost from sight. At night direct a light at the victim.

Maneuver your boat to get to him. Making a circle should bring you to the man. The boat will be best under control by approaching from leeward, getting into a position to windward of him. This will provide a lee with the boat drifting toward him.

Throw him a line. If he is unable to help himself and if you have capable assistance in the boat, then have your assistant put on a life preserver with a line attached to the boat. By going into the water he can assist the victim.

It may be difficult to pull the man into the boat, particularly if he is hurt or exhausted. In small boats the excessive weight on one side can tip the boat. If possible, bring him in by way of the stern or bow. If you have a swim ladder, by all means use it.

There is a legal obligation to exercise reasonable care in the undertaking of operations involved in rescuing a person who has fallen overboard. If the attempt is a grossly bungled one, so that the victim is drowned because of that negligent effort, liability for damages can be imposed against the boat operator and the owner. Should the boat be inadequately equipped in that the statutorily required lifesaving gear is missing and the lack of the life preservers, buoyant cushions, etc., was the proximate cause of the drowning, then again the boat operator and the owner may be held liable.

It is not likely, except perhaps where large ocean-going yachts are involved, that a person can fall overboard without that fact being noticed instantly. But in any event, as soon as the cry "Man overboard!" is heard, every effort should be made toward the prompt rescue of the lost person.

The owner of a large tanker was held liable for damages arising from the drowning of a seaman due to the shipmaster's failure to attempt a rescue operation. The tanker was on her way from New York to Corpus Christi, Texas, sailing along the Florida Keys.

At 11:30 p.m., a seaman was found to be missing from the vessel. He had last been seen on the ship at 6 p.m. At 12:30 a.m., one hour after the captain knew that a member of the crew of his ship was not aboard, he reported that fact to the Coast Guard. The master made no effort to retrace his course to attempt a possible rescue. In advising all ships at the Straits of Florida to keep a sharp lookout for the missing man, an error was made by the Coast Guard in giving the time that he was last seen. The tanker's captain made no effort to correct the error.

In holding the shipowner liable for failing to use reasonable means at hand in attempting a rescue, the court pointed out that at the most the vessel would have lost some time in turning back rather than in proceeding to her port of destination. The duty to rescue a seaman, said the court, includes the positive obligation at least to make a sincere attempt at rescue. When a master disregards that duty by refusing to make even a try at rescue, then the vessel and her owner are liable in damages to the family of the drowned seaman. [Gardner v National Bulk Carriers, Inc., 310 F2d 284, 1963 AMC 29, CA4th 1962, 91 ALR2d 1023, cert den 372 US 913, 9 L ed 2d 721, 83 S Ct 728, reh den 372 US 961, 10 L ed 2d 13, 83 S Ct 1012.]

The owner of a pleasure boat on navigable waters owes to a guest a duty of using reasonable care with regard to his safety. That duty would include an attempt toward rescue should the guest fall overboard. To disregard callously the plight of an individual under these circumstances would most probably result in civil damages against the boat operator.

Capsizing

The capsizing of boats accounts annually for a large

proportion of water accidents which end in loss of life. They may occur suddenly and without warning, giving no time for the boat occupants to don life preservers. In some instances the victims have been trapped in the cabin or underneath the boat or, even worse, knocked unconscious after having been struck by the overturning boat.

A remarkable story regarding a trapped boatsman in an overturned craft is related in the 1961 issue of the United States Coast Guard publication "Pleasure Boat Safety." Two men started out one foggy night in a 21-foot cabin cruiser from a town on the Ohio River. Their destination was another town 23 miles down the river. Shortly after departing, one of the two men "turned in" to get some sleep. He went into the cabin and left his companion operating the boat. About 4 hours later he awoke in a strange position. He found himself out of the cabin and jammed under the floorboards of the cockpit. With difficulty, he finally realized that the deck of the cockpit was overhead.

While he had been asleep, the boat had struck some submerged object and had overturned. Fortunately for him there was a sufficient supply of air trapped in the cockpit which enabled him to stay alive for more than 2 hours while he was below the surface of the water. He cautiously made his way to the edge of the cockpit and then hauled himself out of the boat and up the overturned bottom. His cries for help were heard by someone ashore and he was rescued. His drowned companion was found in the capsized boat, entangled in a manila mooring line.

A capsizing can take place in rough seas when the boat is poorly handled. A boat may also capsize when it is partially flooded and thus loses stability. Loss

111

of stability and rolling in rough seas can bring about the same unfortunate result. If the bilges are not dry and the boat is tender (lacking in stability), try to keep your weights low. The people in the boat should be seated or down with weight centered and placed to make the boat level or trim.

Capsizing differs from foundering; in the latter instance the boat is sunk because an excessive intake of water with resultant loss of buoyancy. In a small overloaded boat, foundering can take place when the wake of a passing boat laps over the meager freeboard.

Stability is the tendency of a vessel to remain upright or the ability to right itself from a roll. Boats are usually designed with a factor of stability sufficient to cover any loading within the limits set by the manufacturer, and with any amount of fuel in the tanks. It is when boatowners make structural changes in the craft that it becomes most probable for the boat to be made unstable. An originally safe and stable boat can be made unstable and dangerous by increasing the size of the water and fuel tanks to permit longer cruises, particularly if the tanks are only partially full.

A highly stable boat is fast-rolling (stiff) and not so comfortable to ride in as a slow-rolling (tender) one, but it is safer. In a very deep roll a point is reached where the force of gravity acting downward and the force of the boat's buoyancy acting upward are in alignment. This point is known as the point of vanishing stability. If the momentum of the roll carries the boat beyond this point, the boat will capsize. The operator has some control of the center of gravity by the placing of weight within the boat. If it is done judiciously, he can influence the point of vanishing stability. Generally speaking, the lower the center of gravity the higher the degree of roll before the point of vanishing stability is reached. An unsecured solid weight in the boat can be a hazardous factor. Not only does it adversely change the center of gravity by moving to the low side during a roll, but there is also the added danger of its stoving the hull by pounding into it.

Weather

No one who engages in boating can afford to ignore weather changes or remain ignorant of the signs which indicate such changes. The simple truth is that the use of common sense and a minimal knowledge of weather patterns and signs can mean the difference between being a smart, safe boatsman and one who finds himself in trouble.

Before starting on your trip or on your day's outing on the water, check the weather—both the weather at the moment and the forecast of weather to come. Have a radio aboard your boat of at least a good transistor type. Learn of the stations which give complete marine weather broadcasts, with information on wind directions, visibility, barometer readings, and detailed forecasts. Tune in on these stations at least once or twice during the day. The presence of static on the radio, particularly when its frequency is being built up, can be an omen of an approaching thunderstorm. Keep a "weather-eye" for thunderheads, those towering clouds with the effect of whipped cream that has been piled high.

The barometer and thermometer are useful instruments aboard your boat. The barometer shows changes in air pressure. Rapid change of pressure can mean high winds and changing weather. It is very easy and simple to set the indicator needle. If the barometer needle remains steady or rises slowly during good

113

weather, then more of that weather pattern can be expected. When you see that the needle is falling rapidly it means that heed must be taken of increasing winds and stormy weather.

Wind directions can have different meanings, depending upon the section of the country you are in. Learn which wind direction spells bad weather for your part of the country. In the northeast section of the United States, the wind coming steadily from the east or northeast usually means several days of rainy and bad weather. During the summer months, in this sector, a steady southwest wind indicates good sailing weather.

Wind force plays an important part in boating pleasure and boating safety. When the breeze is up to 7 miles per hour, safe and pleasant boating should be the order of the day. Calm winds of less than 1 mile per hour is Force 0 on the Beaufort scale; from 1 to 3 miles per hour (Light Air) are Force 1; from 4 to 7 miles per hour (Light Breeze) are Force 2.

There will be a moderate buildup of waves when the wind is from 8 to 12 miles per hour. Crests begin to break. Foam of glassy appearance is seen and there are scattered whitecaps. While the occupants of a very small boat may get wet, there is no danger in a boat properly handled not overloaded. Winds of 8 to 12 miles per hour (Gentle Breeze) are Force 3 on the Beaufort Scale.

A blow of 13 to 18 miles per hour is considered to be a Moderate Breeze. Frequent whitecaps are formed. It is advisable for low-powered motorboats to stay in protected waters. It is Force 4 on the Beaufort Scale.

Winds of from 19 to 24 miles per hour are called a Fresh Breeze and are Force 5 on the Beaufort Scale. The seas are moderately rough with many whitecaps forming and some spray. This no weather to go out in open boats.

At Force 6 on the Beaufort Scale the wind is designated as a Strong Breeze. The wind velocity is between 25 and 31 miles per hour. At sea, waves of 15 inches in height can be expected. Small craft warnings will be displayed at Coast Guard lifeboat stations and at many yacht clubs and marinas. All but the most seaworthy boats should be in protected areas.

In one instance a 17-year-old operator was anxious to "joyride" in his new motorboat. Accompanied by two friends he set out on a cold, rough day although small craft warnings were displayed. Fifteen minutes after they departed, the small craft warnings were lowered and gale warnings were hoisted. The next day the missing boat was discovered, beached and partially awash. All three occupants, who were still in the boat, had perished. They had been drowned in the boat, possibly as a consequence of boarding seas and weakness due to exposure.

Look at the weather maps published in the newspapers each day. Notice the areas of bad weather elsewhere in the country. Remember that weather moves from west to east in the United States. It is not too difficult to figure that bad weather yesterday 500 miles west of you may be your weather today. It may not occur, but at least you'll be on the alert.

Keep in mind that a rapidly falling barometer, abrupt changes of temperature, the building up of huge clouds (either towering or stretched out), and lowering and fast-moving clouds, are signs of oncoming bad weather. Remain alert for the possibility of a line squall appearing with its sudden and violent blow on a hot summer day.

BEAUFORT SCALE
WITH CORRESPONDING SEA STATE CODES

Beaufort number	Wind speed				Seaman's term	U.S. Weather Bureau term	Effects observed at sea	Effects observed on land	Hydrographic Office		International	
	knots	mph	meters per second	km per hour					Term and height of waves, in feet	Code	Term and height of waves, in feet	Code
0	under 1	under 1	0.0-0.2	under 1	Calm		Sea like mirror.	Calm; smoke rises vertically.	Calm, 0	0	Calm, glassy, 0	0
1	1-3	1-3	0.3-1.5	1-5	Light air	Light	Ripples with appearance of scales; no foam crests.	Smoke drift indicates wind direction; vanes do not move.	Smooth, less than 1	1	Rippled, 0-1	1
2	4-6	4-7	1.6-3.3	6-11	Light breeze	Light	Small wavelets; crests of glassy appearance, not breaking.	Wind felt on face; leaves rustle; vanes begin to move.	Slight, 1-3	2	Smooth, 1-2	2
3	7-10	8-12	3.4-5.4	12-19	Gentle breeze	Gentle	Large wavelets; crests begin to break; scattered whitecaps.	Leaves, small twigs in constant motion; light flags extended.	Moderate, 3-5	3	Slight, 2-4	3
4	11-16	13-18	5.5-7.9	20-28	Moderate breeze	Moderate	Small waves, becoming longer; numerous whitecaps.	Dust, leaves, and loose paper raised up; small branches move.	Rough, 5-8	4	Moderate, 4-8	4
5	17-21	19-24	8.0-10.7	29-38	Fresh breeze	Fresh	Moderate waves, taking longer form; many whitecaps; some spray.	Small trees in leaf begin to sway.			Rough, 8-13	5
6	22-27	25-31	10.8-13.8	39-49	Strong breeze	Strong	Larger waves forming; whitecaps everywhere; more spray.	Larger branches of trees in motion; whistling heard in wires.	Very rough, 8-12	5		
7	28-33	32-38	13.9-17.1	50-61	Moderate gale	Strong	Sea heaps up; white foam from breaking waves begins to be blown in streaks.	Whole trees in motion; resistance felt in walking against wind.			Very rough, 13-20	6
8	34-40	39-46	17.2-20.7	62-74	Fresh gale	Gale	Moderately high waves of greater length; edges of crests begin to break into spindrift; foam is blown in well-marked streaks.	Twigs and small branches broken off trees; progress generally impeded.	High, 12-20	6		
9	41-47	47-54	20.8-24.4	75-88	Strong gale	Gale	High waves; sea begins to roll; dense streaks of foam; spray may reduce visibility.	Slight structural damage occurs; slate blown from roofs.			High, 20-30	7
10	48-55	55-63	24.5-28.4	89-102	Whole gale	Whole gale	Very high waves with overhanging crests; sea takes white appearance as foam is blown in very dense streaks; rolling is heavy and visibility reduced.	Seldom experienced on land; trees broken or uprooted; considerable structural damage occurs.	Very high, 20-40	7		
11	56-63	64-72	28.5-32.6	103-117	Storm	Whole gale	Exceptionally high waves; sea covered with white foam patches; visibility still more reduced.				Very high, 30-45	8
12	64-71	73-82	32.7-36.9	118-133	Hurricane	Hurricane	Air filled with foam; sea completely white with driving spray; visibility greatly reduced.	Very rarely experienced on land; usually accompanied by widespread damage.	Mountainous, 40 and higher	8	Phenomenal, over 45	9
13	72-80	83-92	37.0-41.4	134-149								
14	81-89	93-103	41.5-46.1	150-166								
15	90-99	104-114	46.2-50.9	167-183								
16	100-108	115-125	51.0-56.0	184-201					Confused	9		
17	109-118	126-136	56.1-61.2	202-220								

While weather forecasting is not an exact science and the average boatsman is not likely to be an expert meteorologist, nevertheless a comprehension and an awareness of which natural phenomena cause changes in weather can contribute greatly to safe boating.

Distress Signals

Your chances of receiving aid when most needed are immeasurably enhanced when you have the knowledge and the means at hand to send out distress signals. The purpose in sending distress signals, of course, is to attract attention to your plight and to convey the information that help is needed.

All boats, irrespective of type and size, should be equipped with attention-attracting distress signals. Smoke signals for daytime use and flares for night are packaged in kits. They should be stored in a dry place aboard the boat. A Very pistol equipped with red, white, or green distress shells is also a handy device to have on hand.

The radio telephone is a valuable means of calling for help. The code word is "Mayday." Coast Guard ships and stations, and pleasure craft and merchant ships, listen on 2,182 kilocycles. A call on this distress frequency will get help. In an emergency you may use any available frequency to indicate your need for assistance.

Your location when in trouble can also govern the type of signal sent out. When relatively close to shore or in sight of other boats, a visual or audible signal will probably be most effective. On the other hand, if you are several hundred miles offshore, an SOS on your radio sending set, or a "Mayday" on the marine radio telephone, is the required signal to be sent.

Shooting off guns or flares or repeated and prolonged

blowing of your horn, or striking of the ship's bell, can be used as distress signals. Flying the ensign inverted or the alphabet flags "NC" are other methods of getting attention. In fact, any signal that attracts attention is a good distress signal. If it is a commonly used distress signal, then the likelihood of its being recognized for what it is, is greatly increased.

Making flames or smoke by burning oily rags held over the side and away from the boat or in a metal container or bucket are dramatic ways of calling attention to the difficulty you are in. Discretion should be shown in making flames, for obviously your situation will not be bettered by setting the boat on fire.

A distinctive signal of calling for help is by waving your hands from overhead to an outstretched position parallel to your shoulders or sides. This is repeatedly done and can be more effective if flags or other brightly colored and easily visible objects are held in your hands. The highest vantage point on the boat should be mounted to make the signal as effective as possible.

Rule 31 of the International Rules of the Road states that when a vessel is in distress and needs help from other vessels or from shore, the following signals are to be given, either singly or together:

(a) a gun or other explosive signal fired at intervals of about a minute;

(b) a continuous sounding with any fog-signal apparatus;

(c) rockets or shells, throwing red stars fired one at a time at short intervals;

(d) a signal made by radio telegraphy or by any other signaling methods consisting of the group ••• —— —— —— ••• in the Morse Code;

(e) a signal sent by radio telephone consisting of the spoken word "Mayday";

(f) the International Code signal NC;

(g) a signal consisting of a square flag and above or below it a ball, or something resembling a ball;

(h) flames on the vessel (as from a burning tar or oil barrel) ; and

(i) a rocket parachute flare showing a red light.

The comparable rule for boats operating on the inland waters is Article 31 of the INLAND RULES. It states that the daytime signal of distress is a continuous sounding with any fog-signal apparatus or by the firing of a gun.

At night, according to the Inland Rules, the distress signal can be given by:

(a) flames on the vessel as from a burning tar barrel, oil barrel, etc.;

(b) a continuous sounding with any fog-signal apparatus or by the firing of a gun.

WESTERN RIVER RULES regarding distress signals [33 Code of Federal Regulations § 95.39] state as follows:

Daytime:

(a) a gun fired at intervals of about a minute;

(b) the International Code signal of distress indicated by NC;

(c) the distress signal, consisting of a square flag, having a ball or anything resembling a ball either above or below it;

(d) rockets or shells as presented below for use at night;

(e) a continuous sounding with a steam whistle or any fog-signal apparatus;

(f) slowly and repeatedly raising and lowering arms outstretched to each side.

At Night:

    (a) a gun fired at intervals of about a minute;

    (b) flames in the vessel (as from a burning tar barrel, oil barrel, etc.) ;

    (c) rockets or shells, bursting in the air with a loud report and throwing stars of any color or description, fired one at a time at short intervals;

    (d) a continuous sounding with a steam whistle or any fog-signal apparatus.

GREAT LAKES RULES pertaining to distress signals [33 Code of Federal Regulations § 90.15] are as follows:

Daytime:

    (a) a gun or other explosive signal fired at intervals of about a minute;

    (b) the distant signal, consisting of a square flag, having a ball or some object resembling a ball either above or below it;

    (c) a continuous sounding with any fog-signal apparatus;

    (d) slowly and repeatedly raising and lowering arms outstretched to each side.

At Night:

    (a) a gun or other explosive signal fired at intervals of about a minute;

    (b) flames from the vessel (as from burning a tar barrel, oil barrel, etc.) ;

    (c) rockets or shells, throwing stars of any color or description fired one at a time at short intervals;

    (d) a continuous sounding with any fog-signal apparatus.

Reckless Operation

Of the millions of boating enthusiasts who enjoy the waters of the United States there is always that relatively small coterie who comprise the lunatic fringe. They are guilty of stupid and irresponsible acts such as bearing down at high speed on innocent swimmers, cutting trolling lines, and charging close to drifting rowboats.

A particularly tragic outcome of what can be charitably termed as reckless operation took place at Lake Tahoe, California, on a sunny summer day in 1949. A 13-year-old girl and a companion were playing in the shallow waters of the lake close to shore. Suddenly, a speeding motorboat going at 25 miles per hour deliberately navigated between the girl and her companion. Miss Imogene Wittsche, the 13-year-old girl, was struck by the fast-moving boat. The boat's propellers severed both of the poor girl's legs. After striking her the boat operator made a 180° turn, passed close to the two girls, and then sped away without offering assistance. The boat operator was criminally prosecuted in the United States District Court for the Northern District of California, found guilty and sentenced to serve a term of 6 months in a federal prison, and fined $1,500.

Here is a good description of the reckless boat operator which appeared in a government publication. It should provide food for thought for all. It states as follows:

"Some motorboat operators are wilfully reckless or negligent. Others place themselves in the category of reckless or negligent operators by not using common sense and by not being familiar with the requirements of motorboating. In either case the end result may be the death or maiming of some person or persons, and in either case the operator is liable for the full penalty prescribed by the law.

"A typical wilful violator, for example, is a fellow who spots some people in a rowboat and thinks it would be great sport to 'scare the daylights out of them.' He heads his boat straight for the rowboat and roars right at them, veering at the last minute, leaving the rowboat occupants trembling, wet with spray or probably overboard. Another type is one who considers it great sport to see how close he can get to a large commercial vessel. Sometimes he gets too close and tragedy results." [Proceedings of the Merchant Marine Council, July 1948, p. 106.]

Night Boating

A recent article in a popular boating magazine extols the pleasures of boating after dark. Among the advantages of night boating, it states, is the factor of extension of the boat's cruising range by an early weekend start on Friday night and travel on waterways uncrowded by daytime traffic.

Significantly, however, the greater part of the article dwells upon proper planning and preparation for the nighttime journey. A searchlight is essential and the more powerful it is the better. As darkness falls and landmarks disappear, the boatsman should note his position on his chart. A compass course should be selected in order to assure freedom from obstacles. The time of a run should be recorded and dead reckoning of the distance traversed be noted before changing course. Familiarization with the lights for tugs and tows, anchored commercial vessels, other pleasure boats, and government aids to navigation is essential. The night boatsman is advised that if he believes that he is lost or suspects that threatening weather is in the offing, it is best to drop anchor and await daylight, or to stay in a sheltered cove if there is a rising wind.

While the whole idea of boating at night may conjure thoughts of romance and moonlit waters, the plain truth is that nighttime boating in pleasure crafts can have moments of stark terror. Unlike the motorist who can drive his car at night with the road ahead lit up by the automobile's headlights, thus permitting safe operation at relatively high speeds, the boat operator does not usually have a well-defined "road" on the water. Another boat can come at you from any direction. It is not dissimilar, the U.S. Coast Guard has pointed out in its pamphlet on pleasure boat safety, to driving a car continually in an intersection not controlled by traffic lights. Safe operation of a boat under such circumstances requires constant alertness and a sharp lookout.

A continual danger to recreational small boats is the flotsam present on the inland waterways. In one case a 17-foot motorboat with five persons aboard was operating in a river on a clear, dark night. The boat was moving along at 17 miles per hour when unexpectedly a large tree limb was seen only 10 or 15 feet ahead of the craft. The boat operator, almost instinctively, turned sharply to avoid the obstruction, but to no avail. The impact of the collision threw two of the occupants out of the boat. The result: a badly damaged boat and one person drowned.

Another water accident case involved a cabin cruiser in an inland lake. Five people started out on a summer evening to spend a few pleasant evening hours on the water. So calm was the lake that it was unnecessary to throw out the anchor. The boat barely drifted on the quiet waters with scarcely a breeze stirring on this clear, dark night. The boat's occupants were seated

123

in the cockpit, alternately conversing and singing to the accompaniment of a musical instrument. The pleasure boat was well lit up. Suddenly out of the darkness came a tug and her barge. The cabin cruiser was run down and demolished with its occupants thrown into the lake. Two of the pleasure seekers were drowned. It is quite possible that the lights of the cruiser were confused by the tug's helmsman with the many shore lights which formed the background to the craft's position.

Though there are many pleasant aspects to night boating, the fact remains that in a small craft the individual is subjected to more than the normal hazards of boating.

Fueling

The taking on of gasoline in a small boat is a procedure fraught with danger, presently or potentially. A gasoline spill, even if small, can create a dangerous situation. Gasoline evaporates very quickly. Gasoline vapor is heavier than air and when it blends with air in certain proportions an explosive mixture results. Any ignition, such as a spark, in contact with this mixture can bring about a frightful explosion.

Unfortunately, boat explosion accidents following the fueling process occur much too frequently. The explosive force of the gasoline vapor and air mixture is almost incredible. Boats have been completely destroyed and their occupants killed or seriously injured.

Since the gasoline vapor is heavier than air, it seeks to flow down into the lowest point. In small boats this is usually the bilge or some other low and enclosed space. The lethal mixture will lie there like an infernal device, waiting for the spark to set it off.

124

The danger of explosion when fueling can be avoided by following these simple, common-sense rules.

1. Fueling should take place, whenever possible, during daylight. If it is necessary that the boat be fueled at night, electric lights only should be used. The illumination should never come from open flames.

2. The boat should be closed, wherever possible, to prevent fumes from entering the interior. Ports, windows, doors, and hatches should be kept shut. Gasoline vapors can be kept out of the hold by having the entire fuel system free from leaks. All connections must be checked for tightness, since vibrations of the boat caused by engines or rough weather can loosen them.

3. All motors, engines, or fans aboard the boat must be shut off before fueling begins.

4. Under no circumstances should smoking ever be permitted on or near the boat. Do not strike any matches or throw any switches. In fact, avoid the possibility of any spark being created while fueling is going on and until you are absolutely certain that your boat is free of any danger from gasoline vapor.

5. Put out all lights and galley fires.

6. The nozzle of the gasoline hose or the spout from a can must be placed in contact with the fill pipe or tank opening before the gasoline is poured, and the contact should be maintained continuously throughout the time that the fuel is being poured. This is done in order to avoid the likelihood of a spark being formed by the static electricity from the contact of the nozzle and the fill pipe or opening.

7. A tank should not be filled to the brim. Some room should be left in the tank for gasoline expansion. When the fueling has been completed, the fill cap should

be put on as tightly as possible. Any extra gasoline should be carried in an approved safety tank.

8. Fuel spillage should be avoided. See that passengers do not move about and thereby cause fuel to slosh and spill. Immediately wipe up completely any gasoline spill. The rag used for this purpose should be left on shore and should not be thrown into the boat or the water.

9. Open the engine hatch, all ports, windows, doors, and hatches, and permit the boat to ventilate for at least 5 minutes before the engine is started. The bilges and low places in the boat should be well ventilated. The bilge blower should be run for 5 minutes or more.

10. Finally, make certain that there is no odor of gasoline in the bilges, the below-deck spaces, and in the immediate vicinity of the engine before starting.

Types of Installations

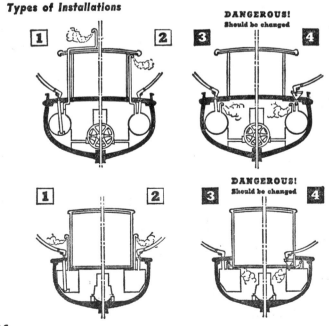

BOAT SAFETY

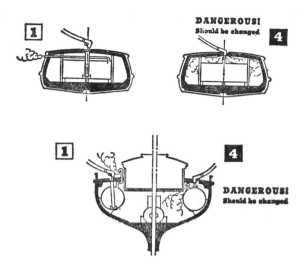

OUTBOARDS,—Permanent Installations

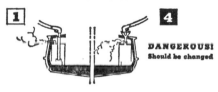

1. BEST INSTALLATION: Fill pipes firmly attached to tight deck plate. Fill pipe extends to bottom of tank, with well to form liquid seal. Vent pipe discharges to open air, away from all hull openings, hatches, doors, windows, ports, etc. Outboard end of vent screened.

2. FAIRLY GOOD INSTALLATION: Fill pipes firmly attached to tight deck plates but not extended to bottom of tank, with liquid seal well. Tank can be exploded from ignited fill pipe. Vent led to open air with screened outboard end. Location of the vent outlet should be kept clear of all hull openings.

3. DANGEROUS INSTALLATION: Fill pipes firmly attached to deck plates, but vent pipes discharge all vapors to inside of boat. Fumes may be ignited by a backfire, a lit match, by electrical apparatus of any kind, or by a fire in the galley stove. Unless vent pipe is led to open air, a tight deck fill pipe is NO protection.

4. VERY DANGEROUS INSTALLATION: Both fill pipe and vent pipe end inside of hull. All vapors escape to interior of boat. Tank will overflow in filling and spill liquid fuel to bilge. Possible static spark from fill connections or funnel may ignite gasoline.

DO NOT place fill pipes inside of deck houses or cockpits.

DO NOT use small diameter tubing for vents. They will cause bubbling and spilling at the fill pipes.

Outboard motorboats which are equipped with portable tanks should be fueled away from the boat. In this way any spillage cannot work its way into the bilge. Where the outboard is equipped with a fixed tank, the fueling should never take place while the engine is hot. Sufficient time should be allowed for the engine to cool off. Should gasoline spill on the engine it should be thoroughly wiped. Make sure that the gasoline has completely evaporated before starting the motor.

This will probably amaze you, but it is a fact: a teaspoonful of gasoline evaporated into the air in the bilge of a small craft will explode like a stick of dynamite. Or if a half pint of gasoline is allowed to vaporize in a confined space so that the percentage of gasoline vapor to air is within the range of 2 to 4 percent, it will have the explosive force equal to 5 pounds of dynamite. The result? A badly damaged, if not totally destroyed, pleasure boat.

There are several law cases which involve fires and explosions caused by bad fueling practices. In one incident at Carter Lake, Iowa, a 17-year-old girl, who was a guest of the boatowner, was badly burned by an explosion. The boat had been brought to a boatyard for a quick charging of its battery and to take on fuel. The fueling was being done by a 15-year-old boy. In doing so, he allowed the tank to spill over. The girl took her place at the stern; the owner at the bow. When he turned on the ignition, the explosion followed. [Nelson v Grimes, 256 F2d 816, CA8th 1958.]

Fire

There are few hazards of the sea which are feared by seamen as much as fire aboard ships. The reason is obvious; if the fire gets out of control there is but

128

one place to go—into the water. In a deep-sea vessel, lifeboats or rafts may be available. In a small pleasure craft the usual means of escape is literally to jump over the side. By contrast, a fire ashore can be less dangerous. Unless you are trapped in a burning building you can walk away from the fire.

Because of the difficulty of reaching its source, fighting a fire at sea can be a most frustrating experience. Unlike firefighting ashore, the fire cannot usually be attacked by approaching it from different angles.

Taking preventive steps against having a fire is far more salutary than having to worry about how to fight it. The boat should be kept in shipshape condition with particular attention to clean bilges. Gear should be properly stowed, and oily rags and paints should not be left lying about. Gasoline or other flammable products should not be used for cleaning purposes. Care should be taken with regard to smoking and the disposal of lighted cigarettes. Thrown from forward over the side of a boat, lighted cigarettes can be blown back into the boat and sometimes smoldering fires have ensued.

Firefighting equipment should be kept handy and in good condition. The boat operator should plan how a fire aboard the boat would be handled long before such an emergency actually exists. The first few moments in fighting a fire are the most important. If the fire can be extinguished quickly or kept under control, then fire damage can be kept within reasonable bounds. When the fire is allowed to get out of hand, total property loss and personal injury can be the consequence. The fire should be stopped or controlled before it reaches the fuel tanks. When the tanks catch on fire the chances of saving the boat become slim.

Fires are extinguished by cooling or smothering. Such solid combustibles as clothing, rags, wood, curtains, kapok, mattresses, and canvas can be best extinguished with water. A bucket or bailer kept in a handy place can be most useful. The supply of water is usually unlimited, so that that aspect provides no problem. Do not hesitate to throw a burning object overboard if that is the quickest and most convenient way of putting out the fire.

Water is not a good means of extinguishing a gasoline or oil fire. The burning fuel will float, and the water can become the means of spreading the fire. Water can be used to cool off heated areas after the flames have been extinguished.

The smothering and cooling action of carbon dioxide, dry chemical, and foam types of fire extinguishers are most effective in fighting an oil or gasoline fire. These fires depend on the combination of the burning substance and of air to spread and do their destructive work. The blanketing or smothering action of these chemicals isolates the oil or gasoline from the air. Without the needed air the fire will die out. The extinguishing agents should be directed at the base of the flames. The vaporizing liquids, such as carbon tetrachloride and chlorobromomethane, when used in confined spaces, are toxic and can be dangerous to life.

If the fire is confined to a relatively limited space, closing the hatches, ports, vents, and doors will be effective in putting out the fire by shutting it off from the air supply. When the fire is localized in the machinery space, the fuel supply should be shut off and the fixed fire-extinguishing system (usually CO_2), if the boat is so equipped, should be discharged.

There are certain actions you can take if your boat is underway. Stopping the boat or slowing its speed will help reduce the blowing effect of the wind. Strong or steady winds—like bellows—can fan the flames. When the boat is moving, then the fire should be kept downwind. That is, if the fire is forward, then the stern of the boat should be put into the wind; with the fire aft, the bow should be headed into the wind.

If abandonment becomes necessary, lifesaving gear should be donned. Before leaving the boat, signal for aid by radio or by any other possible means.

Asphyxiation

The danger of asphyxiation from carbon monoxide poisoning is as everpresent in a boat as it is in an automobile, with this important difference—boats are frequently used as sleeping quarters. If you, your family, and your guests expect to enjoy peaceful repose aboard your craft, common sense dictates that all potential danger from gas poisoning be eliminated.

Any leaks in the exhaust pipes should be corrected at once. A leak in an exhaust line, particularly where it passes through or near sleeping compartments, is a source of certain danger. Be equally alert for danger of asphyxiation from galley stoves using gas. Attention should always be given to good ventilation in closed spaces, particularly of sleeping quarters.

The tragic story of the end of what was to be a pleasurable weekend is told in the published records of the Coast Guard. A family had started on a week-end trip of fishing and cruising. Four young girls were sleeping on the cockpit floor. One of them was sleeping near two ⅞-inch scuppers in the transom near the exhaust pipes. The child never awakened from her sleep. Toxic gases from the pipes were the lethal agents.

Abandoning the Boat

The unenviable prospect of leaving the boat and leaping overboard must be faced when remaining in it no longer becomes desirable or tenable. The impel-

ling force in reaching this decision may be in the form
of capsizing, foundering, or fire.

Most small boats will remain afloat after a casualty,
sometimes indefinitely. If abandoning the boat becomes necessary, quickly put on your life preserver—
that is, if it is not already on. Then stay close to
the boat. An overturned boat often makes an excellent life preserver. Hold on to the boat until help
arrives. A boat in the water can be more easily seen
than a swimmer. If there are several people in the
boat, then stay together. Spirits can be kept up when
in a group, and the possibility of panic avoided. The
chances of being found are also better.

Life preservers should not be stowed in a place
inaccessible or difficult to get to in an emergency.
When not worn they should be in an area where they
can float free in the event of a sudden or unexpected
happening.

Where the abandonment has taken place within
sight of land, the first impulse of most swimmers is
to strike out for shore. But distance over water is
quite deceptive and frequently appears to be much
shorter than it really is. Many lives have been lost
under such circumstances, particularly when a life
preserver was not worn. These needless fatalities
could have been avoided had the swimmer stayed near
his boat. Calm and good judgment is necessary. Keep
cool, and then decide what is best to be done. Nearness
to shore, injury of others, or your strength and swimming ability may be the deciding factors.

A 12-foot aluminum motorboat with four passengers
aboard was cruising down a river one spring day.
The river, fed by fresh spring rainwater, had a swift
and turbulent current. Suddenly the bow dipped
under, swamping the boat and throwing the four occupants into the water. The boat operator told his three

132

companions to stay near the boat while he swam to shore 600 feet away. He never made it. The three clung to the boat until help arrived. Incidentally, the boat was not equipped with life preservers, lifevests, or buoyant cushions.

Search and Rescue

The boatsman's best friend is the United States Coast Guard—there can be no doubt of that. Among its many activities on behalf of the small boat operator, none stands higher in appreciative esteem than the Coast Guard's search and rescue activities.

Notification to the Coast Guard of a boat in distress or missing can come in many ways. If the boat in trouble is equipped with a radio or radio-telephone, a distress call or "Mayday" on 2,182 kilocycles will be picked up by Coast Guard ships and shore stations. A radio-telephone call to the Marine Operator will be transmitted to the Coast Guard. Many calls to the Coast Guard come from merchant ships which have come upon disabled small craft. Merchant ships, as a rule, will not spend much time about a disabled boat. Neither will they be diverted from their port of destination. If danger of loss of life exists, the occupants of the small boat will be taken aboard and carried on to the vessel's port of call. If danger to life is not apparent, the merchant ship will radio to the Coast Guard, giving the position of the distressed craft, and then continue on its journey.

Other small boats which either notice a distress signal or come upon a boat in difficulties will frequently send a message requesting help from the Coast Guard and will stand by until that help arrives.

The Coast Guard will frequently be advised by anxious relatives or friends that a boat is overdue or missing. If the waters where the boat is expected to be is one of the rivers, bays, or inlets near a shore

133

rescue station, the unit stationed there will undertake the search. Where the missing boat is on the high seas, then the larger Coast Guard vessels and planes will take over. If the call regarding the missing boat gives vague, insufficient, or inaccurate information, valuable time may be lost, and what should have been a relatively simple rescue operation can turn out to be a difficult affair.

It is but simple good sense to notify someone of your plans for the day, including your route, destination, stops en route, and estimated time of return. Notify the person concerned of any change in plans. When you reach your destination or your returning place, notify that person of your arrival.

When a missing boat call comes in, a quick telephone check may be made of the families of those on board as well as of marinas, yacht clubs, and harbors of refuge to see whether the boat may have arrived safely at another port.

Your call for aid by radio or radio-telephone will be received by the local Coast Guard Rescue Co-ordination Center. An experienced officer is on continuous duty. Your call for help will get his immediate attention and the machinery for rescue will be set in motion. If the cause for alarm has disappeared, so that the boat is safe and Coast Guard assistance is no longer needed, then call the Coast Guard and *cancel* the request for aid.

In recent years helicopters have been used increasingly to rescue persons from distressed ships and in other situations to take off those who might be injured or sick. Helicopters have also been used, to a limited extent and for limited distances, in towing boats from 400 tons to the minimum of a 16-foot outboard. Smaller boats cannot be properly towed, because of the controllability of the helicopter and lack of sufficient drag.

There are no less than 19 different search patterns used by the Coast Guard in rescue work. Some of these patterns utilize only a boat; in others it is a combination of boat and plane, while in still others several planes are used.

In search and rescue work, if an airplane is available it will be sent out to locate the distressed boat. When the boat is located the airplane will orbit over it. The Coast Guard vessel can home in on it, and thus a more accurate position can be established.

If an airplane is not available, the Coast Guard vessel will head for the estimated position of the distressed craft. If the boat is not immediately located, the pattern of tracking called the "expanding square search" is followed. The track spacing is determined by the searching unit after taking into consideration such factors as the speed of the rescuing vessel, the size of the boat being sought, visibility, the location of the sun, state of the sea, and duration of darkness or daylight.

The "expanding square search" pattern is as follows:

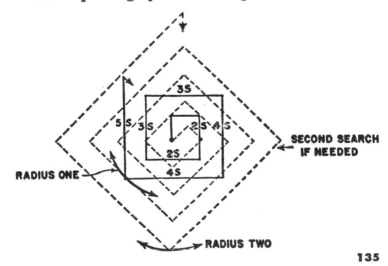

The "co-ordinated creeping line search" is used when an airplane is employed in conjunction with a searching vessel. This type of search pattern is also used when the boat in trouble is believed to be between two points but its exact position is not known. The searching vessel and the plane start at one point. The ship then proceeds at a fixed speed toward the other point. In the meantime the airplane goes back and forth at right angles across her course. If the pattern is completed without finding the object of the search, a new area is selected, unless it is decided to repeat the original pattern with the thought that the sought-for boat may have been missed on the first sweep.

The "co-ordinated creeping line search" would take the following form:

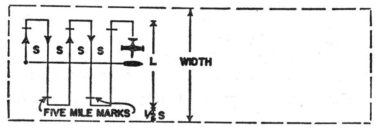

The "Loran line parallel track" method is utilized by a single airplane to search an area when the position of the target is known only approximately or not at all. The Loran coverage permits the flying of tracks by presetting and flying on Loran lines.

The drawing below shows how this pattern is developed:

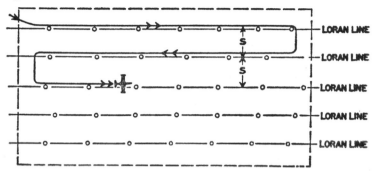

In many instances the Coast Guard is not called in time when a boat is overdue or missing. Such failures adversely affect the probability of successful rescue. In many more cases the calls are made needlessly by persons prematurely alarmed about the safety of others when there are no real reasons for the alarm. They generally cause expensive searches and unnecessarily expose men to the danger of injury and loss of life. Nonetheless, these well-meant but needless alarms are understandable. What is unforgivable is the cruel hoax which sends men and equipment out on a wild-goose chase.

The sending out of a false alarm for aid is an offense which can be punished by a jail term. The federal statute [47 United States Code § 325a] states as follows:

"No person within the jurisdiction of the United States shall knowingly utter or transmit, or cause to be transmitted, any false or fraudulent signal of distress, or communication relating thereto, etc."

The "teeth" are contained in another provision of the federal statute [47 United States Code § 501].

137

It is a general penalty section and provides that any person who wilfully and knowingly "does or causes or suffers to be done any act, matter, or thing, in this chapter prohibited or declared to be unlawful," can be punished by a fine of not more than $10,000 or by imprisonment of a term not exceeding one year, or both. For repeaters, the fine is for not more than $10,000, with imprisonment of not more than 2 years or both.

In the annals of the Coast Guard is the story of the two intelligent and well-educated adults who bought a 47-year-old sloop with the announced purpose of cruising up the Atlantic Coast. They were totally inexperienced in sailing of this kind. The seller of the sloop and friends tried to discourage them. They persisted in their plan and sailed out into a large, open bay. During that pleasant, sunny day the wind was light and southerly. But toward evening it shifted to NW and freshened.

So anxious were they to get sailing that the two adventurers failed to register their boat, so no identifying numbers appeared on her. Since no berthing arrangements had been made at the next boat harbor, no overdue report was made at night when the boat failed to appear. On the next day a passing yacht reported to the Coast Guard that it had sighted a capsized sailboat. The wreckage was recovered, but the boat remained unidentified. Five days later, anxious friends reported that the two men were missing. With the added knowledge gained regarding the characteristics of the missing boat, it was found that the previously recovered wreck was the remains of the missing sloop.

The attitude of the United States Coast Guard with

138

regard to recreational boating and boat safety can be summed up in the following words:

"The records of marine casualties abound with cases of inexperienced boatsmen who put to sea with an abundance of enthusiasm and a minimum of caution and end up as statistics. Discouragement of pleasure boating has never been undertaken by any government agency, and it is strongly hoped that this healthy and satisfying form of recreation will never be dampened by government regulation. Therefore, the safety of pleasure boatsmen must ultimately rest upon their common sense and good judgment. This means a strong measure of reserve in planning and providing for the perils of the sea. The potential strength and fury of the sea must never be underestimated. 'Hope for the best, but plan for the worst' when you are preparing that next trip in your boat. The life you save may be your own."

Artificial Respiration

The need for artificial respiration becomes imperative when breathing has stopped. But because a person has stopped breathing, it does not necessarily follow that he is dead.

For hundreds of years by various methods, attempts have been made to bring the dead, or apparently dead, back to the world of the living. During the Middle Ages, much faith was put in the use of heat as a restorer of breath. The theory was that heat could be restored to a cold body by the external application of heat from an outside source. To restore respiration, warm ashes and hot water were placed on the abdomen of the victim. A favorite nostrum was to burn dried animal excreta on the body of the person. By the sixteenth century the bellows method was employed. Air would be forced into the lungs of the unconscious individual by pumping bellows similar to those used in fanning a fire. The barrel method was extensively used in the eighteenth and nineteenth centuries. The victim would be draped over a barrel, face down. As the barrel was moved forward, pressure was released on his chest, thus allowing for respiration. By moving the barrel backward, it caused the body's weight to compress the chest, which in turn induced expiration.

In 1829 a French physician, Dr. Francois Leroy, introduced a different method of artificial respiration. Pressure was applied to the chest and the abdomen to deflate the lungs. Removal of the pressure caused the inspiration of air.

The Holger Nielson method is featured by lifting the arms of the prone victim, while the Emerson method relies on the lifting of the hips.

Under the newest first-aid technique of artificial respiration, you can do the breathing for the victim until he is enabled to breathe for himself.

Artificial respiration is particularly called for where breathing has stopped due to the following causes: drowning; gas poisoning; smoke suffocation; smothering; stroke; head injuries; chest injuries; foreign objects in the throat; electric shock and poisoning.

The U.S. Coast Guard publication, Recreational Boating Guide, CG–340, gives in detail a description of the mouth-to-mouth technique of artificial respiration. It is repeated here.

In attempting to revive an apparently drowned person, the patient's mouth should first be cleared of any obstruction, such as chewing gum, tobacco, or mucus, so that there is no interference with the entrance or escape of air to or from the lungs.

Artificial respiration should be started immediately.

Every moment of delay is serious. It should be continued at least 4 hours without interruption, until normal breathing is established, or until the patient is pronounced dead by a medical officer.

The victim's clothing should be loosened and he should be kept warm. However, this cannot be allowed to interrupt the administering of artificial respiration.

Frequently, the patient, after temporary recovery of respiration, stops breathing again. The patient must be watched and if natural breathing stops, artificial respiration should be resumed at once.

There are several approved methods of administering artificial respiration. Scientific organizations interested particularly in methods of artificial respiration have concluded that the mouth-to-mouth method is more effective in most cases than any of the other manual methods. For added protection, boatsmen are encouraged to familiarize themselves with a pressure technique, such as the Holger Nielson or Shaffer method. A description of the mouth-to-mouth technique follows:

1. Place the unconscious victim on his back, since you must be able to see his face.

2. Move an injured victim cautiously.

3. If there is foreign matter visible at the mouth, turn his head to the side, force his mouth open and quickly clean the mouth or throat with your fingers or a piece of cloth.

4. Place the victim's head in the "sniffing position," placing the head as far back as possible so that it "juts out" (it is most important that the jaw be held in this position).

5. Hold the jaw in this position in one hand, approach the victim's head from his left side.

6. Insert the thumb of your left hand between the victim's teeth and grasp his lower jaw at the midline.

7. Lift the lower jaw forcefully upward so that the lower teeth are higher than the upper teeth.

8. Hold the jaw in this position as long as the victim is unconscious.

9. Close the victim's nose with your right hand.

10. After taking a deep breath, place your mouth over the victim's mouth *with airtight contact*. Do not hold the victim's mouth open widely, as you must take the entire mouth of the victim inside your lips.

11. Blow into the victim's mouth, forcefully if adults, and gently if children.

12. While blowing, watch the victim's chest. When the chest rises, stop blowing and quickly remove your mouth from the victim's mouth.

13. Let the victim exhale passively by the elasticity of his lungs and chest.

14. When the chest does not rise, improve the support of the air passageway and blow more forcefully.

15. Repeat these inflations 12 to 20 times per minute.

4

personal injuries

Introduction

I have read recently in a book devoted to small boat operation that the incidence of personal injuries is not large. How incredible! The frequency of injury claims and lawsuits involving guests of the boatowner, bathers and swimmers run down by negligent helms men, victims of boat collisions, mechanics and other workers seriously injured while repairing recreational and other small craft—all belie this sophomoric concept.

When we consider, too, that employees of boatowners can be regarded under maritime law as seamen and the beneficiaries of the liberal Jones Act, the doctrine of maintenance and cure, and the rule of seaworthiness with its tenet of liability without fault, the responsibilities of boatowners and operators for personal injuries on vessels are awesome indeed. It should be readily understood that the average landsman who is accustomed to a world of accepted norms by way of shore-side regulations and legal rights and responsibilities leaves much of this behind at the moment he steps into his boat. It is at this point that he must perforce accept the rules and the laws of the sea, most of which will appear strange and incomprehensible to him. Accept them, he must, for better or for worse.

Seamen Employed on Boats

It is, of course, most unlikely (but not at all impossible) that the owner of a 15-foot outboard motorboat will employ a crew—even a crew consisting of one person. [Norton v Warner Co., 321 US 565, 571, 88 L ed 931, 64 S Ct 747; Loverich v Warner Co., 118 F2d 690, 1941 AMC 604, CCA3d 1941, cert den 313 US 577, 85 L ed 1535, 61 S Ct 1104, 1105.] The presence, however, of a professional captain and a large paid crew among the bigger yachts is not infrequent. The famous millionaires' yachts—the Corsair, Hi-Esmeralda, and the Nourmahal—carried large crews. In the more modestly sized ones a crew of about a dozen seamen is not unusual. A suit for wages [The Marie Anna, 1941 AMC 321, DC ED NY 1941] by the crew of the yacht Marie-Anna disclosed that she employed a company of 10 mariners, consisting of the captain, mate, engineer, steward, cook, and five seamen. If we include in the term "small craft" company-owned yachts, tugs, commercial and sport-fishing boats, scows, barges, derricks, etc., and accept the fact that they regularly employ workers to man and navigate them, then the boatowner must realistically face the peculiar legal problems connected with seamen who are injured or who become sick.

Even the single paid hand on a recreational boat can be regarded as a seaman—a member of the boat's crew—and is therefore entitled to all the benefits and protective care which the admiralty law affords seamen.

In the case of the yacht Revenge [Walliser v Bassett,

144

33 F Supp 636, 1940 AMC 510, DC Wis 1939] a shore
employee of one of the owners of the sailing yacht
was taken along as the boat's cook. Unfortunately for
the poor man, he fell overboard and was drowned. It
was held that he had been employed as a seaman. His
widow was not restricted to workmen's compensation
benefit payments. Since he had been a seaman, she had
the right to sue his employer for his alleged wrongful
death.

The person whom you have agreed to take along
to assist you in running your boat may be regarded,
in contemplation of the maritime law, as a seaman
entitled to the remedies of the Jones Act, unseaworthiness, and of maintenance and cure.

The two-masted auxiliary yacht Meridian was in
Miami for the Miami-Nassau race. A young man who
had always been interested in boats and boat races
journeyed from his home to Miami in the hope of
getting on one of the boats participating in the race.
He came aboard the Meridian and asked to be taken
along. The yacht was owned by two men. Seven
friends of the owners were serving as a crew for the
race. Because of the young man's prior racing experience he was accepted. He had not been promised nor
did he receive any payment in money for his services.
In fact, he was being taken only to Nassau, after which
he was expected to make his own arrangements for
the return trip to Miami. During the race he was
struck and seriously injured by the handle of a defective winch. He had helped with the sails. At the time
of injury he had been taking in the Genoa sheet to
trim the luff of the sail.

The court held that because of the services which
he was rendering he was a seaman. The two owners
sought relief under the limitation of liability statute.

Their right to limit their liability to the value of the boat was granted. The injured young man was awarded damages in the amount of $43,000, the entire value of the boat. [In re Read's Petition, 224 F Supp 241, DC Fla 1963.]

Maintenance and Cure

The rights and benefits given to seamen have their roots in ancient sea laws going back about a thousand years. Among them is the right of maintenance and cure. This means that a seaman who is injured or who becomes sick while in the service of the ship is given medical treatment and the cost of board and lodging until he is fit to return to work or until that time when he has reached the maximum cure which medical science can afford him. In addition, the law also allows him wages to the end of the voyage.

Where boats of the inland waters are involved with seamen most frequently being hired on a monthly basis, the seaman who is entitled to maintenance and cure would receive his wages to the end of the month. Maintenance and cure thus takes the place of workmen's compensation, so far as the sick or injured seaman is concerned.

Sea Codes

The old French code, The Laws of Oleron, which were brought to England by the Norman conquerors and introduced into that country by Richard the Lion Hearted, are the common antecedents of our present law of maintenance and cure. The Laws of Oleron provided that if a seaman became sick during a voyage the master was to set him ashore where he would receive lodging, subsistence, and nursing care. The ship did not have to tarry for the sick mariner but could continue on her voyage. If the sick man recovered, then he was to receive his full wages. But if he died, then his wages were to be paid to his widow or to the next of kin. Considering that this law was in effect during the Middle Ages when human life and human rights were afforded but little consideration, it was remarkable that such humanitarian rights were given to the seafarer.

Wards of the Admiralty Courts

For the past two centuries in England as well as in America, seamen have been regarded as the wards of the admiralty courts and are given solicitous and liberal treatment. While they are in most instances mature individuals and are considered capable of making their own contracts, nevertheless their dealings with shipmasters and owners are watched as carefully by the courts as though the seaman were a child. To this day he is regarded in admiralty as improvident and incapable of protecting his rights.

Beginning in 1790 with the statutes passed by the first Congress of the United States, seamen have received legislative attention accorded to no other class of workers. Governed by law are the payment of his wages, his subsistence, medical care, the comfort of his lodging aboard ship, and his protection from shanghaiers, parasitic crimps, and shady boardinghouse keepers. Like the welfare state with its cradle-to-grave format, the seaman's working life is regulated from the very time he signs his contract of employment to the distribution of his wages and effects upon his decease. The beneficent attitude of the courts is also reflected in his favor when suits are brought for negligent injury and for maintenance and cure.

Contributory Negligence

Fault or contributory negligence on the part of the

147

seaman do not affect his right to maintenance and cure, provided his injury or illness is not due to his wilful misbehavior. The usual examples of wilful misbehavior are disability due to venereal disease and intoxication. There is, however, a tendency of the courts not to deprive a seaman of maintenance and cure by a finding of intoxication unless he is virtually in a state of drunken stupor. [Warren v United States, 340 US 523, 95 L ed 503, 71 S Ct 432, 1951 AMC 416, 1951.] If it is found that his injury or illness was caused by his own wilfulness, then he loses his right to compensation, cost of lodging, and subsistence and medical care at the expense of his employer.

One other fact which may deprive a seaman of maintenance and cure is his failure to disclose a pre-existing physical condition which subsequently becomes disabling while he is in the employ of the boatowner. When the seaman knows that he is afflicted with a disabling disease (tuberculosis, as an example), and conceals that fact and holds himself out as fit, he will be denied the right of maintenance and cure. [Tawada v United States, 162 F2d 615, 1947 AMC 947, CCA9th 1947.] When he has a latent physical condition and is without reasonable ground to suspect its disabling effect during his employment on the boat, deprivation of maintenance and cure will not be his lot. [Lindquist v Dilkes, 127 F2d 21, 1943 AMC 1202, CCA3d 1942.]

How Maintenance and Cure Works

How does maintenance and cure really work? Here is a typical example. Jack James signed the articles of the SS American Science at Philadelphia as an able-bodied seaman at wages of $392 per month. The vessel was making a voyage to several European ports and then back to Philadelphia. On the homeward-bound leg of the voyage, the vessel stopped at Barcelona, Spain. While on shore leave, James, who had been doing some shopping, made a misstep and badly injured his ankle. Wilful misbehavior was not involved in his accident. He was taken to a Barcelona hospital where his ankle received medical care. James returned to the SS American Science before she left for home. Because of the intense pain which the injured ankle was causing him, he was unable to work for the remainder of the voyage. At Boston, the ship's first port of call in the United States, Jack James left the ship and entered a United States Public Health Service hospital. The ship finished her voyage at Philadelphia 5 days later. After 2 weeks the injured seaman was discharged from the Boston hospital. He returned to his home near Philadelphia and continued to receive out-patient treatment at a United States Public Health Service hospital in that city. One month after the out-patient medical care began, he was declared by the hospital to be fit for duty.

James was entitled to receive his wages for the time he was aboard ship. Although his was not a shipboard accident, the maritime law recognizes liability if a seaman on shore leave is injured while he is still in the service of the ship. [Aguilar v Standard Oil Co. of N.J., 318 US 724, 87 L ed 1107, 63 S Ct 930, 1943 AMC 451, 1943.] Jack James will also receive his wages for the 5 days from the time he was compelled to leave the ship at Boston to the end of the voyage at Philadelphia. This portion of his pay is commonly called "unearned wages."

The shipowner must pay for James' medical treatment at the Barcelona hospital as well as doctors', nurses', or druggists' bills which may have been incurred on his behalf. This is the "cure" portion of maintenance and cure. The United States Public

149

Health Service hospitals admit working American seamen free of charge. Shipowners do not have to pay for the medical services rendered to their vessel employees. The Public Health Service hospitals are indirectly supported by shipowners through revenue derived from tonnage taxes exacted from deep-sea freighters and passenger ships entering American ports. James will also be reimbursed by his employer for his transportation expenses from Boston to the port of final discharge, Philadelphia.

Lastly, James will receive his cost of maintenance from the time he left the ship (excluding his stay at the Public Health Service hospital) until the date when he reached his maximum degree of cure. This is usually determined to be the time when he is declared fit for duty. The amount of maintenance is fixed by the court. At the present date it is about $8 per day.

An engineer aboard the yacht Truelove slipped while climbing a ladder and broke his ankle. He had received medical care and treatment at the expense of the yacht owner. The owner died and thereupon his executor declined to go on with the medical treatment. (The executor was perhaps unacquainted with the maritime law.) A lawsuit followed in which the engineer charged the yacht with negligence and unseaworthiness, alleging that he had been furnished with a defective ladder. After trial the judges found the ladder not defective and the boat not negligent. As to the engineer's right to maintenance and cure, the judge stated that "there is no question" but that he was entitled to it. He received maintenance for approximately 130 days at $3.50 per day, the then prevailing rate. [Michaelson v Yacht Truelove, 1940 AMC 1171, DC SD NY 1940.]

Please note that in admiralty law the boat is personalized. Therefore, such phrases as "the boat was negligent" or "the vessel was held not to be liable" is the accepted form.

Jones Act

The Jones Act is well known among lawyers but I suspect that it is relatively little known to owners of small boats. First, as to its title; it was named after Senator Wesley L. Jones of Washington, who in 1920 sponsored and guided the bill through its passage in Congress. The Jones Act gave to ship's officers and crewmen the right to sue the owner of the ship involved for damages arising from personal injuries due to negligence. There is no workmen's compensation law for seamen. As a result of the act, seamen were given liberal rights previously accorded only to railroad workers.

It may be asked, "What is so special about the Jones Act? Doesn't everyone have the right to sue for personal injuries?" Well, it is not so simple as that. Prior to the enactment of the Jones Act, the admiralty courts did not give seamen much comfort in the way of money damages for personal injuries.

Justice Story, a great admiralty judge, made it clear more than a hundred years ago that the extent of the seaman's remedy for injury caused by ship negligence was maintenance and cure. When the cure was completed, the shipowner was freed from all further liability. [Reed v Canfield, F Cas No 11641, CC Mass 1832.] Under the general maritime law, when the seaman's injury resulted in death his cause of action died with him. His widow and children—if such he had—were left without legal recourse by way of damages arising as a result of his injury and death, whether or not it was caused through negligence or because of the unseaworthiness of the vessel. [The

151

Harrisburg, 119 US 199, 30 L ed 358, 7 S Ct 140, 1886.] Later, the admiralty courts began to recognize the seaman's right of damages for injuries caused by defective appliances and faulty equipment while serving on an unseaworthy vessel. [The Osceola, 189 US 158, 175, 47 L ed 760, 764, 23 S Ct 483, 1903.] But with respect to injuries caused by fault of the ship, the strict fellow-servant rule of the common law (non-statutory) was sufficient to defeat every claim. The negligence of the ship's officers and of the crewmen—fellow servants of the injured seaman—were not regarded as acts for which the shipowner was responsible.

In 1920 there was in existence the Federal Employers' Liability Act, [46 United States Code §§ 51 et seq.] which gave to railroad workers the right to sue their employers for personal injury. The Federal Employers' Liability Act (commonly called FELA) is liberal and remedial legislation. By the Jones Act, Congress merely applied all of the benefits of the FELA to seamen. The Jones Act thus abolished the defense of the fellow-servant rule and made the shipowner responsible for injuries to a seaman caused by a fellow worker. Contributory negligence of the injured person did not bar his right to recover a judgment; but the admiralty rule of comparative damages was applied. As a practical measure, this meant that if the injured seaman contributed, for example, 30 percent of the fault which brought about the accident, then the amount of damages awarded to him would be the total damages less 30 percent.

Prior to the enactment of the Jones Act, it was a general defense of the shipowner to assert that the injured seaman had assumed the risk of his employment or, in short, that the risk of injury was part of

152

the normal risk involved in the employment. The Jones Act abolished the defense of assumption of risk.

If the injury resulted in death, the Jones Act permitted the deceased's personal representative to bring suit for damages for the death. Thus, death no longer put an end to the employers' liability, but the cause of action was continued by the personal representative for the benefit of certain survivors. They are: (a) the surviving widow or husband and children of the deceased; (b) if there is no widow or husband and children of the deceased, then the seaman's parents; and (c) if there are no survivors of the first two classes, that is (a) and (b), then the survivors are the next of kin of the deceased seaman who were dependent upon him for support.

The suit against the shipowner must be brought within 3 years from the day of the injury.

It should always be remembered that the Jones Act remedy is open only to seamen; that the relationship of employee and employer must exist between the injured plaintiff and the defendant; and that the basis of the cause of action must be the alleged negligence of the defendant.

Just what constitutes negligence is a factual question which is left to a jury or to a judge to decide. The United States Supreme Court has indicated [Jamison v Encarnacion, 281 US 635, 74 L ed 1082, 50 S Ct 440, 1930 AMC 1129, 1930] that the interpretation of what is negligence should not be given a narrow or restricted reading. The meaning of negligence has been left to the courts, to be construed liberally and remedially in the light of the peculiar hazards of the seafaring profession.

There are literally hundreds of examples of fact situations under the Jones Act in which the shipowner has been held liable for negligent conditions aboard ship which may result in personal injuries. Some are obviously due to neglect in failing to make the ship a reasonably safe place in which to work.

Some fact situations, however, border on the ludicrous and the bizarre. Here are but a few examples: An intoxicated seaman was left lying on a dock by a sober shipmate while he went to notify a ship's officer. During his absence the intoxicated seaman fell off the dock and drowned. The shipowner was held liable for failing to safeguard him properly. [McDonough v Buckeye SS Co., 103 F Supp 473, 1951 AMC 2042, DC Ohio 1951, affirmed, 200 F2d 558, 1953 AMC 343, CA6th 1952, cert den 345 US 926, 97 L ed 1357, 73 S Ct 785.]

It was held to be negligence and improper medical treatment to use cupping on a sick seaman. [Allardice v Isthmian Steamship Co. Inc., 1954 AMC 315, 205 Misc 541, 129 NYS2d 197, City Ct NY 1954, affd 206 Misc 755, 136 NYS2d 707, affd 285 App Div 927, 139 NYS2d 884.]

A large fish was dropped on a board by a fisherman, causing the board to rise and strike a fellow fisherman in the eye. He recovered damages against the shipowner. [Petricich v Devlahovich, 107 F Supp 871, DC Cal 1952.]

Other examples of negligence and liability follow: delay in calling a doctor for a seaman suffering from a perforated gastric ulcer [Poindexter v Groves, 197 F 2d 915, 1952 AMC 2083, CA2d 1952]; a bargemaster injured when he fell through a rotted deck [Williamson v Roen Steamship Company, 149 F Supp 787, 1957 AMC 1344, DC Wis 1957]; a ship's officer knew or should have known of ice on the deck and failed to sand it [Vareltzis v Luckenbach Steamship Company, Inc.,

258 F2d 78, 1958 AMC 1848, CA2d 1958]; assault on a seaman by a fellow crewman of known vicious character [Kyriakos v Goulandris, 151 F2d 132, 1945 AMC 1041, CCA2d 1945]; seamen bitten by dogs allowed to run at will about a vessel [McGee v Sinclair Refining Co., 47 F Supp 912, DC ED Pa 1942]; broken railing of a catwalk from which a seaman fell and drowned [Pollard v Seas Shipping Co., Inc., 146 F2d 875, 1945 AMC 119, CCA2d 1945]; fall on a greasy deck [Cervo v Isbrandtsen Co., 178 F2d 919, 1950 AMC 251, CA2d 1949]; and a seaman contracting asthma because of the use of a defective spray gun [Darlington v National Bulk Carriers, Inc., 157 F2d 817, 1947 AMC 315, CCA2d 1946].

The shipowner is not required to maintain an accident-proof ship. The accident must be caused by some fault, or act of neglect, of the ship. There are hundreds of maritime personal injury Jones Act cases which have been dismissed for failure to prove negligence. [See 2 Norris: "The Law of Seamen" 2d ed pp. 858–863 for a listing of them.]

Unseaworthy Boats

In the early days of shipping, seaworthiness meant a vessel staunch and sound in hull, and with gear and sail free of defects. Within recent decades, however, under a series of court decisions in cases involving personal injury, the concept of unseaworthiness has had some startling and fantastic changes. A boat or vessel might appear to be in perfect shape; but should there be a spot of oil or grease on a deck and should that condition result in injury to a seaman, then the craft will be held to be unseaworthy.

So strictly is the boatowner or shipowner held to an obligation to provide a seaworthy vessel that the injured party need only show that his injury was caused

155

or brought about by this unseaworthy condition. This is known as the doctrine of liability without fault. In those cases (other than unseaworthiness) where negligence is the applied standard, the injured party must show that his injury was brought about by a negligent condition which could have been eliminated or prevented by the exercise of due diligence, and of reasonable care on the part of the boatowner. Due diligence and reasonable care, however, play no part in those cases involving unseaworthiness. If the spot of oil has been on the deck for only a brief time—so brief, in fact, that the boat operator was not informed of its presence or had sufficient time to eliminate it—it nevertheless cannot be a successful defense to the injury suit. The fact that the boat was temporarily or transitorily in an unsound condition can still result in a finding of unseaworthiness and of liability. [Mitchell v Trawler Racer, Inc., 362 US 539, 4 L ed 2d 941, 80 S Ct 926, 1960 AMC 1503, 1960.]

The doctrine of seaworthiness has been applied where there have been defects in the ship's structure, machinery, appliances, furnishings, equipment, appurtenances, tackle, and gear. The owner's obligation is to supply and to keep in order these items on the boat. They should be in sound and proper condition, free of defects, and of the type and capacity normally used aboard ships and boats. The simplest example of an unseaworthy piece of equipment could be the ladder which breaks under the weight of someone using it. A sound ladder aboard the ship should not break when used in the normal fashion; its giving way under these circumstances constitutes unseaworthiness.

The boat need not be in perfect condition. The shipowner is not obliged to furnish an accident-proof craft. What is his obligation *is* the duty to furnish a boat and

156

appurtenances reasonably fit for its intended use. Thus reasonable fitness becomes the test of seaworthiness. Since the determination of reasonable fitness becomes a question of fact, it is left to a jury or a judge to decide.

Seaworthiness is a relative term. What may be regarded as unseaworthiness on a large ocean liner is not necessarily unseaworthiness where a small boat is concerned. The lack of a deck rail will make a vessel sailing on the high seas unseaworthy, while the lack of such a rail in a harbor boat operating in protected waters or in a boat undergoing repairs will not constitute unseaworthiness.

A motor yacht used in New York harbor had been brought to a drydock for repair. An electrician employed by the repair contractor was working on the running-light panel. To determine whether the boat's running lights were operative, he left the pilothouse, walked aft on the trunk-top roof, lost his footing and fell overboard to the floor of the drydock. He was seriously injured. The weather was clear; there was no oil, grease, or other foreign substance present on the trunk top. The repairman had fallen from an unobstructed, virtually level, canvas-covered surface across the main deck. The trunk-top roof was some 18 to 24 inches above the main deck.

In deciding in favor of the boatowner, the court pointed out that while the absence of guardrails might constitute unseaworthiness for some of the purposes to which a vessel may be put, it did not mean that the rails were necessary to make the vessel seaworthy while motionless in a drydock. The test of liability is whether this motor yacht was reasonably fit for the purpose for which she was being used. The trunk-top roof of the yacht, it was held, was a reasonably fit place

157

for the electrician to perform his work aboard a boat in drydock with reasonable safety, and therefore she was seaworthy. [Lester v United States, 234 F2d 625, 1956 AMC 1885, CA2d 1956, cert dismd 352 US 983, 1 L ed 2d 366, 77 S Ct 384.]

Although a boat may be in an unseaworthy condition and personal injury has occurred as a consequence of that condition, it does not therefore necessarily follow that the boatowner will be held liable in damages. The reason for this lies in the fact that in order for there to be liability, the duty to supply a seaworthy boat must be owed to the injured person. If the boatowner has a seaman in his employ, then that individual could be the beneficiary of this liberal law.

From time immemorial the maritime law has required as an absolute obligation that the owner provide the crew with a vessel reasonably sound in hull and gear and one which could be expected to meet the normal hazards of the forthcoming journey.

In 1946 the United States Supreme Court expanded its interpretation of the doctrine of seaworthiness so as to include coverage of longshoremen. [Seas Shipping Co. v Sieracki, 328 US 85, 90 L ed 1099, 66 S Ct 872, 1946 AMC 698, 1946, reh den 328 US 878, 90 L ed 1646, 66 S Ct 1116.] The holding was based on the theory that longshoremen do certain work in connection with the handling of cargo which years ago sailors were obliged to perform. The Supreme Court reasoned that since longshoremen faced the same hazards as seamen do, of working aboard an unseaworthy ship in port, they were entitled to the same degree of protection.

It is extremely unlikely that the doctrine of seaworthiness as it pertains to longshoremen will be of concern to recreational boatowners, with the possible exception of large ocean-going yachts, which may require services of shoreside workers.

The seaworthiness doctrine has not at present been applied to cases of personal injuries to guests, passengers, and repair-yard workers. Generally, when a boat is brought into a yard for repairs, it is not expected that the craft will be in seaworthy condition. There has been one exception to this rule. When a vessel has been brought into a repair yard for periodic inspection and repair between voyages, a court has held that the repair-yard workers are entitled to the benefits of the seaworthiness doctrine. [Socony-Vacuum Oil Company, Inc. v Lawlor, 275 F2d 599, 84 ALR2d 613, 1960 AMC 716, CA2d 1960, cert den 363 US 844, 4 L ed 2d 1728, 80 S Ct 1614.]

This branch of American maritime law is in a state of rapid change and expansion. New decisions and new trends of the courts may mean new concepts with respect to the boatowner's obligation and liability. It is quite possible that the severe obligation of seaworthiness with its harsh rule of liability without fault will, in the near future, be applied to those holding the status of passengers. It is also possible that in the foreseeable future, the inclusion of invited guests among those to whom the duty of furnishing a seaworthy boat is owed will be an accomplished fact.

Guests

Undoubtedly one of the great pleasures of boat ownership is that of being the host to invited guests. When guests come aboard the boat, the problem is always present of an accident or injury occurring to them and of consequent liability of the boatowner. Certain precautions can be taken to avoid or at least to minimize the possibility of accidents. These include the keeping of the boat and its equipment in excellent shape and free from dangerous and defective conditions. An ancillary step would be the giving of proper instructions to the guests regarding their conduct, dress, and avoidance of areas where dangerous and working machinery is located.

The boatowner can be held responsible for any negligent or reckless conduct on his part which may result in injury to the guest. The guest is owed a duty of reasonable care and if he is injured by the failure of the boatowner to exercise that care properly, then the guest is entitled to recover damages.

Basically the position of the guest in a boat is no different from that of the invited passenger in an automobile. The automobile owner or operator must use reasonable care in the handling of the conveyance, and can be held legally responsible if the guest is injured as a result of negligent operation.

In state common law there is a distinction made between a "licensee" and the "invitee." There is a further distinction made with respect to a "trespasser." A trespasser is one who enters upon the property of another without invitation, express or implied, or against the wishes of the owner. The owner owes him no duty of care and can be liable only for wilfully harming him. [Ribeiro v United Fruit Co., 284 F2d 317, 1961 AMC 514, CA2d 1960, cert den 365 US 872, 5 L ed 2d 861, 81 S Ct 905.] A licensee is a visitor by sufferance. An example of this class would be a person who is visiting an invited guest of the boatowner. Under the common law the owner's duty would be to warn the visitor of a dangerous condition within the owner's knowledge. On the other hand, the boatowner's duty to a guest or business visitor, the "invitee," is to use reasonable care for his safety.

In a recent case in the United States Supreme Court,

the distinction between "licensee" and "invitee" was
wiped out so far as maritime injury cases are concerned. A passenger vessel was moored to her pier
in New York City. A man named Kermarec was the
friend of a seaman who was a member of the crew
of this vessel. The seaman invited Kermarec to visit
him and in anticipation of the visit obtained a pass
from the steamship company which owned the vessel.
Kermarec came aboard the ship and spent several hours
visiting his friend. In order to leave the ship it was
necessary for him to descend a certain stairway. This
stairway was carpeted and in order to keep the carpet-
ing clean a canvas runner was laid on the stairway
temporarily. (This is a customary practice on fine
ships when in port.) At the time Kermarec was descending the stairway the canvas runner had become
detached and therefore was in a potentially dangerous
condition.

Kermarec fell down the stairway and was severely
injured. The trial judge instructed the jury that it
was to consider Kermarec as "a gratuitous licensee"
and one who could recover damages only if he proved
that the shipowner had failed to warn him of a dangerous condition within the shipowner's actual knowledge. Therefore, it would have been necessary for
Kermarec to show that some ship's officer had noticed
that the canvas runner had become disarranged and
had failed to do anything about it.

In spite of the instruction, the jury returned a verdict in favor of Kermarec. Thereupon the trial judge
granted a motion to set aside the verdict, and dismissed
the complaint. Eventually the case reached the United
States Supreme Court, which held that the distinction
in the common law of the standard of care owed to
licensees and invitees was incompatible with the mari-

time law's traditions of simplicity and practicality. The Supreme Court concluded, and laid down the rule, that the owner of a ship in navigable waters owes to all who are on board for purposes not inimical to the owner's legitimate interests (as a burglar aboard ship) the duty of exercising reasonable care. [Kermarec v Compagnie Generale Transatlantique, 358 US 625, 3 L ed 2d 550, 79 S Ct 406, 1959 AMC 597, 1959.] The jury's verdict in favor of Kermarec was restored.

The same duty applies to boatowners whose boats operate on navigable waters. The law places a duty upon the boatowner of not causing harm to anyone aboard the boat because of negligence on his part; but this duty does not apply toward a trespasser. The class of invitees would include, in addition to invited guests, such persons as a deliverer of a package, a visitor of the invited guests, a would-be purchaser of the boat, a repairman or mechanic, a boat club official or employee, etc. The persons who may fall into the class of "invitees" are numerous indeed.

Whether or not the boatowner or the boat operator is negligent is usually a question of fact. The fact-finder, either a jury or a judge sitting alone, must pass on the circumstances of each particular case in order to determine if there is negligence involved and who is responsible for that negligence. It can readily be seen that there are literally hundreds of fact situations which can constitute negligent conduct.

Accidents to Guests

Thoughtlessness, recklessness, and dangerous operation and navigation of a boat can cause injury to guests and can constitute negligence. High speed with sharp turns or imprudent maneuvering in the face of large waves or in heavy seas can be fruitful sources of injuries and injury claims.

162

Contrasting two cases which involved injuries to adolescents as a consequence of riding on the bow of the boat should prove a good primer regarding reckless or imprudent maneuvering. In the first instance a 14-year-old girl swimmer was given a lift by a passing speedboat operator. She was allowed to sit on the polished, crowned bow of the boat. The operator started off at a high rate of speed and then made a quick and violent turn. The girl could not retain her grip on the bow and slid off. She was seriously injured by the boat's propellers and lost her life. The boat operator was held to have been negligent in the boat's operation while the owner was permitted to limit liability. [Petition of Liebler, 19 F Supp 829, 1937 AMC 1006, DC WD NY 1937.]

The second case involves a 17-year-old boy who, with the owner's permission, borrowed a 14-foot Champion Sabre motorboat powered by a 40 horsepower outboard motor. He took aboard three boys, one of whom was the plaintiff, Scheiner, aged 16. The boat was being operated in San Francisco Bay. Scheiner was sitting on the bow in a straddling position with his feet in the water. As the boat made a turn to starboard Scheiner fell off. His arm and hip were cut by the boat's propeller. The boat operator's father was sued for damages. Scheiner contended that the young operator was negligent, since he was making a sharp turn while traveling at a high rate of speed and failed to give Scheiner any warning of the intended maneuver. The trial judge found that Scheiner was guilty of contributory negligence, because of the manner and place in which he sat in the boat, but that under the maritime law (which is applicable here since San Francisco Bay is navigable waters) his contributory negligence did not bar him from recovery, but could be considered with respect to diminution of damages. However, the trial judge also found that there was no evidence that the boat operator made a sharp turn or that the boat was going at a high rate of speed. Since the speed was not excessive, Scheiner was not entitled to any warning. The boat was being operated in a reasonably prudent manner. The court gave judgment to the defendant. [Scheiner v St. Jovite, 180 F Supp 452, DC Cal 1960.]

Boats were being rented at a winter resort. Two honeymooning couples chartered or rented an 18-foot inboard motorboat. They were engaged in sightseeing and taking pictures on Biscayne Bay. Gas fumes had accumulated in the bilge. When the motor was started, an explosion and fire resulted, injuring several of the boat's occupants. The renting company was held to be negligent for allowing its boat to get into bad condition. This unseaworthiness was the sole proximate cause of the accident. The court disregarded a signed agreement entered into by the renter in which he had stated that he had examined the boat, found it seaworthy, and released the renting company from all liability. The court held that one who deals with the general public cannot escape liability under the maritime law by placing the responsibility on the renter to examine the boat for an unseaworthy condition. [Rothman v U-Steer-It, Inc., 247 F2d 803, 1957 AMC 2077, CA5th 1957.]

Water-skiing is a sport which has become increasingly popular. Also on the increase are the skiing accidents and resulting personal injuries which are the consequence, logical or otherwise, of this sport. A young man was water-skiing on Fort Loudon Lake, Tennessee. His friend was operating a 23-foot Owens Craft Cruiser. The libelant, the skier, claimed that his friend made a sharp turn to the left and that the waves from the boat plus the waves from nearby speedboats caused him to fall and suffer an eye injury. He asserted, too, that the boat operator was negligent for having failed to arrange signals with him for his skiing maneuvers. On the other hand, his friend contended that he had been steering a straight course down the lake; that the boat had not been changed from a straight line; and that at the time the libelant fell he had been going over the crest of merely small waves from his boat and the speedboats. Faced with these conflicting versions, the court decided that the water skier failed to show by the greater weight of the believable evidence that the boat operator was negligent. As to the failure to arrange for signals, the court concluded that the lack of signals had nothing directly to do with the accident. [King v Testerman, 214 F Supp 335, 1963 AMC 2054, DC Tenn 1963.]

The owner of an outboard motorboat invited a friend and his wife to go water-skiing. The owner asked the plaintiff (the friend) to start the motor. It seemed that the motor was equipped with an electric starter, which was not working. It was also equipped with a hand-operated starting rope, which had a handgrip on the end. Instead of using the handgrip the plaintiff wrapped the rope around his hand and then jerked it in an effort to start the motor. At this particular time the boatowner was standing in the water and did not see what the plaintiff was doing. On the plaintiff's third attempt the motor misfired, causing the rope to recoil, thus pulling him against the motor where he was injured. The evidence further showed that the plaintiff was an experienced garage mechanic and that he owned an outboard motor himself. The owner testified that in using the handgrip it would be harm-

165

lessly pulled out of his hand whenever the motor mis-fired. Whether the accident took place on navigable waters (which would have enabled the court to apply the federal maritime laws) is not clear in the reported case. Since Florida law was applied, it is most prob-able that the injury occurred on state nonnavigable waters. Under Florida law, the court held, the plain-tiff was a licensee. The duty which the boatowner owed to him was to refrain from wanton negligence which would injure him, to refrain from intentionally exposing him to danger, and to warn him of a defect or condition known to the owner to be dangerous when the danger could not be apparent to the injured person. However, the injury to the plaintiff was caused by his act of wrapping the rope around his hand and not by the failure to warn of danger. The plaintiff lost the case. [Wagner v Owens, 1964 AMC 689, 155 So 2d 181, D Ct of App Fla 1963.]

It should be noted that in both of these water-skiing cases the courts applied the rather strict rules used in negligence cases and properly placed the burden on the injured persons of proving that not only was the defendant negligent but that the negligent act was the proximate cause of the accident. In seamen's neg-ligence cases, it may be observed in passing, the deter-mination of what constitutes negligence has been so greatly liberalized that in similar fact situations it is not at all improbable that the plaintiffs—seamen—would prevail.

Fishing Accidents

Fishing-party boats, to the probable surprise of no one, provide many accidents, some of the freakish kind. A passenger on a public fishing boat was injured when he was struck in the eye by a lead sinker cast by a fellow fisherman. The injured passenger claimed that the boat proprietor had the duty to protect him from the negligent acts of fellow fishermen while engaged in fishing. He lost the case. The judge declared that there is no law that requires the adoption of rules governing the manner in which fishing on boats may be carried on. In short, the boat operator was held not negligent merely for the failure to set up rules with regard to casting. [Anderson v Ocean Sport Fishing, Inc., 1938 AMC 1513, D Ct of App Cal 1938.]

A freak wave was encountered by a chartered fishing boat. Seven seconds after the boat operator sighted the wave, it struck. The plaintiff, who was injured when the wave washed over the boat, was only a step or two from the trunk cabin, which offered shelter at the time the wave broke. He was engaged in "shooting the breeze" with his fellow fishermen and did not see the freak wave. The judge held that because of the suddenness of the peril, the boat operator's failure to warn the passengers of the impending danger was not negligence as a matter of law. The personal injury damage suit was dismissed. [Washburn v Ensley, 1959 AMC 1585, S Ct Wash 1959.]

The boat Sport Fisher had, to no one's surprise, a party of sport fishermen aboard. The captain of the boat announced that he was going to move it. The plaintiff proceeded to reel in his line, preparatory to placing his fishing pole in a rack. When the boat made a sudden movement the plaintiff stepped forward on an anchovy which had been used as bait. He slipped and injured a knee. The court was of the opinion that the sudden movement of the boat was caused by a wave that hit it. It was this natural phenomena, it was held, rather than any negligent act or omission in the operation of the boat, which caused the fisherman to fall. The judge then made the following statement which should be handbook law regarding accidents of this type. The court stated:

"It is a matter of common knowledge that the movements of fishing boats and other small water craft are constantly affected by the waves and thereby made unsteady, and that this is true without regard to the care exercised in their operation. The bigger the waves the more vigorous is the impact on the boat and the more severe and sudden the lurch or jerk caused thereby. Anyone who has ever been on such a boat or who has observed their movements from the shore, particularly when the tide was coming in, has observed how the waves upon occasion cause these boats to pitch and churn. Such vigorous and unpredictable movements may readily cause a person to lose his balance and fall as did the plaintiff here. This is simply one of natural hazards of this type of venture." [Lockhart v Martin, 1962 AMC 1076, 159 Cal App 2d 760, 324 P2d 340, D Ct of App Cal 1958.]

Injuries to Workingmen

Probably the very last thing a boatowner will think of in connection with personal injury liability is that he may find himself responsible for providing compensation payments to an injured employee. If a person is hired by you to navigate the boat or to work as a steward he may be considered in law to be a seaman. And if you hire a worker to repair or paint your boat while it is in the water or when drawn up on land and he is injured while doing so, it is likely that he will come under the benefits of either the Longshoremen's and Harbor Workers' Compensation Act or a state compensation act. [See: Norris: Maritime Personal Injuries, 1959.]

Of course, you may avoid workmen's compensation

168

complications by dealing with a reputable boat repairman. As a contractor and an employer he will be initially and solely responsible for coverage under workmen's compensation laws. But a boatowner may still not be out of the woods. Should the workman be injured as a consequence of an unseaworthy or negligent condition on your boat, he could sue you as the owner of the boat. This is known as a "third-party action."

When this happens the boatowner would then attempt to bring the repairman into the action as a "third party defendant." Should the boatowner find himself with a judgment against him, he would wish to have the repairman make good or "indemnify" him. All this is highly technical legal procedure. The techniques involved are not within the scope of this present work. [See: Norris: Maritime Personal Injuries, 1959.]

If you are insured, then this will become the headache of your insurance company and its lawyers.

•

5

insuring
pleasure boats

On Carrying Insurance

As an automobile owner and operator of many years' standing, I would no more think of driving my car to the local shopping center without insurance coverage than of walking into a bank clothed only in my underwear. Through the years the amount of my insurance coverage has been progressively increased until it sometimes appears to me to be an astronomical amount. Whether you care to call it caution or phobia, nonetheless, I am convinced that driving an uninsured automobile is an obliging way of courting financial disaster. Interestingly enough, I have avoided accidents for the past 30 years.

I hold the same conviction with respect to the operation of a pleasure boat. Unless a boatowner is financially and mentally prepared to make good on all boating casualties, serious or slight, carrying boat insurance makes but simple, good sense. With the number of boats increasing rapidly on our inland and restricted waters the possibility of being involved in a boating accident—with the resultant personal injury

171

and property damage claims—becomes progressively more probable. Whether insurance coverage is sought with the emphasis placed on the value of your boat or on exposure to liability as the criterion must depend upon the desire of the individual owner.

To rely on the limitation of liability law (see chapter six on Limitation of Liability) as a form of protection from a large damage claim can be foolhardy. In the overwhelming percentage of instances pleasure boats are operated either by the owner or the operating conditions are known to him. To be denied by the courts the right to limit liability and at the same time to be uninsured will most certainly leave the financially responsible owner in an exposed and bereft position.

When You Are Insured

An insurance policy is a form of contract whereby an insurance company agrees, for a stipulated premium, to compensate the party insured for a loss or damage to property or persons by specified perils. You, the boatowner, are called "the insured," "the policyholder," or "the assured." The insurance company is also known as "the insurer," "the underwriter," or "the assurer."

Before you can obtain insurance you must have a pecuniary or moneyed interest in the property sought to be insured. This is known as an "insurable interest."

Having obtained insurance on your boat, you have a certain amount of protection. I say "a certain amount" advisedly, for like any other contract it covers only those things specifically mentioned in the contract or policy. Don't be naive! Don't imagine that because you have paid your premium the insurance company is now prepared to undertake the maintenance of your boat for you. If you do, it is a foregone conclusion that you will be rudely jolted when you discover, as I have, that the facts of insurance life are so totally different.

Reputable insurance companies will make good on losses as they have agreed and specifically set out to do in their policies, and except in rare instances where the claim is minor and customer good will is involved, only for those losses. The admonition to "read your policy" is not meant to be an idle or vapid phrase.

The first thing that a claims adjuster will do when he receives your claim of loss will be to check your policy and see whether the damage or loss resulted from one of the named perils or is otherwise within the policy coverage. If the loss does not come within the terms of the policy, then the likelihood is that your claim will be turned down. Insurance companies do not regard themselves as charitable institutions. It is expected that the premiums received will constitute a part of the insurance "pool" to be used to pay off those losses contemplated by the policy. No insurance company can for long stay in business if it also pays for those losses either not covered by the policy or only remotely related to it.

Marine insurance can be an involved and tricky subject. Fortunately for owners of recreational boats, such technical matters as "general average" and "particular average" are applicable, in the main, to cargo-carrying vessels. Nevertheless, there is much about marine insurance which can trap the unwary. A knowledgeable broker who is a specialist in marine insurance can be helpful. But the fact that you place reliance on your broker should not deter you from diligently reading your policy. Generally, only you will have a clear picture of what type of protection you need or desire. Be sure to talk this phase over with your broker.

Types of Policies

It is important that you be aware of the types of policies which are currently provided by the insurance industry so that you will know which policy features are best suited for your needs.

Basically there are two types of boat policies—the yacht policy and the outboard motorboat policy, having different terms and conditions. Much of the discussion in this chapter will be concerned with the provisions of the yacht policy. Remember, however, that the really important provisions appear also in the outboard motorboat policy and therefore the essential meaning of the yacht policy provisions applies equally as well to the outboard policy.

The title "yacht policy" is something of a misnomer and an unfortunate descriptive term. While the word "yacht" will conjure to some a picture of Mr. Morgan's palatial ocean-going pleasure boat, it is really intended as a word of wide inclusion when used in connection with marine insurance. To insurance companies, a yacht policy is used in connection with all sorts and sizes of pleasure boats, both powered and sail. Some companies, strangely enough, include outboard motorboats in their yacht policy coverage.

The principal features of the yacht policy are contained in those categories designated as hull, protection and indemnity ("P & I" or bodily injury insurance), federal longshoremen's and harbor workers' compensation insurance, and medical payments. These provisions are of importance to boatowners, since accidents in the form of collision, injuries to employees, guests, and others, can occur at any time. Each of the policy provisions will be discussed in detail in this chapter.

It should always be remembered that the specific

details of coverage vary from company to company, and indeed from the same company's many different forms of policies. The wording of marine insurance policies is not controlled by law. The terms of the policies are further varied by riders and indorsements which are attached to the policy. Some companies will cover risks which others do not. It is therefore important to you that your policy should contain that coverage which *you* feel is essential for your financial protection.

The Application Form

In order to obtain marine insurance on your boat you will most likely be asked to fill out and submit an application form. One printed form which I have examined is comprehensive indeed. It contains no less than 125 questions. The most detailed information regarding the boat is requested. The queries cover, among others, the cost of the boat; where and when built; whether used commercially or chartered; waters to be navigated; where she lays up and where she may be inspected; particulars regarding the dimensions and features of her hull; her propulsion and machinery and equipment, etc.

A material fact should not be concealed or misrepresented. In marine insurance all material facts should be disclosed by the insured, that is, all facts material to the risk known to him and not known to the insurer should be stated. This includes facts whether inquired for or not. Whether the failure to disclose material facts is due to accident, oversight, or error, its consequences will be grave, for it can void the policy. Such an outcome is justified on the ground that the risk assumed is not the one which the parties intended.

Marine insurance has been founded on the fullest good faith between the parties. Both the insured and

175

the insurance company are expected to disclose all material information whether known by knowledge or by information. Thus, a shipowner applying for insurance who knows that the vessel has met with a mishap, no matter how slight, must make this fact known. Likewise the underwriter who knows that the vessel has completed her voyage on which the insurance is sought is obliged to tell the applicant of it.

The application form sets forth that the boatowner is in no way bound to accept any quotation which the underwriter may make and that the underwriters are not bound to accept the risk.

Usually the underwriter will issue a "binder" pending the issuance of the policy. If the underwriter knows nothing about the boat and is uncertain of the risk, a binder will not be issued until an inspection of the boat is made. A binder issued "subject to inspection" *may* have no force and effect until the inspection has been made and the risk is finally accepted by the underwriter. From the underwriter's point of view there is no certainty, however, that the courts will rule to this effect. The underwriter may well be held liable if a loss occurs after the binder has been issued and before an inspection has taken place. It is not at all improbable that a court will reason that the binder was not intended to be issued as a mere idle gesture and that it must therefore have been intended to cover the assured at least until such time as an inspection made cancellation by the insurance company desirable.

An insurance underwriter is under no compulsion to grant a policy. The usual reason for refusing to insure is the poor condition of the boat as found by the survey. Extreme old age of the craft may be a cause for refusing coverage. If the risk is accepted on such a boat, the premium rate may be higher.

The Language of the Policy

There is no standard form of marine insurance policy for pleasure-boat owners. Please keep this fact in mind. Policy features discussed in this chapter are not necessarily contained in all policies. Check your policy to see whether anything important is missing. Some companies may have similar or even identical forms but others issue policies which are variants in that they contain either differently worded clauses or exclude some clauses or include others. In short, one cannot speak of a boating policy as though it were a uniform statute or ordinance contained in a code of laws.

Since an insurance policy is a form of contract it can take any of the multitudinous forms which exist in the many differing types of contracts.

Like all contracts the insurance policy must have the requisites of a valid contract. It must be an agreement resulting from an offer and acceptance. To be a binding agreement the contract must be in the form required by law. There must be two parties legally capable of contracting. The agreement must be supported by a valuable consideration, unless the consideration is dispensed with by the use of a seal. The purpose of the contract must be legal and must not contravene public policy. Finally, the insurance contract must be fairly made with the consent of the parties given upon full knowledge of all the material and relevant facts known to the other.

Since the words in the policy are the words of the insurance company any ambiguities will be construed against it and in favor of the insured. [Royal Insurance Co. v Martin, 192 US 149, 48 L ed 385, 24 S Ct 247, 1904.]

While ordinarily contracts are construed by the courts so as to give effect to the intention of the parties, in insurance policies any doubt created by ambiguous language is always resolved strictly against the insurer. When the language is clear and understandable there is, of course, no necessity for judicial scrutiny.

Marine insurance is the oldest form of indemnity. There is evidence that marine insurance was in use in the twelfth century and dealt in by the Jews banished from France at that period. It was also engaged in by the Lombard merchants. Near the close of the seventeenth century the coffeehouse of Edward Lloyd became the meeting place of the insurance fraternity. Marine insurance, as we know it today, has its roots in the rapid development of this form of indemnity in the eighteenth century among the English underwriters who formed the insurance body known as Lloyds of London.

Some of the boating policies contain a clause regarding sea perils in language which might have been written in Edward Lloyd's coffeehouse. It reads as follows:

"Touching the adventures and perils which we, the assurers, are content to bear and take upon us in this voyage, they are of the Seas, men of war, fire, enemies, pirates, rovers, thieves, jettisons, letters of marque and countermarque; reprisals and taking at sea, arrests, restraints and detainments, of all Kings, Princes and Peoples of what Nation, condition or quality soever, Barratry of the Master, and mariners and of all other losses, perils and misfortunes that have or shall come to the hurt, detriment or damage of the said goods and merchandise or any parts thereof."

Small wonder then that recently a judge remarked that a policy issued to cover barges operating on inland creeks in the twentieth century was anachronistically worded in Elizabethan, if not Chaucerian, English. The judge held that the insurance company could not now be heard to say in effect that the policy was meaningless on the ground that the ancient and antiquated language used did not apply to the barge and those on it. [Russell Mining Co. v Northwestern Fire & Marine Ins. Co. 207 F Supp 162, 1963 AMC 130, DC Tenn 1963, set aside on other grounds (CA6) 322 F2d 440.]

Of the "touching the adventures" language another jurist made the following remarks: "The words of the policy smell of the tang and the salt of the sea. They bring up pictures of the Spanish Main of the Sixteenth Century. We expect to see Captain Kidd or Sir Francis Drake jump out of the pages. It illustrates the 'cake of custom' to see how the old marine policies written four centuries ago persist to the present day." [Lind and Gaffney v Boston Insurance Company, 1953 AMC 1047, Sup Ct Wash 1953.]

It is readily apparent that the manner in which insurance policies are drafted leaves much to be desired. The use of stylized and stilted language is defended by those in the insurance business on the assumption that it has been used for centuries and that therefore each word and phrase has been carefully gone over and construed by the courts. It is feared that any change in the language of the policy might invite a new and differing view by the courts.

Some of the present-day policies which I have examined show a modified version of this granddaddy clause, while others have eliminated it entirely. I think that if the insurance people really know their business there is no reason why a marine insurance

179

policy cannot be written in plain, basic English. Insurance companies, however, generally rely on hallowed printed forms and, therefore, interpreting an ambiguous or unclear policy provision in favor of the insured is but an act of simple justice. There is a present trend toward greater clarity in the wording of marine insurance policies.

Policy Exceptions

In reading an insurance policy I have always been intrigued (and sometimes disturbed) by the listed exceptions or exclusions. In other words, I can readily accept and absorb those happenings which the policy will cover in the event of a loss or damage, but my blood pressure rises when I read the exceptions. However, policy exclusions, like death and taxes, are always with us.

Natural deterioration of the boat, such as dry rot, is generally excluded from coverage. Also excluded is wear and tear.

Destruction or damage caused, or contributed to, by war, revolution, rebellion, insurrection, piracy, civil strife, and riots, will—if so stated in the policy—mean that the loss will not be covered. One company now includes loss or damage caused by strikes, riots, and civil commotions, as part of its policy coverage. This subject is discussed in somewhat more detail later in this chapter.

Other exclusions which may be found in the usual yacht policy are: loss of individual pieces of equipment by theft unless the boat itself is stolen; loss or damage to spars, sails, and rigging while racing (some companies will accept this risk with a deductible provision, but still will exclude loss of or damage to a spinnaker) ; wages and loss, damage, or expense caused by or in consequence of ice or freezing while afloat.

Special indorsements may be obtained by payment of higher premiums to vary the exclusion if the insurance company agrees. This means that by paying an additional premium the company will include a risk which is usually excluded.

A "named perils" policy provides indemnity for loss or damage only when the incident is specifically provided for in the policy. An "all risks" policy is a more comprehensive type of policy intended to cover many losses not provided for in the "named perils" policy. However, the term "all risks" is in itself a contradiction, for that kind of policy carries the usual exclusions mentioned in this section.

Cruising Limits

Your policy may have written into it certain specific geographical limits. If the limits are set for the Great Lakes you will find that you do not have the protection of your policy when you take your boat down the Atlantic Coast. Should you contemplate such a trip it is advisable to notify your underwriter or your broker of your plan. An additional premium may have to be paid for the "extended navigation limits." Depending upon locality, it is possible that the extension of cruising limits may be granted without the payment of an additional fee.

An owner of a yacht which was outside the geographic limits specified in his policy found himself sustaining a total loss when the yacht was destroyed by fire. The policy had a clause which read as follows: "Warranty confined to the waters of the Great Lakes and tributaries not below Quebec." The yacht was taken to Florida where she was lost in a repair yard fire. In denying recovery to the yacht owner on the policy the court said:

"As I construe this entire policy, I am satisfied that

the parties never contemplated that this policy would embrace a fire loss on an unknown and unfamiliar Marine Railway at a point considerably over a thousand miles distant from the only waters where the vessel might float and be covered by the policy." [Rosenbaum v Standard Insurance Co. of N. Y., 1949 AMC 716, Cir Ct Fla 1949.]

If a boat has gone beyond her cruising limits but then has returned within them when a loss occurs, the owner is covered.

A clause in a marine policy covering a boat used in Florida coastal waters stated that the insurance applied only within "the limits of the continental United States of America." The boat had gone to the Bahama Islands and was en route to West Palm Beach, Florida, when the loss occurred. The court considered as being unrealistic the argument that 3 miles off the coast was intended as the geographical limit contemplated by the policy. Finding the phrase "continental United States of America" ambiguous in view of the various interpretations given to it by the courts, the doubt was resolved in favor of the insured. Said the court, reasonably enough: "Had the insurance company whose scrivener prepared the subject policy of insurance desired to restrict the coverage to an area within three miles of the coast of the United States or within any other prescribed area it would have been a simple matter to have so stated." [Winter v Employers Fire Insurance Company, 1962 AMC 1972, Civil Ct Fla 1962.]

Private Pleasure Warranty

It is essential, from the point of view of the underwriter, that the insured boat be used for the purpose intended or contemplated by the parties. When a recreational boat is insured at a rate usually applied to

182

boats used for personal pleasure, it is not expected that the owner will use it as a craft for hire. The risks involved when the boat is operated for private pleasure by the owner can be made more numerous, or the opportunity of loss or damage greatly enlarged, when the boat is placed in the hands or under the direction or purpose of strangers whose only interest in the boat is the money paid for its use. When there is a greater risk involved due to the altered use to which the boat is being put, then the insurance company, if it wishes to continue the coverage under that circumstance, is entitled to impose a different rate.

To guard against the imposition of liability should the type of boat use be changed by the insured, the underwriter places an express warranty in the marine policy which states that the policy shall be null and void while the boat is used as a public or livery conveyance for carrying passengers or property for hire, or where it is rented or leased to others. Some policies state that the policy terminates upon the use of the boat for other than private pleasure purposes unless previous consent of the underwriter has been obtained and has been indorsed on the policy.

If you are tempted to make "expense money" by hiring out your boat, at least be aware that you jeopardize your insurance protection when you do so.

As previously noted in this chapter, the insured must disclose all facts material to the risk. When the owner failed to disclose the fact that the boat was to be used for excursion purposes while carrying paying passengers, it was held to be a concealment of a material fact which voided the policy. [Fireman's Fund Insurance Company v Wilburn Boat Company, 300 F2d 631, 1962 AMC 1593, CA5th 1962, cert den 370 US 925, 8 L ed 2d 505, 82 S Ct 1562, reh den 371 US 854, 9 L ed 2d 92, 83 S Ct 17.]

In an unusual case, an insurance company was estopped from the defense of breach of the private pleasure warranty when it knew that the boat had been chartered for a week and was under charter at the time of the accident. The underwriter, although it possessed this knowledge, allowed the owner to proceed with the making of repairs and did not deny liability until months later. [Reliance Insurance Co. v Yacht Escapade, 280 F2d 482, 86 ALR2d 1236, 1961 AMC 2410, CA5th 1960.]

Water-skiing

Insurance companies are aware of the fact that water-skiing, aquaplaning, and similar sports are a fruitful source of accidents and productive of collision and personal injury claims. Their awareness is shown by a policy clause limiting liability for loss of life and bodily injury to any one person to $10,000 and for any one accident to $20,000.

Property damage arising from this form of towing is restricted to $10,000 for any one accident. That is, the amount of protection named in the policy is reduced to these respective amounts. If an additional premium is paid, the water-skiing limitation will be removed at the discretion of the insurance company.

Transfer of Ownership

The marine underwriter (who is concerned with the moral aspects of the hazard) wants to be certain that the individual who obtained the policy is the one who is the owner at the time of the loss. The possibility of paying the loss to the wrong party, with legal complications which undoubtedly would follow, is another factor.

For these reasons the policy will contain a clause similar to the following: "This insurance shall be void in case of transfer of ownership of the property insured by this policy without the previous consent in writing of this Company." Another insurance company form goes still further and includes the assignment, transfer, or pledge of the boat in this interdiction.

Normal caution would dictate that the boatowner should know the terms of his policy and that if there is any variance in fact with those terms the underwriter should be notified promptly in writing.

No Thirds Off

In the old days of wooden ships the repair to the hull of a damaged vessel often left the ship in better condition than it was before the accident. The underwriters followed a practice of deducting one-third from the cost of repairs to equalize the increase in value to the owner. The theory underlying this course was that the underwriter should not bear the whole burden of repair.

The yacht policies of today usually provide that repairs are to be paid by the insurer without deducting "new for old." The modern policies therefore contain a "no thirds off" clause.

However, claims for damage to canvas or sails are adjusted on the basis of its depreciated value at the time of the loss or damage.

Sue and Labor

If your uninsured boat has been damaged in an accident, what would you do? Or perhaps, to be more accurate, what wouldn't you do? Well, in all likelihood you wouldn't abandon your boat and allow her to sink. You would undoubtedly seek a tow to a safe berth, after which you would arrange for the necessary repairs.

When your boat is insured your underwriter expects you to show the same interest and application of common sense in salvaging and repairing her in order to prevent any further loss than that arising from the initial occurrence. In return, the insurance company will pay all of your reasonable expenses incurred therefor up to the amount for which the boat is insured. This, in its simplest terms, is the meaning of "sue and labor."

The usual wording of this clause is as follows:

"And in case of any loss or misfortune, it shall be lawful and necessary for the Insured, their factors, servants and assigns, to sue, labor and travel for, in and about the defense, safeguard and recovery of the property insured or any part thereof, without prejudice to this insurance, to the charges whereof this Company will contribute their proportion as provided herein."

The object of the sue and labor clause is the diminishment of the amount of loss; it is designed for the benefit of the insurance company. [See: Reliance Insurance Co. v Yacht Escapade, 280 F2d 482, 86 ALR2d 1236, 1961 AMC 2410, CA5th 1960.]

Latent Defects

During the transitional period in ship transportation from sail to steam a serious question arose as to whether the traditional "perils" of the sea in marine policies would apply to loss by damage of the ship's machinery. A test case involving the breaking of an air chamber of a pump operated by a donkey engine on the steamship Inchmaree was taken up to the House of Lords. The machinery damage was brought about by the negligence of the ship's crew. The House of Lords (England's Supreme Court) held that a machinery breakage loss was not occasioned by a cause of the same nature as a peril of the sea. The underwriters, it was declared, were not liable under the terms of the policy.

To avoid the limitation imposed by this decision and to give needed protection to shipowners, a clause was written into marine policies to cover this type of contingency. It is known as the "Inchmaree clause" after the vessel which figured in the test case.

The inclusion in a marine insurance policy of the "Inchmaree clause" or "negligence clause" or "latent defects clause," as it is variously known, is of great importance to boatowners. The effect of it is that the underwriter assumes the liability for any loss or damage to your boat if it is caused by explosion, breakage of shafts, or by a latent (hidden) defect in the machinery or hull, etc. If your boat carries a master and crew, your boat is covered if the loss or damage was caused by their negligence. The loss covered is the damage caused by the breakage but not the cost of replacing the broken part.

The condition, however, must not have resulted from lack of due diligence on the part of the owner. For example, if a machinery part has become worn and its condition is known to the owner and because of procrastination he has failed to replace it, upon an ensuing loss, the insurance company will undoubtedly decline to accept liability.

The clause as contained in one particular policy is satisfyingly broad. It reads:

> "This insurance also specially to cover loss of or damage to the subject matter insured directly caused by the following:
> "Accidents in loading, discharging or in taking on fuel, or in hauling, launching or in going on

187

or off, or while on drydocks, graving docks, ways, gridirons or pontoons;

"Collapse of buildings or other structures including collapse of shoring, blocking or staging;

"Explosions on shipboard or elsewhere;

"Bursting of boilers, breakage of shafts or any latent defect in the machinery or hull (excluding the cost and expense of replacing or repairing the defective part);

"Negligence of Masters, Mariners, Engineers or Pilots;

"Contact with aircraft (including articles falling therefrom) or with any land conveyance;

"Provided such losses or damages have not resulted from want of due diligence by the Owners of the insured yacht or any of them, or by the Managers."

A "Sunday skipper" employed a captain. Due to the master's negligence in winterizing the boat, water entered some holes in the exhaust line and the boat sank. The captain knew of these defects in the line and had decided to replace it but had failed to do so. The owner, however, did not know of this, and in fact knew nothing about the operation and maintenance of the boat. The owner, it was held, was not lacking in due diligence in relying upon the competence of the captain under the circumstances of this case. The insurance company was held to be liable by virtue of the "Inchmaree clause." [Founders' Insurance Company v Rogers, 305 F2d 944, 1963 AMC 116, CA9th, 1962.]

When the owner and his friends lay up the boat and a sinking occurs through their negligence it is not a sea peril and not negligence of "masters, mariners, engineers or pilots." [Wigle v The Aetna Casualty and Surety Company, 177 F Supp 932, 1959 AMC 2270, DC Mich 1959.]

Similarly, the negligence of an independent contractor (such as a boat repairman) is not covered by the "Inchmaree clause" in the policy. The negligence of the contractor is not the negligence of the "master or other officer acting professionally in the handling of the vessel at sea." [Read v Agricultural Insurance Co., 219 Wis 580, 263 NW 632, 1936 AMC 25, 1935; Baggaley v Aetna Insurance Company, 111 F2d 134, 1940 AMC 583, CA7th 1940.]

The yacht Sea Cat was hauled up on a repair yard's marine railway. The marine railway collapsed and the yacht was badly damaged. The owner was held to be entitled to recover under the policy for the cost of repair and restoration of the boat. [Boyce-Harvey Machinery, Incorporated v The Standard Fire Insurance Company, 1955 AMC 563, DC La 1955.]

Should a building collapse and damage the boat then the underwriter would be liable under a clause such as the one illustrated. But there would be no liability for the collapse of a boathouse when the boat is not in it. [Vosges v Travelers Fire Insurance Co. of Hartford, 1954 AMC 457, City Ct NY 1954.] The collapse must result in damage to the boat.

Personal Negligence

The yacht policies usually provide that the personal negligence or fault of the owner or assured in the navigation of the boat, or the owner's complicity or knowledge of such negligence, will not excuse the insurance company from indemnifying for the loss or damage. Nevertheless, loss, damage, or liability caused or brought about wilfully or intentionally by the owner or the assured will not be covered.

There can be a fine line of demarcation between

gross negligence and wilful conduct. Reckless conduct
can often be regarded as gross negligence and still not
be a deliberate, wanton, or intentional act. It is certain that if the underwriter refuses to accept liability
on the ground of wilful or intentional harm, it would
have the burden of proving such an allegation to be
a fact. Such a burden would generally be very difficult to sustain.

The word "assured" as used in the collision and protection and indemnity part of the yacht policy includes,
in addition to the individual named in the policy, members of his immediate family, friends, guests, or any
"firm, corporation or other legal entity" who may be
operating the boat with the prior permission of the
person named in the policy. Not covered in the yacht-
type policy is the negligence of a paid master or a
paid member of the boat's crew. Neither is there
coverage for the negligence of persons connected with
a shipyard, boat repair yard, marina, yacht club, sales
agency, boat service station or any similar organization.

Some policies define the assured to include those persons who are residents of his household. Suppose the
person using the boat is a distant cousin not residing
in the household of the owner, would there be liability
on the part of the insurance company? Since this type
of policy also includes "any person or organization
legally responsible for the boat" as coming under the
heading of "assured" or "insured," any barring of the
relatives outside of the immediate family or household
of the named insured appears to be specious.

Privileges Clause

Your policy covers your boat while she is afloat, in
dry dock, on ways, ashore, and in shipyards. The owner
is also permitted by this clause, so far as coverage

is concerned, to sail his boat whether she carries a pilot or not, to go on trial trips, to be towed, and to engage in salving ships and boats in distress.

Some policies include in the enumerated privileges, transportation of the boat by conveyances. Other policies prudently carry a proviso that the enumerated privilege is not to apply if it conflicts with warranties, clauses, and indorsements elsewhere mentioned in the policy.

An owner of the yacht Muskateer held a policy which limited the cruising range to the Great Lakes and their tributaries. The policy also had a privilege clause which extended coverage to include her presence on a dry dock or a marine railway. She had been hauled out in a shipyard in Florida. The yacht became a total loss as a result of fire. Her owner admitted that he had exceeded the geographical limits stated in the policy, but contended that the boat was covered by the privileges clause. In this instance the court ruled against him. [Rosenbaum v Standard Insurance Co. of N. Y. 1949 AMC 716, Cir Ct Fla 1949.] The issue, however, is not free of doubt, for when there are two conflicting clauses the dispute should not be resolved against the insured. Perhaps it is for this reason that the aforementioned warning regarding conflicts with warranties, clauses, and indorsements has been inserted.

Continuation Clause

Should you be cruising on the date your policy expired (assuming, of course, that you had failed to renew it), would you be covered in the event of an accident after the expiration date? Most boat policies contain a continuation clause and therefore you would be.

The clause would read somewhat as follows: "Should

191

the Yacht at the expiration of this Policy (other than by cancellation) be at sea, the risk may be continued until arrival at her next port and for 24 hours while moored thereat at prorata monthly premium, provided request for continuation be made to the Company prior to expiration of this Policy."

If you have started on a long cruise and then remembered that you had failed to make the necessary arrangements to renew the policy you should act promptly. If you have a radiomarine telephone, then put in a call to your underwriter or your insurance broker. If not, notify them as soon as you reach the first intermediate port.

Workmen's Compensation

The usual yacht policy carries federal longshoremen's and harbor workers' compensation insurance coverage in conjunction with protection and indemnity insurance (bodily injury). Should you engage a plumber, electrician, rigger, painter, carpenter, etc., to do repair work on your boat as a salaried or part-time worker you may have a compensation claim on your hands in the event that the worker sustains personal injury.

The Longshoremen's and Harbor Workers' Compensation Act was enacted in 1927 to give compensation protection to a class of employees who are usually engaged on or near water in work activities. Since their navigable water or waterfront activities placed them in a category where they were neither seamen nor shoreside employees—and therefore state compensation acts did not ordinarily apply to them—an act of Congress became necessary. While for many years it was thought that state compensation laws applied in some borderline cases, it is now settled that this act applies when the work activities take place on or about nav-

192

igable waters. [Calbeck v Travelers Insurance Co., 370 US 114, 8 L ed 2d 368, 82 S Ct 1196, 1962 AMC 1413, 1962.]

Protection and Indemnity Insurance

This feature of the yacht policy is much like the comprehensive personal injury and property damage policies familiar to practically every automobile owner. The coverage includes protection and indemnity for loss of life or bodily injury to guests and to other persons. It excludes any liability under any workmen's compensation law.

It may include coverage for loss of life, for personal injury, and for illness of the yacht's captain and members of the crew. Also included is the yacht's liability for transportation, wages, and maintenance and cure under the General Maritime Law. [This aspect is covered in detail in Norris: The Law of Seamen, 2d ed 1962.]

The provision with respect to the master and the crew is not a standard one. I have seen such coverage included in one yacht policy form and missing entirely in another.

The property damage part of the protection and indemnity protection section of the yacht policy pertains to losses not ordinarily covered in the collision clause. It specifically covers:

(1) Loss or damage to other vessels, or to their merchandise, goods and freight, caused by the insured yacht.

(2) Damage to fixed objects, such as a harbor, dock (including a graving dock, dry dock, etc.), slipway, way, gridiron, pontoon, pier, quay, jetty, stage, buoy, telegraph cable, etc.

(3) The cost of attempting to raise, remove, or the

193

destruction of the wreck of the insured yacht, whether successful or not.

(4) Loss or damage to any goods or merchandise, etc., whether on board the insured yacht or not, which may arise from any cause.

Medical Payments Insurance

Many a yacht owner feels that he owes a moral obligation to a guest injured aboard his boat even though there may not be a legal obligation involved. Guests or business invitees may become injured in many ways indeed. In innumerable instances the accident may be due simply to the negligence or clumsiness on the part of the injured person.

Payment of the medical costs is provided by the medical payments clause contained in most yacht policies. This type of coverage can also be of benefit to the underwriter for it may serve to forestall the bringing of expensive injury claims and litigation. There are many people who are entirely satisfied to have their medical bills taken care of and, if so, would then consider the matter closed.

The insurance company agrees to pay the reasonable expense of necessary medical, surgical, ambulance, hospital, and professional nursing services incurred for those injured while in or upon the boat, or in boarding or alighting from it. Should there be a death resulting from the accident, then the underwriter will pay the reasonable funeral expenses. The time limit for these incurred expenses has been set by the policy as within one year from the date of the accident.

The injured person must furnish written proof of claim setting forth the details regarding the expenditures. The insurance company also may require a physical examination of the injured person by a physician selected by the company.

194

The coverage does not apply to a trespasser. Neither is it applicable to one who is covered by workmen's compensation; an employee of the owner (other than a domestic) ; to the owner himself; or for any liability assumed by the owner under any contract or agreement. It is intended to apply to guests and other invited persons. For an additional premium, coverage can be obtained for the owner, his wife, and his children.

Perils of The Sea

The perils clause of the usual marine policy with its quaint and archaic language of "Touching the adventures and perils which we, the said Assurers, are content to bear and take upon us, they are of the seas, etc.," has caused grief to many an unknowing boatowner. The reason, readily enough, is that the peril spoken of in the policy refers to a misfortune caused by the sea and not necessarily one which has taken place on the water. Should you be unfortunate enough to have aboard an unsophisticated and curious guest who turns open a sea cock, the resultant sinking would not be covered by the "perils of the sea" clause. [Founders' Insurance Company v Rogers, 305 F2d 944, 1963 AMC 116, CA9th 1962.]

The "perils of the sea" against which underwriters insure mean "those perils which are peculiar to the sea, and which are of an extraordinary nature or arise from irresistible force or overwhelming power; and which cannot be guarded against by the ordinary exertions of human skill and prudence." [The Giula, 218 F 744, CA2d 1914.] They are extraordinary occurrences such as stress of weather, winds, current, tides, waves, lightning, accidental stranding, grounding, shipwreck; collision with other boats, docks, reefs, rocks, submerged objects, pilings, debris; and damage from hail, snow, ice, etc. They are the mishaps and calamities associated with or peculiar to the sailing of ships on the seas, unusual and extraordinary, but not necessarily catastrophic.

Damage to a boat caused by swells from a passing vessel may not be considered to be a peril of the sea, particularly if the insured boat is not in a seaworthy condition. Much depends upon the circumstances. Where a derrick barge was engaged in a delicate salvage operation, swells from a passing ship which caused the derrick to buckle were considered to be "unanticipated and extraordinary" and therefore a peril of the sea within the meaning of the policy. [Allen N. Spooner & Son, Inc. v Connecticut Fire Ins. Co. 314 F2d 753 (CA2 NY, 1963) cert den 375 US 819, 11 L ed 2d 54, 84 S Ct 56.]

Engine damage in a motorboat due to the propeller's striking a cable, followed by an explosion, was found not to be damage caused by stranding. [Cohen v Agricultural Insurance Company, 1961 AMC 2408, DC NY 1961.]

When a packing nut on the packing box around the drive shaft of a Higgins Runabout boat on an inland lake in Georgia allowed water to enter so that the boat sank, it was not occasioned by some unusual occurrence, so held the court, and therefore was not a peril of the sea. [Dwyer v Providence Washington Insurance Company, 1958 AMC 1488, Ct of App Ga 1957.]

Other examples of damage or loss not judicially regarded as a peril of the sea are the following:

(1) The collapse of an improvised derrick on land just as a boat was being hauled out of the water. [Lind v Boston Insurance Company, 1953 AMC 1047, Sup Ct Wash 1953.]

(2) The sinking of an unattended yacht which had a break in the exhaust outlet, leak in the intake valve of the toilet, and a break in the chine board. There was no evidence of unusual weather. [Fine v American Eagle Fire Insurance Co., 178 Misc 27, 32 NYS 2d 21, 1942 AMC 96, City Ct NY 1941, aff'd 180 Misc 789, 46 NYS2d 512.]

(3) A repaired boat at a boatyard, which was launched with a valve open thus allowing sea water to come into the hull. [Read v Agricultural Insurance Co., 1936 AMC 25, Sup Ct Wis 1935.]

(4) High tide, not of an unusual kind, raising a boat stored in a shed above a wet dock so that her superstructure came in contact with a beam and the boat was damaged. [Glover v Philadelphia Fire and Marine Ins. Co., 1956 AMC 1210, Balt. City Ct Md 1956.]

Laid Up and Out of Commission

In the northern states of the United States it is the usual practice to place recreational boats out of commission for a period of about 6 months. In this area the insurance rates are set having this factor in mind, for when a boat is out of operation the risk of loss is greatly reduced. Policies generally specify the layup period as from November 1 to April 1. In the southern states boats are kept in use throughout the year and therefore the layup condition is not prevalent in that region.

When a boat has been damaged during the layup period, a controversy may arise as to whether the loss comes within the coverage of the policy. If the boat has been hauled up on land or properly winterized and placed out of commission no dispute should ensue. It is when the boat has been left in the water, although the owner had previously taken steps to have the craft placed out of commission, that an area of conflict between the insured and the underwriter comes to the fore. It then often becomes necessary for the courts to determine the dispute and ascertain what the parties to the contract (policy) meant by the term "laid up and out of commission."

To reach this understanding recourse can be made to local usage and custom with respect to putting a boat out of commission. Protected waters, unexposed boatyards, etc., may be regarded by local custom as a proper place to keep a boat—at least before there is danger of ice damage or the arrival of the season of wintry storms. In some areas (Chesapeake Bay, James River, etc.) it is customary to lay up the boat in wet storage. In the northeastern part of this country (New England) and in the Great Lakes area, boats are usually hauled ashore. Many policies contain an ice-damage clause excluding damage caused by ice or by freezing conditions while the boat is afloat.

The owner of the yacht Edward James left it at a boatyard at City Island, N. Y., on September 28, 1945, after removing ship's papers, the compass, and personal belongings, and turning the keys over to the yard. The policy called for a layup from November 1. The boat was not hauled up but was left afloat in open water moored to two dolphins about 500 feet offshore until November 29, when she sank. A northeaster blew up, there were heavy seas, and apparently the yacht suffered her damage when she broke loose from her moorings and hit a barge tied up astern of her. A jury found in favor of the insurance company, which had resisted paying the loss on the ground that the boat had not been in a laid up and out of commission status at the time of the loss. The court, on appeal, held that the jury's verdict was right and that there was evi-

198

dence that in this particular locality the customary procedure for laying up such a boat was to haul her on shore rather than to leave her afloat. [Gelb v The Automobile Co. of Hartford, 168 F2d 774, 1948 AMC 1257, CA2d 1948.]

The layup story of the 40-foot yacht Braemer had a different ending. According to the policy the layup period was to run from November 1, at noon, to May 1, at noon. At the end of October the owner had ordered a marina located on Providence River, R. I., to haul up his yacht for the winter. At this time the ship's papers, wet batteries, fresh water from the bilges, pumps, and motors, and the gasoline were removed. The Braemer was kept in wet storage when she was damaged and sank at her moorings on November 25. It was shown that in the area of this marina it was the practice to haul up boats on shore prior to November 1, and to winterize them on land; but if this were not possible, to winterize them in wet storage and to haul up not later than December 15. The marina was found by the court to be a reasonably safe place to lay up boats in wet storage during the period from November 1 to December 15. The Braemer was held to be "laid up and out of commission" when she sank on November 25, 1950. [Providence Washington Insurance Co. v Lovett, 119 F Supp 371, 1955 AMC 384, DC RI 1953. See also: Gehrlein's Production Tooling Corp. v The Travelers Fire Insurance Co., 1957 AMC 1029, DC SD NY 1957.]

An Owens cabin cruiser was stored at the Alpine Boat Basin at Palisades Park, New Jersey. The basin was closed for business about November 15 each year. It had no facilities for winter storage nor did it have a marine railway to haul boats out of the water. The policy warranted that the boat would be laid up and out of commission from October 1 until April 1. During the month of September the owner had removed foodstuffs, silverware, new life preservers, charts, barometer, ship's clock, etc., but gasoline had been left in the tanks. The owner had made arrangements to winter-store the boat at another yard.

The Owens cruiser was still at the Alpine basin on November 7, when a severe storm arose. Due to the abnormally high tides and strong winds the boat rubbed against a spike with the result that she holed and sank. The court held that the phrase "laid up and out of commission" must be interpreted according to the well-established custom and practice at the place where the damage to the boat had occurred. A boat left at this basin at the time of the damage could not be said to be in a laid-up and out of commission state. The removing of the various items from the boat, it was held, did not indicate the taking of steps in anticipation of a layup, but rather that it was to prevent the stealing of easily removable articles. [Kane v Aetna Insurance Company, 1955 AMC 2346, Sup Ct NJ 1955.]

Along the same lines is the case of the 16-foot open-cockpit inboard motorboat moored between two pilings at a public marina in Long Island Sound, New York. She sank during a storm on December 7, 1959. According to the policy she was to have been laid up and out of commission beginning at noon on November 1. Said the court: "Leaving a small open boat, uncovered and completely exposed to the elements, tied up at a public marina during the winter months can scarcely be considered safe practice within the terms of the policy." Recovery of the loss was denied. [Poulos v Fireman's Fund Insurance Co., 231 NYS2d 206, 1962 AMC 1979, Sup Ct NY 1962.]

You may wonder how a law court with a judge or

jury perhaps not versed on the local custom and practice can arrive at a decision. Their deliberations are aided by expert testimony. The attorneys for the boat owner and the insurance companies will call as witnesses experts who have particular knowledge of the custom and usage respecting the placing of boats in a laid-up and out of commission state. These witnesses may be boatowners, boat repairmen, mariners, marina operators, surveyors, and authors of books and articles in periodicals on the subject of small boats. They should have a knowledge of the practice, custom, and usage in the locality where the incident has occurred.

Collision Clause

The collision clause of a marine policy is also known as the "running down clause." It is the property damage feature of the policy so far as collision with another boat is concerned.

The clause usually provides that the underwriter will pay the damages incurred up to the amount called for in the policy. Any amount in excess of the insured value of your boat will be for your own account, unless you have been sufficiently foresighted to have arranged for increased liability coverage.

The underwriters agree to pay for the costs of litigation and attorneys' fees should you decide to litigate the question of who was at fault in the collision, but they will do so only when they have consented in writing to such a contest. If necessary or desirable, an attorney will be provided by the insurance company to conduct the litigation.

A maritime collision differs greatly in the negligence aspect from a collision on land. When two automobiles collide neither owner can collect if both are at fault. The contributory negligence of each driver nullifies his right to collect damages from the other. In marine collisions the rule of "divided damages" or "mutual fault" applies.

Should your boat collide with another and the court holds that both boats were at fault—a "both-to-blame" situation—each owner is compelled to pay one-half the damage to the other. If in such a casualty your boat sustained damage amounting to $5,000 and the other boat was damaged to the extent of $1,000, you would collect $2,500 and you would pay $500.

When both boats in the collision are owned by the same person the insurance company agrees to pay the damages as though both boats were owned by separate policyholders.

The collision clause usually states that the company will not pay for damages, or for your incurred costs, in connection with injury to harbors, piers, stages, and "similar structures." Also excluded is the cost of removing your sunken boat when it obstructs a channel. In some P & I policies, however, the cost of removal is included.

The collision clause of the hull part of a marine policy is not applicable to liability for loss of life or personal injury.

F. C. & S. Clause

The letters "F. C. & S." stand for "free of capture and seizure." Insurance companies are prepared to engage in the usual risks and perils of their business. Sudden and unexpected catastrophies such as acts of war and civil strife, however, are abhorrent to underwriters. These unforetold occurrences can quickly exhaust and deplete the insurance fund which had been built up to provide for the claims arising from the normal and therefore expected risks of the insurance business.

The F. C. & S. clause is in reality an exclusion clause. It states specifically that the policy is warranted free from any claim for loss or damage due to a variety of causes. These causes are specified as warlike acts, such as capture, restraint, arrest, seizure, or detainment. Included too, are the consequences of civil war, revolution, rebellion, insurrection, acts of piracy, and damage caused by the atomic bomb.

War risk insurance is written and furnished to those who want it, and who are willing to pay the high rates which this type of policy demands.

Boats and Launches

The yacht policy covers any damage or loss to the yacht's tender, should your boat be large enough to have one. The boats and launches clause in one particular yacht policy form reads as follows:

"The Boats and Launches of the Yacht including their outboard motors are insured also while afloat, whether under way or not, subject to all of the terms and conditions, including the collision clause, of this Policy."

Some policies will cover the tender provided that the value of the tender is included in the "amount of Insurance" valuation.

Equipment on Shore

When equipment belonging to the boat is removed and stored ashore during the term of the policy, it is covered; but a ceiling on the amount of loss has been set. Yacht policies provide that the loss paid will be up to 20 percent of the face amount of the policy. In one particular policy which I have read, the loss that can be paid is up to 50 percent of the face amount of the policy.

The policy of a certain underwriter provides that

203

the provision regarding equipment on shore does not apply to loss by theft.

The equipment-on-shore clause does not appear in the usual outboard motorboat policy.

Theft

You should examine your policy to see whether or not you are covered for theft of the boat and theft of its equipment. Perhaps, to be more realistic, you should make arrangements to obtain coverage for loss by thievery, if that is what you wish. The all-risks yacht policy insures for the loss of the entire boat by theft, but excludes mysterious disappearance of equipment.

Theft implies forcible entry, such as breaking a window, forcing a lock, cutting through canvas, etc. Casual taking of loose equipment not under lock and key is pilferage and therefore differs from theft. Theft or mysterious disappearance of equipment or accessories is not covered by some policies unless it occurs in conjunction with the theft of the entire boat or unless there is visible evidence of forcible entry.

At a marina in the Neponset River in Dorchester, Massachusetts, within range of a floodlight, lay the luxurious twin-screw Chris-Craft cabin cruiser Mariposa. One morning the yacht was found about 90 feet away in a sinking condition. It was discovered that the sea cock or drain plug had been unscrewed and removed. Although there was no evidence of a forced entrance into the yacht, personal property in the form of cases of liquor, fishing tackle, guns, ammunition, and a TV set had been removed. Smudges, fingermarks, and scuff marks on the river side of the hull indicated that the property had most probably been carried away by a small boat which had been brought alongside of it. The insurance company refused to pay the loss contending that the "entire vessel" had not been stolen. The pertinent clause in the policy read: "Touching the adventures and perils which this Company is content to bear, and does take upon itself, they are . . . theft of the entire yacht . . . and of all other like perils, losses and misfortunes, that have or shall come to the hurt, detriment or damage of said yacht or any part thereof."

While it was clear that the entire vessel had not been stolen the court laid particular stress on the phrase "other like perils." The phrase could not simply be brushed aside as being essentially a flourish. A literary embellishment has no place in an insurance policy, stated the court. The clause must have been included in the policy to serve a purpose. The court reasoned that the purpose was to include in the coverage all losses which, although not technically or strictly speaking covered in the specific perils enumerated, are losses very much like the enumerated perils. What had happened to the Mariposa, while not a "theft" of the entire yacht, under the law of Massachusetts, nevertheless was so very much like a theft that the court held that the harm which came to her was covered by "all other like perils" clause. [Feinberg v Insurance Company of North America, 260 F2d 523, 1959 AMC 11, CA1st 1958.]

Had the words of the policy ended with the words "theft of the entire yacht" there would have been a contrary result. The additional words of "other like perils" rightfully gave the court an opportunity to apply a rule of reason.

If the policy covers loss by "assailing thieves" then there must be proof of the use of force by the thief.

Most insurance companies will compensate for the loss of boat equipment such as dinghies, outboard motors, radiotelephones, barometers, depth finders, fire extinguishers, searchlights, compasses, tools, charts, anchors, lines, life jackets, etc. Reasonable evidence of theft must be provided with the claim of loss.

Generally items not associated with the operation and safe navigation of the boat will not be covered. These include such articles of convenience as cameras, watches, jewelry, guns, money, food, liquor, etc.

Payment of Loss

The usual clause regarding the payment of loss states that it will be paid within 30 days after satisfactory proof of loss and of interest in the boat has been submitted. When your boat has been damaged or sunk you just cannot sit idly by and expect to be compensated. The burden of establishing the loss is upon the assured. Therefore you must notify the company promptly of the damage, file your claim of loss and give the necessary details of the occurrence. Unless the damage is trifling the underwriter will have its marine surveyor (or adjustor) examine the boat to ascertain the extent of damage and the cost of repair.

If the assured owes any money to the insurance company, the amount of the indebtedness will first be deducted from the proceeds of the claim.

When the insured boat has been so completely destroyed that she has no residual value then it is said to be an "absolute total loss." One such example is the sinking of the boat in waters hundreds of fathoms deep.

A "constructive total loss" is one where the cost of repairing the damaged property together with the cost of recovering it (salvage) exceeds the insured value less her scrap value (salvage). The word "salvage" has a double meaning here. Recovery of damaged property is known as "salvage" in maritime law. The amount an insurance company can realize on property surrendered to it is also known as "salvage" in insurance circles.

The definition of "constructive total loss" given above is known as the English rule. It has been established by English statute. Most marine insurance policies follow it and have a clause to that effect. In the absence of such a policy clause either defining "constructive total loss" or specifying that the English rule should prevail, there is a "constructive total loss" when the cost of repairs exceeds one-half the repaired value of the vessel. [Jeffcott v Aetna Insurance Company, 129 F2d 582, CA2d 1942, cert den 317 US 663, 87 L ed 533, 63 S Ct 64.]

The repaired value, generally speaking, may be the market value after repairs have been completed.

If the underwriter pays you for a total loss, the title to the boat—or whatever is left of it—goes to the underwriter. The insurance company will attempt to realize whatever it can by finding a buyer. In many instances the former owner will buy back his boat.

If the cost of repairs exceeds the insured value but the assured nevertheless wants to repair his boat, the insurance company will pay the total loss as called for in the policy and the owner can then proceed to repair at his own expense. If he sells the boat without repairing it he is entitled to the face value of the policy less its "salvage value", namely, the sale price. [Delta Supply Co. v Liberty Mutual Insurance Co., 211 F Supp 429, DC Tex 1962.]

Partial Loss

The yacht policy may be in the form of a valued contract or valued policy, that is, the value of the boat has been agreed upon by the insured and the underwriter.

207

In such case partial losses will be paid in full. For example, if my boat has a reasonable value (replacement cost) of $6,000 and I wish to insure it for that amount, upon acceptance by the insurance underwriter, the agreement then becomes a valued policy. If a particular damage to my boat amounts to $1,500, I will be paid $1,500 if the loss otherwise comes within the provisions of the policy. A total loss would, of course, be paid in full.

Should I wish to insure my boat for less than its reasonable value, any loss will be paid in proportion to what the insured value is to its agreed value. Example: I may wish to save money on insurance premiums. I decide to insure my $6,000 boat for $3,000. A damage claim of $1,500 will be met by a payment by the insurance company of $750, since I had insured the boat for one-half its value. In the event of a total loss I would receive the value insured for, namely, $3,000.

Trailer Transportation

Yacht policies normally do not cover damage to the yacht while being transported on land. Some yacht policies provide for this coverage when a separate premium rate has been paid. An "all-risks" yacht policy which I have examined does include land transportation if the boat is conveyed within a radius of 250 miles of her home port. The included risk also pertains to the process of loading and unloading the boat, but excluded is the marring, scratching, denting, and chipping of the craft.

The land transportation clause in the yacht policy covers the boat while in transit by land conveyance for loss or damage when it is caused directly by loading and unloading, fire, lightning, windstorm, flood, collision of the yacht or conveyance, upset of the yacht or conveyance, collapse of bridges or wharves or other structures, or for the theft of the entire yacht.

The trailer itself can be insured upon the payment of a separate or additional premium.

The outboard motorboat policy usually includes trailer transportation in the scope of the coverage. In this type of policy the trailer too can be covered for loss or damage at a determined rate.

The insurance companies are careful to state in their policies that the coverage is not intended either directly or indirectly to benefit any carrier or bailee. This provision is intended to be directed against anyone who is conveying your boat for a stipulated fee.

Other General Conditions

There are other clauses in the yacht policy not heretofore mentioned. They are not necessarily unimportant and, as usual, they become of greater moment after being overlooked or misunderstood by the policyholder.

If you are dissatisfied with the actions of your insurance company and contemplate bringing suit, then do so as promptly as possible. The time limit placed in the policy for the bringing of a suit against the company for the recovery of a claim is 12 months. Whether this restriction will always be upheld by the courts is doubtful; much may depend on the circumstances of the case or on delay or "lulling to sleep" by the insurance company. But, to repeat, if you, as the holder of a policy, wish to bring suit against the insurance company, then by all means act without undue delay.

When an insurance company pays you for your loss or damages, then any legal rights which you may have against the party who caused your loss or damage goes to the insurance company. This is the meaning of

209

the subrogation clause of the yacht policy. Presumably, the underwriter will try to recoup all or part of the money paid to you from that other party. One thing further: do not give a release to the person who caused this loss or damage, because you may find that it has had the effect of making your policy null and void.

If your boat contains plywood, plastic, or fiber glass portions, the cost of repairs is limited to the customary and generally accepted repair practices; or the cost of making those repairs by following the boat manufacturer's recommended repair specifications, whichever amount is less.

Homeowners' Policies

What has a comprehensive homeowner's policy to do with marine insurance? The answer is—considerable. The standard type of homeowner's policy which contemplates a "package deal" on private home coverage—fire, bodily injury, property damage, and medical expenses—extends also to include small boats.

A boat owned by the holder of the comprehensive homeowner's policy is automatically covered by that policy. The coverage (without the payment of any additional premium) is confined to inboard motorboats not exceeding 50 horsepower. Also included are sailboats not over 26 feet in length and outboard motorboats.

The limit of liability for bodily injury and property damage caused by the insured boat is the amount listed on the face of the policy for the bodily injury category. The boat is also covered for damage or destruction by fire, explosion, smoke, or smudge; but liability in this category is limited to $500. The medical payments feature calls for the payment of reasonable medical expenses up to the policy limit. Where the accident results in death the insurance company will pay the reasonable funeral expenses. A separate application form need not be supplied by the boatowner under this policy in order to have coverage.

If your inboard motorboat exceeds 50 horsepower or if your sailboat is over 26 feet in length, coverage can be obtained upon the payment of the necessary premium.

Since this type of policy, so far as boats are concerned, is written in the language of shoreside policies, it must be read and analyzed carefully in order to determine whether it provides adequately for the protection which the boatowner requires. The homeowner's comprehensive policy may be a bargain if the protection which you desire is met. On the other hand, inadequate coverage can turn out to be a bad bargain indeed.

Other boat insurance policies similar to the homeowner's policy are provided by mutual insurance companies which specialize in automobile coverage and also by companies which sell policies through boat clubs and associations.

*

6

limiting liability

Desirability of Limiting Your Liability

Owners of pleasure boats are accorded an extraordinary privilege under the maritime law of being enabled, under certain conditions, to limit their liability, in the event of accident, to the value of their boat. This right is peculiar to maritime law and does not have its counterpart ashore with respect to ownership of personal property, as, for example, an automobile. However, efforts of man to limit his financial liability for injuries caused to others are not new in the law or in the field of commerce. Limitation of liability is an accepted and commonplace feature of stock corporations and limited partnerships. But maritime exoneration from, or limitation of, a shipowner's liability, with its enjoinment of pending suits, concourse of claims, establishment of a limitation fund and its distribution amongst claimants, is indeed unique.

Historical Background

The statute relating to limitation of liability originated in the United States in 1851. The passing of this law occurred during the period of sail and before the arrival of the age of steam, which was to bring with it greater relative safety in ship operation and the successful termination of the maritime venture. Limiting liability had been practiced heretofore by the leading maritime nations of Europe, that is, England, France, and Germany. It was the feeling of Congress that our merchant shipping should be placed upon an equal footing with our European competitors, particularly England, and that American shipowners and the shipbuilding industry should not remain in a state of economic disadvantage.

Chief Justice Taft, in an opinion many years later, stated:

"The great object of the statute was to encourage shipbuilding and to induce the investment of money in this branch of industry, by limiting the venture of those who build the ship to the loss of the ship itself or her freight then pending, in cases of damage or wrong, happening without the privity or knowledge of the shipowner, and by the fault or neglect of the master or other persons on board." [Hartford Accident & Indemnity Co. of Hartford v Southern Pacific Co., 273 US 207, 71 L ed 612, 47 S Ct 357, 1927.]

In sum, the purpose of this important statute was to encourage investments in ships and their employment in commerce [American Car & Foundry Co. v Brassert, 289 US 261, 77 L ed 1162, 53 S Ct 618, 1933 AMC 749, 1933]; to give our shipowners a chance to compete with those of Europe [Liverpool, B. & R. P. Steam Nav. Co. v Brooklyn Eastern Dist. Terminal, 251 US 48, 64 L ed 130, 40 S Ct 66, 1919]; and to place American shipping upon a footing of equality with that of other maritime nations [The Main v Williams, 152 US 122, 38 L ed 381, 14 S Ct 486, 1894].

Applying Limitation to Small Boats

What have shipbuilding, commerce, and trade to do with pleasure boating? You may well ask this, and undoubtedly there will be many who will reply, "Very little, if anything!" The opposing views of two jurists on this interesting proposition are of moment. Judge Foley has stated that it is difficult "to relate the principle of limitation to encourage investment in shipping and shipbuilding with the happening of these small boat accidents where the owner is a private individual usually covered by Insurance. I am sure the ever-growing number of purchasers of these small pleasure craft do not check the limitation statutes before they purchase and never will. The financial protection and regulation necessary to alleviate the burden of society where the widow and orphan, marred and crippled, are with us as a result of unfortunate highway accidents seem to me just as important in these boating accidents. Much of the complexity in this respect is for the legislative wisdom to solve, with realization that the general legislation on limitation may have harsh and oppressive impact in certain circumstances that may fairly and equitably be removed." [Petition of Madsen, 187 F Supp 411, DC ND NY 1960.]

The other side of the coin is indicated in the views of Judge Anderson. He said: "There is reason behind a policy of encouraging the building of pleasure craft as well as larger commercial vessels. It gives additional work to shipyards whose men are thus enabled to preserve their skills; it gives experience to those who operate the vessels on the seas and in navigable water and, as occurred in the early part of World War II, it provides a source of small craft available for patrol and picket duty in guarding harbors and important water-front facilities in time of war or

215

other emergency." [Petition of Colonial Trust Company, 124 F Supp 73, 1955 AMC 1290, DC Conn 1954.]

I suppose that the simple answer to this question is that the statutes permit the owners of pleasure boats to limit liability, and this permission is spelled out from the fact that application is made to "any vessel." [46 United States Code § 183a.]

This statute regarding limitation states that the liability of the owner of any vessel, whether American or foreign, for any loss, damage, or injury by collision, or for any loss or damage occasioned or incurred without the privity or knowledge of the owner, shall not exceed the amount or value of the interest of the owner in the vessel. Another part of this statute refers specifically "to all vessels used on lakes or rivers or in inland navigation." [46 United States Code § 188.]

While a shipowner's limitation of liability is usually thought of by the general public as applying to large deep-sea passenger liners, freighters, and tankers, it is well to remember that the right of limitation is not based upon the engagement of the vessel in maritime commerce, or upon the size of the craft. [Petition of Ferguson, 39 F Supp 271, 1941 AMC 1147, DC Mass 1941; Petition of Liebler, 19 F Supp 829, 1937 AMC 1006, DC WD NY 1937.]

Relief under the limitation of liability statutes has been accorded to an 18-foot craft propelled by two sets of oars. The rowboat was being used as a ferry. Six of the 10 passengers were lost. Thus, large death claims were met by a picayune limitation fund. [Grays Landing Ferry Co. v Stone, 46 F2d 394, 1931 AMC 787, CA3 1931.]

Likewise, in The Mistral, [50 F2d 957, DC WD NY 1931] claims against a yacht owner of about $150,000 were met by his petition to limit liability in the amount of $7,500, the yacht's value. Argument by counsel for the injured parties that the limitation of liability statute did not apply to pleasure boats was unavailing. Other small boats which have been permitted to limit liability include sailing sloops which collided in Lake Michigan off the Chicago shore [Petition of Rapp, 255 F'2d 628, 1959 AMC 1144, CA7 1958]; a 15-foot motor speedboat [Feige v Hurley, 89 F2d 575, 1937 AMC 913, CA6 1937]; a 19-foot motorboat [Petition of Liebler, 19 F Supp 829, 1937 AMC 1006, DC WD NY 1937]; a yacht club's station tender [California Yacht Club of Los Angeles v Johnson, 65 F2d 245, 1933 AMC 943, CA9 1933]; a yacht loaned to a friend [The Pegeen, 14 F Supp 748, 1936 AMC 667, DC Cal 1936]; and a 30-foot gasoline launch [Warnken v Moody, 22 F2d 960, CA5 1927].

In the case of the speedboat Francesca, a 14-year-old girl swimming in Lake Erie off the Buffalo beaches was given a ride by the operator of a speedboat. She was permitted to sit forward of the windshield on a deck crowned and smooth. The boat operator started the craft at a high rate of speed and then made a turn. The girl fell or slid off the deck and was so badly cut by the propeller that she died. Since the operator was not the owner (the latter did not have privity or knowledge of the negligent act), limitation of liability was allowed, with the court holding that although the boat was small and used for pleasure it came within the meaning of the limitation statutes. [Petition of Liebler, 19 F Supp 829, 1937 AMC 1006, DC WD NY 1937.]

Jurisdiction

As it is with jurisdiction of salvage cases in the admiralty courts (see Chapter 7), a boatowner's petition for limitation of liability can only be effective if the accident or occurrence has taken place in navigable waters. Unless admiralty has jurisdiction, there cannot be relief by way of putting a ceiling on the owner's liability to the injured party.

This factor was emphasized in the case of Petition of Madsen. [187 F Supp 411, DC ND NY 1960.] A pleasure speedboat owned by Madsen and operated by his son struck and injured a water skier being pulled by another motorboat on Lake Pleasant. Lake Pleasant is a small landlocked lake in the center of the Adirondack Mountains. Madsen's efforts to limit his liability went for naught, for the court held that it did not have the necessary jurisdiction. Lake Pleasant was not "navigable waters" in law. It did not form, either by itself or by uniting with other waters, a continued highway over which commerce is carried on with other states or foreign countries.

If we could use our imagination and picture Lake Pleasant in the center of the Adirondack Mountains, but with a navigable river flowing from it and emptying into the Hudson River, then Lake Pleasant would be navigable in law, and boats operating on it would be subject to the limitation of liability statutes. And that would be so because the connecting river flows into the Hudson River, which, in turn, flows into the Atlantic Ocean after passing the states of New York and New Jersey. We then would have the necessary waterway over which commerce is carried on with other states or foreign countries.

There are lower court decisions which hold that the limitation of liability statutes apply to boats which have been drawn out of the water and stored on land. [Petition of Colonial Trust Company, 124 F Supp 73,

1955 AMC 1290, DC Conn 1954; Petition of Ferguson, 39 F Supp 271, 1941 AMC 1147, DC Mass 1941.]

These holdings, in my opinion, are questionable, for it is apparent that under those circumstances jurisdiction is lacking in the admiralty courts.

Privity or Knowledge

A boatowner is permitted to limit his liability to the value of the boat at the time of the incident which has caused claims for injuries to be made against him. The injuries may be in the form of property damage (as holeing another boat) or of damage caused to a person (as running down a swimmer).

The right to limit liability is given to the boatowner with, however, one big proviso. He can limit his liability to the extent of the value of his boat in her condition immediately after the casualty, provided the damage or injury has occurred without the privity or knowledge of the owner.

"Privity" has been regarded as some fault or neglect in which the owner personally participates, and which fault or neglect caused or contributed to the loss or injury. [Coryell v Phipps, 317 US 406, 87 L ed 363, 63 S Ct 291, 1943 AMC 18, 1943.] "Knowledge" means personal cognizance which the owner has of the condition which brought about the accident. [The Cleveco, 154 F2d 605, 1946 AMC 933, CA6 1946.]

The burden of proving that the accident was caused or brought about because of negligence is upon the one who is making the claim against the boatowner. When the boatowner seeks to limit his liability, he then has the burden of proving that the accident was caused without privity or knowledge on his part. [The John H. Starin, 191 F 800, CA NY 1911.]

Whether or not the boatowner had privity or knowledge is a question of fact depending upon the circumstances of each happening. [Coryell v Phipps, 317 US 406, 87 L ed 363, 63 S Ct 291, 1943 AMC 18, 1943.]

Rarely, if ever, are the facts precisely alike in any two casualties.

"Privity and knowledge" means being a party in the fault which was the cause of the accident. A large oil tanker was held, by a court, to be solely at fault for colliding with the stern of a pleasure boat. A guest in the pleasure boat was injured. A co-owner of the small boat, who was at the wheel at the time, was granted exoneration from liability. [Petition of Landi, 194 F Supp 353, 1961 AMC 690, DC SD NY 1960.]

Negligence and Privity

The owner who is not actually operating a boat may be liable for the negligence of his agent just as the automobile owner may be liable for the damage caused by his car which had been loaned to a friend. But unlike the automobile owner, the boatowner can limit his liability to the value of his boat, provided he was not a party to the accident. This point is illustrated in the case of the speedboat Francesca, previously mentioned. The boat was being run by the husband. His wife, who owned the boat, could not operate it. The man, his wife, and several guests were cruising on Lake Erie. The husband gave a lift to a 14-year-old girl swimmer. She was permitted to sit immediately in front of the windshield on a crowned and highly polished forward deck. The boat started off at high speed, then made a turn, the girl slid off and was killed by the propeller. The boatowner was seated behind the boat operator. The court held that her husband was acting as her agent and therefore she, as principal, was liable for

220

his negligent acts. She could have prevented or protested the taking on of the swimmer. She could have directed that the girl be placed in a safe place at the stern of the boat. She could have given directions regarding the craft's speed and movements. The operator, said the court, was subject to the control of the owner. Although the wife-owner was held liable for her husband's negligence, she was permitted to limit her liability to the small value of the boat. She did not personally participate in any fault or act of negligence; she did not contribute to the injury; she gave no direction with reference to the operation of the boat. She had no knowledge regarding the operation of the craft, leaving that to her husband, an experienced operator. [Petition of Liebler, 19 F Supp 829, 1937 AMC 1006, DC WD NY 1937.]

The palpable injustice of serious injury to persons with resultant limitation of the damages to an amount which frequently reflects the small value of the offending boat has been characterized rather severely as "a general license to kill and destroy." [Gilmore and Black: "The Law of Admiralty", p. 700.]

Refusing Limitation

Boatowners should never make the mistake of believing that the right of limitation of liability has precluded the necessity for adequate insurance coverage. The simple truth is that after a casualty, when a boatowner needs financial protection the most, the courts may deny to him the right of limiting his liability to the value of the boat. This type of situation—denial of the right to limit—is most frequently brought about by the very nature of recreational boating, since the owner is usually either at the helm at the time of the accident or at least present in the boat. When this has occurred it is difficult for the owner to sustain the burden of proving that the accident was caused without privity or knowledge on his part.

An owner of a speedboat had sought to limit liability to $4,000, the value of his boat. He had run down a girl swimming in Lake Tahoe, California. The boat's propellers had so severely cut both of the girl's legs below the knees that amputation was required. Damages were sought in the amount of $321,399.50. When it was shown as an uncontroverted fact that the owner himself had operated the boat at the time of the accident, limitation of liability was denied by the court. [Petition of Davis, 1950 AMC 1029, DC Cal 1950 affd Davis v U. S., 185 F2d 938, 1951 AMC 93, CA9 1950, cert den 340 US 932, 95 L ed 673, 71 S Ct 495; see also: Petition of Dilbert, 1961 AMC 539, DC SD NY 1960.]

In The Inga [33 F Supp 122, DC SD NY 1940] a pleasure cruiser on a Hudson River outing ran into a series of difficulties. She stranded in shoal water and had to be pulled by a tug over a bar. Apparently this mishap started a leak in her gasoline tanks. She also developed motor and ignition trouble. The motor commenced to sputter and the boat could proceed only at slow speed. She put in at Catskill, where a mechanic sought to adjust the carburetor. A hundred gallons of gasoline were taken on. At this point the owner left the boat, while his brother and 16-year-old son and a guest remained on the boat, which proceeded down the river to Nyack. By this time she had run out of gas and the motor was again giving trouble. The owner, advised of the situation by telephone by his brother, directed that a mechanic be obtained and consented to his son's and the guest's remaining on the boat. The brother followed these instructions and then left. The mechanic had not been told of the prior

222

difficulties nor that the presence of gasoline had been detected in the bilges. While trying to start the motor, the mechanic and the guest were injured by an explosion which followed. Limitation was denied to the owner, for he had knowledge of the boat's defective conditions and had consented to the procurement of the mechanic at Nyack.

Another case of defective equipment and failure to inspect the offending boat properly involved a cruising houseboat yacht and two lady guests. The ladies had been assigned to a double stateroom located at the stern, directly above the bilge. The exhaust pipes from the houseboat's twin gasoline motors passed through the bilge. Unfortunately, there were several holes in the pipes and as a consequence carbon monoxide gas collected in the bilge. The gas passed through vents into the stateroom. As the houseboat yacht was nearing Miami, the ladies were discovered unconscious in their berths. The owner, who was on board at the time, had been told when he purchased the boat that the port exhaust pipe should be renewed, but this had not been done. It was also shown that twice before, to his knowledge, persons aboard the yacht, including his two sons, had been overcome in the same stateroom. The right to limit liability was denied to him. [The Friendship II, 113 F2d 105, CA5 1940 revd on other grounds Just v Chambers, 312 US 383, 85 L ed 903, 61 S Ct 687, reh den 312 US 716, 85 L ed 1146.]

The boatowner who employs a professional skipper doesn't necessarily gain the protection of the limitation statute by that circumstance—particularly if the owner is aboard ship at the time of collision. The Winem II, a 40-foot twin-screw cabin cruiser, was proceeding on automatic pilot ("Iron Mike") when she collided with a party fishing boat carrying 29 passengers. The collision caused the party boat to go down in a matter of minutes. Most of her passengers were thrown into the water. They were picked up by the Winem II, which had received little damage. Since the owner was aboard, said the court, he had the burden of showing that he did not participate in, and was in no way privy to, her negligence. The owner asserted that he had been below, with the skipper in full charge of the boat. The court found that the skipper had left the wheel unattended until the Winem II was only 18 feet from the fishing boat. The owner was held to be privy to the fact that the cruiser was proceeding without an adequate lookout, the very factor which had caused the collision. [Petition of Robertson, 1958 AMC 1697, DC Mass 1958.]

Lack of Privity or Knowledge

The question whether the accident was caused with the privity or knowledge of the boatowner requires an examination of the facts in each particular case. Boatowners will undoubtedly be interested in the following cases where limitation has been granted.

The yacht Trillora II, owned by the copper magnate Guggenheim, exploded while being put into shape after having been laid up during World War II. The explosion caused considerable property damage as well as loss of life. Guggenheim had turned over many personal matters, including the operation of the yacht, to an associate, one Clarence Rothschild. The work of recommissioning the yacht had been assigned to Captain Gott, a licensed master. It appeared that the cause of the explosion was due to the negligence of Gott, who cranked the engine after it had been discovered that gasoline was leaking from one of the tanks into the bilge. Guggenheim was allowed limi-

224

tation, since the negligence of Captain Gott could not be imputed to him. [Petition of Guggenheim, 76 F Supp 50, 1948 AMC 132, DC SC 1947.]

Similarly, in The Spare Time II, [36 F Supp 642, DC ED NY 1941] where the owner had delegated the procurement of maintenance and repair work to his handyman Lewis, limitation of liability was granted in view of the owner's lack of privity or knowledge. Lewis had engaged two mechanics to make repairs on the engine. An explosion was caused by a spark from an electric bilge pump igniting gasoline which had leaked from a break in a gasoline feedpipe. The owner did not know of this leak and it was not proved that the feedpipe break occurred through any fault, neglect, or want of care on his part.

In one case the owner had been charged with knowledge of faulty wiring and short circuits on the yacht Ronar as evidenced by the batteries losing their charge. While undergoing repairs at Nuta's Yacht Basin, fire broke out aboard the Ronar, causing considerable damage to the basin and to nearby vessels. The yacht owner had ordered a repair contractor to replace the wiring and to check the batteries. There was evidence that the failure of the batteries to hold a charge was due to age rather than to a short circuit. The suspicion that the fire had been caused by faulty wiring, said the court, was mere speculation. Since the Ronar's owner did not have privity or knowledge respecting the cause of the fire, limitation of liability to the value of the damaged yacht was permitted. [Rooney v Nuta, 267 F2d 142, 1960 AMC 1212, CA5 1959 cert den 361 US 884, 4 L ed 2d 120, 80 S Ct 156.]

Corporation-Owned Boats

Corporations, like individuals, owning small boats, may limit liability. However, when the boat is owned by a corporation, the privity and knowledge of a managing officer or agent of the corporation is regarded as the privity and knowledge of the corporation, thus preventing limitation of liability. [The Cleveco, 154 F2d 605, 1946 AMC 933, CA6 1946.]

Generally, the knowledge or privity of an ordinary servant or employee not having a managerial function will not be ascribed to the corporate owner. [United States v Eastern Transportation Co. 59 F2d 984, 1932 AMC 964, CA2 1932.]

A plant manager's privity or knowledge of a negligent condition in the operation of a motor launch, owned by a corporation engaged in the manufacture of linseed oil, resulted in a denial of limitation of liability. The corporation used the 45-foot launch as a ferry to bring workmen across the Hudson River from New York City to the factory at Edgewater, New Jersey. Although a safe load called for not more than 60 passengers, she took on almost 80 workmen on the morning of December 20, 1926. There was drift ice in the river. On the trip to Edgewater, a cake of ice stove a hole in the port bow of the boat, causing her to fill and sink in about 2 minutes. More than 35 men lost their lives. The launch, the Linseed King, was admittedly unfit to run through ice. The corporation's executive officers knew of this fact and had instructed the manager in charge of the Edgewater plant that the boat should not be run in the river when ice was present. The decision rested with the manager regarding the conditions under which the launch should be withdrawn from its ferry service for the winter. It was apparent that ice had appeared in the river several days before the casualty and, indeed, this fact was known to an assistant to the manager. The manager knew, or should have known,

226

of the ice. The manager's position as head of the Edgewater plant and the scope of his authority rendered his privity or knowledge that of the corporation. [Spencer Kellogg & Sons v Hicks, 285 US 502, 76 L ed 903, 52 S Ct 450, 1932.]

The president of a corporation who took a 22-foot cabin cruiser into dangerous waters with an improperly secured anchor and defective mechanical equipment was instrumental in having limitation denied to his corporation. The tug Columbia Queen had grounded on the beach at Siletz Bay, Oregon. After she had been freed, it became necessary to ascertain whether the mouth of Siletz Bay was passable. The cabin cruiser Curlew, owned by the corporation, was used for this purpose. During part of the trip the corporation president was at the helm, and was actually on board when the Curlew encountered disaster. Two employees who were aboard at the time met death by drowning. The court held that the corporation officer had such supervision of the operation as to make his participation and knowledge binding upon the corporate owner. [Petition of Sause Bros. Ocean Towing Co., Inc. 193 F Supp 14, 1962 AMC 1782, DC Or 1960.]

Limitation Procedure

A boat accident may involve injury to property, personal injury, or both. The accident may involve only a single suitor or there may be many.

After the happening of the accident or incident which gives rise to tort or contractual liability of the boat, the owner of that boat may either admit or deny liability, and if he so wishes, he may seek to limit his liability by filing a petition of limitation. If he denies liability he will also seek exoneration therefrom. If he is exonerated from liability there is, of course, no further necessity to limit liability.

227

If the owner is found by the court to be at fault and therefore liable, he may still seek and obtain a limit of that liability, and that limit would be the value of the boat at the time of the accident or incident.

The owner's petition to limit liability must be filed in a District Court of the United States.

If there is but a single claim—as, for example, the bather who is run down and injured by a negligently operated boat—the lawsuit can be brought in a state court or in a Federal District Court on the civil side. The owner can plead the limitation of liability statutes as a defense to the court action and the matter need not be drawn into the admiralty court. The state court is obliged to recognize the benefits of the limitation statutes. The liability issue will be determined by the state court, but the ultimate question of the right to limit liability is reserved for the admiralty court.

When separate suits have been filed against the boatowner, he can invoke the protection of the admiralty court by filing his petition to limit in that court. Thereafter all separate suits against the boatowner, whether in the state courts or in the Federal District Courts, are stopped by injunction, and those who have brought suit must then file claims in the admiralty court limitation proceeding.

This last procedure is known as "a concourse of claims." All claims are thus before one judge for disposition.

If limitation of liability is granted, then all claimants must share prorata in the fund established by the value of the boat involved. For example: Smith, Brown, and Jones were injured by the pleasure craft Happy Times and recovered judgments in their favor. Smith's judgment amounted to $20,000; Brown's $10,000; and Jones' $5,000. The value of the Happy

228

Times was $7,000. The three judgments amounted to $35,000. Smith's prorated share would be in the ratio of $20,000 to $35,000, or four-sevenths of the limitation fund of $7,000, which would give him $4,000. Brown's share would be two-sevenths or $2,000, and Jones would get one-seventh or $1,000.

Value at Limitation

The value of the boat with respect to which limitation of liability is being sought is its value after the accident. The boatowner can surrender his boat to a trustee appointed by a United States District Court in connection with the limitation proceedings. If he wishes to keep the boat, the owner must then furnish the court with an approved surety company agreement to pay to the court the cash value for which the boat has been appraised. If the boat is a total loss with no wreckage of value, the boatowner will state the facts to the court and no surety company agreement, payment of cash, or transfer follows.

Where there is an admission of liability by the owner, or a finding of liability by the court, with a grant to the owner of the right to limit liability, either the surrendered boat, the surety company agreement, or the cash deposit becomes the source of the limitation fund.

When the boat is a total loss—as by her complete destruction by fire or by her sinking in deep water—then it is tantamount to the extinguishing of the owner's liability (provided limitation of liability is granted). [California Yacht Club of Los Angeles v Johnson, 65 F2d 245, 1933 AMC 943, CA9 1933.]

Time to Limit

A petition to limit liability must be filed by the boatowner, if he so decides, within 6 months after receiving a claim, or after such a claim has been filed in court in the form of a lawsuit. The notice of claim can be as informal as a letter from the injured party or from his counsel. The 6-month limit is strictly enforced. Delay beyond that point can mean that the boatowner has lost his valuable right of limiting his liability.

7

boat salvage

A Television Rescue

During a violent storm one early winter morning
in 1962, a cabin cruiser broke from her moorings at
a marina in New Jersey, and before long was seen
to be drifting across the Hudson River. A motorist
driving along the Henry Hudson Parkway observed
the derelict craft, now but a few dozen yards off the
New York City shoreline, bobbing about in the choppy
waters. He parked his automobile alongside the road
and boarded the boat. He was then able to attach
a line from the helpless boat to his car and to a nearby
tree, thereby succeeding in placing the cruiser in a
position of safety. After boarding her he started bailing operations and before long, with a relatively dry
boat and with tight mooring lines, he was enabled
snugly to sit out the storm.

It was at this juncture that a television newsreel
cameraman caught the interesting sight. The motorist announced to him that he expected to get a liberal
salvage award for his rescue efforts.

Later that morning I received a telephone call at
my office from a perplexed television news commentator

inquiring whether the motorist could really expect to be legally rewarded for his efforts.

After giving him the time-honored caveat of all careful lawyers who are asked to render a curbstone opinion, I told him that "based on the given facts" the rescuer certainly was entitled to a salvage award. The facts involved fitted the classic pattern of a meritorious salvage situation. The work was performed by a volunteer (the motorist) who had no legal obligation to perform the service; marine property (the boat) was in peril on navigable waters (the Hudson River); and the effort ended in success.

That afternoon TV viewers in thousands of homes were told that the motorist, still ensconced on a pleasure boat which a few hours earlier he had never seen, was legally entitled to look to the boatowner for a substantial reward for the services rendered—services of which the owner, most likely, was still wholly unaware.

Salvage Is Encouraged

Small boatowners and operators almost instinctively abhor the thought of one seeking a monetary award for rendering help to a disabled boat. In the fraternity of sailors and boatsmen the giving of aid under such circumstances is merely an expression of an act of good-neighborliness. Almost invariably help is offered or sought without a thought being given to material gain. While this spirit is much to their credit, nevertheless, it runs counter to the hard realism of the laws of the sea. Marine salvage has deep roots and a firm foundation in maritime law. As with many other nautical laws it is equally applicable to the tiniest outboard motorboat as it is to the largest ocean liner.

Recently on a Sunday afternoon a large cabin cruiser was lazily sailing along on one of the Great Lakes not far offshore when suddenly an explosion occurred below decks followed by quickly enveloping flames. Fortunately for the boat's occupants the cruiser was passing a yacht club when the mishap took place. About twenty of the club's members jumped into their boats and went to the aid of the stricken craft. So prompt and able were their efforts that the fire was put out before the yacht was near to destruction. The lives of those aboard the craft were saved. Shortly thereafter the club members retained counsel to press their claim for salvage. The hitherto grateful boatowner became violently indignant at the thought of recreational boat owners seeking a salvage reward. Indignant or not, the insurance company lawyer, after researching the law, wisely concluded that their claim was a meritorious one and arranged for a mutually satisfactory settlement.

Salvage law is probably as old as the sailing of commercial vessels. It dates back to the days of the Romans and Rhodians. The laws of those ancient countries permitted an award to the salvors of derelict, wrecked, or sunken property. The amount of the award was proportioned to the dangers which the salvors had to meet. Penalties were also provided for the looters of the goods of shipwrecked vessels.

The present laws of all seafaring nations encourage the activities of salvors, for they recognize that salvage serves a most useful purpose. It is designed to turn what could be a total loss to the owner of distressed property into a partial loss.

On Navigable Waters

Salvage is a service voluntarily rendered in relieving property from an impending peril at sea or other navigable waters by those under no legal obligation to do so.

Please note that in the definition of salvage just stated mention is made of the fact that the service must take place on navigable waters. The term "navigable waters" has a peculiar connotation in American admiralty law. It will be better understood perhaps when we are aware that only the admiralty courts—that is, the admiralty parts of the United States District Courts—have jurisdiction over a salvage case and have the authority and power to grant a salvage award. The admiralty jurisdiction of the United States District Courts extends to happenings occurring on the high seas and the navigable inland waters of the United States.

The navigable waters must be navigable in law as well as navigable in fact. Waters which are navigable in law are those which serve the means of international or interstate commerce. For example, the Atlantic and Pacific Oceans and the Gulf of Mexico are navigable waters. Not only are they navigable in fact but because they are bodies of waters which we recognize and commonly refer to as "the high seas," they are navigable in law and admiralty has jurisdiction. Inland waters which flow into the sea or which go through or touch the borders of states are also navigable in law. Examples of these are: the Hudson River, the Mississippi River, the Columbia River, etc.

The test of admiralty jurisdiction is the public navigable character of the water, no matter how the water originates. If a river flows into one of the Great Lakes, the admiralty courts have jurisdiction although the river itself is all in one state. On the other hand, if a navigable body of water is wholly within one state and does not flow into the sea or into a navigable body of water that lies in more than one state, the admiralty courts have no jurisdiction.

234

The rescue of a distressed pleasure boat on Lake George, which lies wholly within the state of New York, could not be rewarded by a salvage decree given by an admiralty court. Lake George, not being in interstate commerce, is not navigable in law. However, Oneida Lake, also located within the borders of the state of New York, is. It is navigable in law because the Erie Canal connects its waters with one of the Great Lakes and with the Hudson River.

Since state courts cannot grant a salvage award and admiralty courts do not have jurisdiction over waters not in interstate commerce, a voluntary service to imperiled marine property remains just that—the service of a good Samaritan.

Salvage Law Is Different

There is sound reason under the common law (law based upon precedents and not upon statutes) for the fact that a state court cannot give an award for a purely voluntary service. By common law a person who performs a voluntary service can expect only to be thanked for it. He cannot legally expect payment. On the contrary, under admiralty law none but a volunteer can be rewarded for rendering a salvage service. Voluntariness with respect to a salvage operation does not necessarily imply, in an academic sense, a service rendered solely from one's free will—rather the word connotes performance under circumstances where the performer is not legally obligated to render the act.

The following illustration should make this point clearly understood. Your automobile has skidded off the road and landed in a ditch. While you are off to call the AAA, a farmer passing by has seen your hapless car. In the belief that a car should not be left lying in a ditch, and to be of help to its owner, he proceeds to haul it out. Through his efforts your car

235

has been restored to driving condition. When you return from your telephone call you are surprised and pleased to see your vehicle once again in a driveable state. If the farmer seeks to be paid for his services you are under no obligation to do so. You made no contract with him, either in writing or orally. It was simply a voluntary act on his part. Should he sue you for the service his suit must be dismissed, because under the common law (which state courts follow) a voluntary service bestowed does not constitute a cause of action.

But how different is the maritime law! If your boat should break from its mooring while on navigable waters and drift onto a rocky ledge, the first person who gets to it and moves your boat to a place of safety is regarded as a meritorious salvor and can be rewarded as such.

It is this basic difference between the maritime (or admiralty) law and the common law which impelled Chief Justice Marshall of the United States Supreme Court to say:

> "If the property of an individual on land be exposed to the greatest peril, and be saved by the voluntary exertions of any persons whatever; if valuable goods be rescued from a house in flames, at the imminent hazard of life by the salvor, no remuneration in the shape of salvage is allowed. The act is highly meritorious, and the service is as great as if rendered at sea. Yet the claim for salvage could not, perhaps, be supported. It is certainly not made. Let precisely the same service, at precisely the same hazard, be rendered at sea, and a very ample reward will be bestowed in the courts of justice." [Mason v The Blaireau, 2 Cranch 240, 266, 2 L ed 266, 1804.]

Types of Salvage Services

The form which the salvage service takes is varied indeed. A common type of salvage service is the towage of a damaged or disabled boat. If there are persons on the boat who request the aid, or who do not refuse it when proffered, a salvage service ensues. If the distressed boat is unattended, and therefore derelict, the salvor need not seek consent but can proceed immediately with what must be done for the boat's safety.

A pleasure cruiser, the Happy Times II, was found one August day adrift in Long Island Sound one hour outside of Bridgeport, Connecticut, by the Two Brothers, a commercial fishing boat. The wind was from 12 to 15 miles per hour and the waters choppy. The fishermen took the cruiser in tow and brought her safely to harbor in Bridgeport. By doing so they missed the early morning catch and lost a day's fishing. The tow was held to be a salvage service. The court observed that the pleasure craft had been in danger, for while she was a considerable distance off shore when found, she would nevertheless have fetched up on shore or on a reef with possible extensive damage had she not first been rescued. In making a salvage award of $2,250, the judge took into consideration, among other circumstances, the fishermen's loss of probable earnings by reason of their being diverted from their fishing enterprise. [Kacprzynski v Lenhart, 1957 AMC 1121, DC Conn 1957.]

Relieving a stranded boat is a salvage service. A stranded craft usually finds herself in that predicament by grounding fast in shoal waters, on a beach, bar, reef, or rocks, and in general, going wherever a vessel shouldn't. The usual method of getting a stranded vessel free is to attach, or "bend," a towing line to her and pull until she comes off. When large-sized vessels are stranded, other methods are used. Sometimes the salvage operation is aided when the stranded vessel uses her own machinery while the salving vessel is pulling. Another method is the placing of anchors a distance away from the distressed vessel and then connecting them to the ship's winches. Pulling on the anchors by the use of her own machinery will often free the vessel. If the stranded ship has been driven far up on the beach, "high and dry," and is some distance away from deep water, it may require laborious efforts of canal digging to free her. Recently, a tug which had the misfortune of having her tow stranded in sandy-bottomed shoal water attempted to create a channel to deep water by "washing" the soft sand with her propellers. Her engines were speeded up and her stern was rocked from side to side during the "washing" process. [Caillouet v The Jackie G., 196 F Supp 951, 1961 AMC 2256, DC La 1961.]

A court case involving a pleasure boat concerned the yacht Escapade, formerly known as the Thor II, which stranded in the Bahamas. Her owner contracted by letter with a Miama boatyard to perform the salvage operation. It was stipulated that a fair and reasonable sum in payment of the salvage contract was $2,700. After the yacht had been relieved from her strand she was brought into a harbor and at the request of her owner, she was repaired at another boatyard. In a dispute between the salvor and the repairman it was held that the claim of the salvors was superior to and of a higher order of priority than the claim of the repairman. [Hempstead v The Escapade, 173 F Supp 833, DC Fla 1959.]

"Saving a ship from imminent danger of destruction by fire is as much a salvage service as saving her from the perils of the seas." [The Connemara, 108 US 352, 27 L ed 751, 2 S Ct 754, 1883.]

Putting out a fire on a boat generally increases the risk to the salvors and calls for promptness and skill, if the effort is to be successful and the property saved from total loss. The possibility of explosion is often present. The fire may be fought by playing a water hose upon it, using the contents of a chemical extinguisher, beating down the flames, or by sinking the boat in shallows. A salvage service may also be rendered by towing a threatened boat from the scene of conflagration, or by throwing off her lines when moored to a burning pier.

The 45-foot yacht Kiki, valued originally at $16,000, caught fire while in the Hudson River. Before long, flames 20 to 30 feet high were seen shooting from her. Fortunately for the Kiki and the people on her, the tug F. I. Robinson was nearby. The fire was extinguished quickly by the tug's hose. The fire damage was severe, since the Kiki's value dropped to $500. For the few minutes of work involved, the tug and her crew were awarded $300. [The F. I. Robinson, 2 F Supp 644, 1933 AMC 567, DC ED NY 1933.]

Still another type of salvage service is the raising of sunken vessels, parts or equipment of a sunken craft, cargo, and other property. With the present popularity of skindiving, this type of salvage work may become increasingly common, particularly in the inland waters and in the relatively shallow coastal waters.

After an explosion, the motorboat Mist-Chief sank quickly at her pier at Watch Hill, Rhode Island. The pier owner, on his own, raised the wreck, removed the engines, and cleaned and reassembled them. For his efforts in retrieving the valuable engines from the corrosive salt water, the pier owner was declared to be a rightful salvor. [The Mist-Chief, 57 F2d 875, DC RI 1931.]

Life Salvage

The saving of human life when connected with the saving of marine property is in the nature of a salvage service. When the salvage service involves the saving of both life and property, the salvor of human life is entitled by statute to share with the salvor of property in the award. [46 United States Code § 729.]

The saving of human life without the associated saving of property does not entitle the salvor to an award. Thus, if while cruising in your boat you rescue a drowning swimmer, your reward in heaven will be great indeed; but for the life-saving effort there is no law which requires monetary payment. However, if that drowning swimmer came from an imperiled boat, the picture would be quite different if you or someone else also rescued the boat. The fact that human life was saved would be recognized as a contributing factor when deciding on the amount of the salvage award. If you saved a life while the other salvor saved the boat, you, as a life salvor, would be entitled to a share in the award.

Other Types of Salvage Services

Other types of salvage service are recovery of cargo from a disabled ship, wreck, or sunken craft, or picking up cargo afloat; standing by a distressed ship at her request or by bringing aid to her; supplying manpower to a dangerously short-handed vessel; recapturing a vessel from an enemy, pirate, or privateer; and giving advice which aids a distressed ship.

Volunteers

Since a salvage service must be one voluntarily rendered, then all who are under no legal obligation to do so can be considered to be salvors. The crew of the vessel of a professional salvage company is not eligible to be rewarded as salvors. The same restriction applies to Coast Guardsmen. They engage in salvage services not as volunteers, but within the line of normal duty for which they are compensated.

The position of a passenger is somewhat peculiar. He is to a certain extent bound to the ship by the contract of carriage (his passage ticket) and he is obliged, in moments of distress, to join the crew in attempting to save the vessel. However, he is not—like the crew—obliged to stand by the ship to the last, and if he performs extraordinary services to the vessel in which he is being transported, he is entitled to a salvage award. I have no doubt but that the same principle would apply to nonpaying guests on pleasure boats.

The salving of the Great Eastern by one of her passengers is one of the great sagas of the sea. This gargantuan vessel of the 1860's, a steamer with sails, was almost as large as today's Queen Mary. While on a voyage from Liverpool to New York she suffered an incapacitating injury to her rudder which left her helpless in the rough seas. For several days she wallowed in the trough of the waves being buffeted about while her engineroom crew was ineffectually working to repair the injured rudder. Towle, a passenger aboard the Great Eastern and a civil engineer by profession, observed some of the crew, under the direction of the ship's chief engineer, loosening a large nut which held the rudder shaft in place. Fearing that the damaged rudder would be dropped into the sea, Towle went to the captain and explained his plan of rigging a jury rudder so that the vessel could be temporarily steered. By this time the master had become discouraged at the chief engineer's futile efforts and gave his consent to Towle's plan. Towle had devised an ingenious method of making the damaged rudder operate by means of a combination of chains wrapped around the rudder shaft. Towle worked day and night supervising the operation until the job was done. The Great Eastern was able to be turned about and was brought to her home port slowly but safely. The passenger's expert and extraordinary services undoubtedly saved the liner and the lives of hundreds of passengers from destruction. Towle was held to be a salvor and was handsomely rewarded. [Towle v The Great Eastern, F Cas No 14110, DC SD NY 1864.]

Public officers, pilots, and ships' agents can be recognized as salvors when their services are rendered beyond the call of duty and are in the nature of extraordinary services.

Ordinarily, the master and crew of the distressed ship cannot be rewarded as salvors for saving their own vessel. They are obligated, under the general maritime law and the shipping articles pursuant to which they sail, to stand by their ship in fair weather and foul; in good fortune and in distress. But seamen may be salvors of their own vessel and be rewarded as such where:

(1) The vessel has been abandoned by all, or all except the salvors, under circumstances which show conclusively that the abandonment was absolute, without hope or expectation of recovery.

(2) The master has unmistakably discharged the seaman from the service of the shipowner and their contract of employment.

(3) The vessel has been wrecked and a total loss with the ship either going to the bottom or leaving her bones on the shore.

(4) The ship is recaptured after it has been captured by a hostile power.

Success Is Essential

Success is essential if an award is to be earned by the volunteer salvor. Without success there can be no salvage reward. It does not matter how daring is the attempt to save the imperiled property or how arduously or skilfully the would-be rescuers may have labored. If the property is lost, so is the salvage award; for salvage money is allowed only for property saved.

The property need not be saved solely by the efforts of the person seeking the award. It is sufficient if his efforts *contributed* in some way to the ultimate success.

It may well be asked, "What *is* success with respect to a salvage service?" In a broad sense it can be said that salvage success means any service or labor which restores, or aids in the restoration, of the distressed property to its owner. It does not necessarily follow that the property restored will be in as sound a condition as before the imperilment. For the service to be successful, it does not mean that the property be restored in even a slightly damaged condition. The lack or the severity of damage does not govern the requirement of success. So long as the property is saved for the owner in a state where it can be converted into money—where something more beneficial than total loss results from the salvor's services—then can it be said that the salvage service has been rendered successfully.

Abandoning the Effort

Where the distressed property has been voluntarily abandoned by those who have attempted to save it, they

cannot be rewarded for their efforts to the time of
the abandonment although the property is preserved
by the subsequent efforts of others. However, when
the salvors are prevented from completing their efforts
due to causes beyond their control, as stress of weather,
fog, darkness, being ordered away by the master of
the salved ship, leaving in compliance with orders or
to seek assistance, etc., and where there has been no
wilful disregard of duty on their part to the aided
property, forfeiture of their right to a salvage reward
will not be imposed.

The Salvor's Motive

If aid is successfully given to property in distress
on navigable waters, the motive, if lawful, which impelled that person, no matter how crass or selfish it
may be, is immaterial to the right to be regarded as
a salvor. The amount of the award, whether it be
decreased or forfeited because of improper motives,
may be affected, as in the case of misconduct on the
part of the salvor. I have said "lawful" with respect
to the salvor's connection with the salved property, for
it appears unlikely, under principles of public policy,
that he would be rewarded as a salvor when he first
came to the property for an illegal purpose. For
example: the man who boards a vessel and commits
a robbery, but stays to help put out a fire, should not
be given a salvor's reward.

That the salvor has been motivated in the salvage
service by a desire to profit financially is no ground
whatever for barring him from the status of salvor,
for one of the hallmarks of the law of salvage is
the appeal to the cupidity of the salvor in the hope
of encouraging the saving of life and property on
navigable waters.

Acts of Misconduct

The law of salvage deals kindly with the meritorious salvors, giving them, when successful, a reward sometimes far out of proportion to the value of their services if figured on actual time spent. But the same law deals firmly and strictly with those individuals who transgress and engage in acts of misconduct. The distress and helplessness of a victim of the sea or other navigable waters should not provide the occasion for rapaciousness on the part of the would-be salvor. The salvor who will not aid the victim until his exorbitant terms are met first, who demands the abandonment to him of the distressed property as a condition before rendering service, who makes untruthful statements in order to obtain consent to salve the endangered property, and who does not deal fairly, will receive the disapproval of the admiralty courts.

Specific examples of acts of misconduct are: the stealing or misappropriation of the salved property; refusing, or refraining from participating in, the salvage service; exaggerating the peril involved and the value of the services rendered; forcing aid on the unwilling; compelling the posting of a bond in an excessive amount; the salvor being the cause of the distress; taking the salved property to a distant point for the purpose of extending the duration of the salvage operation; failure of the salvor to take proper care of the salved property; the negligence of the salvor in failing to exercise ordinary care and thereby damaging the salved vessel and goods; giving false information; undue delay in going to assist the distressed property; and unreasonably detaining the salved vessel and cargo. For these offenses an admi-

245

ralty court may diminish the reward or declare an entire forfeiture.

For a more detailed discussion of this and other topics on salvage law see: Norris, "The Law of Salvage," (1958).

The Right of Possession

The title of the owner of distressed property on navigable waters is not lost because of the mishap although that property becomes the subject of salvage services. The salvor gains a lien on the property salved and the right to hold it in his possession until the lien is satisfied; he does not acquire ownership or title to the salved boat.

When the salved property has been brought to a place of safety by the salvor, it has been saved for the benefit of the owner. It is the salvor's obligation to bring the salved property before an admiralty court (unless amicable agreement is reached with the owner) where the owner will be given an opportunity to come in and claim the property. The salvor, by suing for the salvage reward and by having possession of the recovered property taken by the federal marshal, is enabled to take the necessary steps for securing his reward. Thereafter (particularly if the owner fails to appear and to claim his property, or make suitable arrangements for the salvor's compensation), the property can be sold by the marshal on order of the court. The proceeds of the sale is placed in the registry of the court (after deduction of legal expenses and fees) for distribution to the salvor and the owner of the salvaged property. The salvor can purchase the property at the sale, if he so wishes, and can acquire title like any other purchaser in good faith.

The right of the salvor to hold the salved property pursuant to his claim or lien is something which most boatowners have difficulty in comprehending. That right, however, is not peculiar to maritime law; it has its counterpart in the bailee's lien. For example, the tailor who alters a suit can retain the garment if the bill is not paid.

Recently a New York City police detective attached to a harbor boat squad asked me whether certain fishermen who had come upon a cruiser drifting along the Atlantic shoreline and had brought it safely into harbor had the right to retain the boat, pending settlement with the owner. The irate boatowner had demanded that the police arrest the fishermen for unlawfully retaining private property. When I told the detective that the fishermen were acting in accordance with their legal rights, he exclaimed, "You don't say so! And for years I've been telling salvors to return property or risk arrest."

An example of erroneous concepts on this phase of salvage is seen in The Snow Maiden. This fishing schooner went aground near Plymouth, Mass., in 1955. The owner and his two-man crew were taken off her by a Coast Guard rescue unit.

Immediately after coming ashore the owner engaged a boatyard repairman to salvage the craft. However, early next morning, Powers, a fisherman, heading out to sea, spotted the wreck on Brown's Bank. He rescued the engine and a pump and brought them into Plymouth. The owner, who was on the dock, demanded the return of his engine. Powers refused to give it up without first receiving a salvage award. Following the advice of local harbor and police authorities, Powers turned the engine over to the boat repairman. A few weeks later, acting on the advice of his counsel, Powers instructed the boat repairman to return the engine to the schooner's owner.

The fundamental error here of the local harbor and police authorities and of counsel lay in their apparent complete misconception of the legal rights of the salvor. Powers, as the salvor of marine property on navigable waters, had the right of possession. By virtue of the salvage service which he performed he did not become the owner of the rescued property but he did automatically receive a salvage lien on that property. That lien gave Powers the right to hold the salved property even against the demands of the owner. The owner could regain his property either by agreeing to a satisfactory reward or, in lieu of that, by posting security such as a surety company bond, cash, collateral, etc. If payment of a reward or the posting of security is not obtainable, the salvor must, within a reasonable period of time, file a suit or libel in the Federal District Court of that area. The property is then taken into possession by a United States marshal pending disposition after trial.

The error in The Snow Maiden was further compounded in court when the judge mistakenly ruled that the maritime law did not recognize or grant a salvage lien. Fortunately, the error was corrected in a second opinion, after this author had called it to the attention of the court. [The Snow Maiden, 159 F Supp 30, 1958 AMC 272, DC Mass 1958.]

Contract Salvage

A voluntary salvage service not undertaken or completed pursuant to a contractual arrangement is called "pure salvage." A typical example: the salving vessel on navigable waters comes upon a drifting cruiser, helpless because of motor trouble. The owner of the stricken boat states that he needs help. The salvor throws him a line (or receives the cruiser's line) and the disabled boat is taken in tow and brought to a place

248

of safety.   No arrangements have been made with respect to compensation.

Unless the owner of the salved property and the salvors come to an understanding as to the amount of compensation to be paid, in cases of "pure salvage," it is fixed after lawsuit by a Federal District Court judge sitting in admiralty.   The compensation so determined is called a "salvage award."

There is a type of service called "contract salvage." In this form of service the parties involved may agree, either orally or in writing, for the service to be rendered.   They may also agree that the salvor is to be paid for his efforts whether or not those efforts result in ultimate success.   The contract may also provide that the compensation is contingent upon the success of the enterprise.   This type of contract is called "no cure, no pay."

A valid salvage contract will be enforced by the admiralty courts.   The amount of compensation paid to the salvor will be the amount agreed upon by the parties.   The Federal District Court Judge does not grant a discretionary salvage award when a valid contract is involved.

It is not every agreement which will be regarded as a valid and binding one.   Loose talk or general expressions will not make a binding salvage contract.   Such statements as "I'll be reasonable in my charges," or "we will leave it to arbitration," in the absence of a definite and explicit bargain, will not meet the test of a binding salvage contract.   Neither will an implied agreement (that is, an agreement by inference) be regarded as an enforceable salvage contract, for the reason that unless an agreement is clearly and specifically set out with respect to the amount and there is mutual understanding that the services involved

249

are in the nature of salvage, the courts will not infer that a contract exists.

A contract made under compulsion or duress will not be enforced. A salvor cannot assume a "take it or leave it" attitude toward the unfortunate victim. A classic case is that which involved the barge Bolikow when she was in distress about 120 miles from Tampico. The tug George C. Greer with a tow behind her was sighted by the Bolikow and assistance was requested from the tug's master. The Greer's master demanded $20,000 for the tow. The captain of the Bolikow turned down this demand, stating that he would pay anything within reason. After further negotiations the master of the Greer demanded $15,000 and said that he was going to leave and proceed on his way if an agreement in that amount was not made. Under these compelling circumstances the master of the Bolikow signed an agreement to pay $15,000 for the Greer's services. The Greer simply added the Bolikow to her tow and brought her in. The tow was uneventful with fine weather and smooth seas prevailing. The United States District Court refused to enforce the contract and made a salvage award of $3,000.

On appeal, this amount was reduced to $1,700, with the Court saying:

> "The refusal of the master of the Greer to render assistance and his threat to leave the Bolikow unless his exorbitant demand was acceded to amounted to moral compulsion and the contract which he procured by the methods adopted is not protected or made binding and valid." [Magnolia Petroleum Co. v National Oil Transport Co., 286 F 40, CA5th 1923.]

The Salvage Award

It is the spirit of the maritime law, based on public policy, to reward salvors liberally in order to overcome all unwillingness on their part toward assuming additional labor and risks in the saving of life and property on navigable waters. In the language of a court: "The very object of the law of salvage is to promote commerce and trade, and the general interests of the country, by preventing the destruction of property, and to accomplish this by appealing to the personal interests of the individual as a motive of action, with the assurance that he will not depend upon the owner of the property he saves for the measure of his compensation, but to a court of admiralty, governed by principles in equity." [Seven Coal Barges, F Cas No 12677, CC Ind 1870.]

The voluntary salvor is never treated as a mere creditor for work and labor done and the courts in considering compensation do not look solely to the exact amount of services performed in the salvage operation.

In determining the amount of the award, the court considers the various elements to be found in the salvage service. They are:

1. The labor expended by the salvors in rendering the salvage service.

2. The promptitude, skill, and energy displayed in rendering the service and saving the property.

3. The value of the property employed by the salvors in rendering the service, and the danger to which such property was exposed.

4. The risk incurred by the salvors in securing the property from the impending peril.

5. The value of the property saved.

6. The degree of danger from which the property

was rescued. [The Blackwall, 77 US 1, 10 Wall 1, 19 L ed 870, 1870.]

Some Odd Salvage Cases

Three men in a rowboat were held to be salvors of a vessel and a canal boat. The vessel, with a canal boat attached to her, broke from her moorings and drifted through the turbulent Hell Gate at New York. Just at dark the captain of the canal boat, who was the only man on board, succeeded in attracting the attention of the three men in the rowboat. The vessel and the canal boat were then nearing shore. The men took the vessel's hawser and made it fast ashore. Their shouts attracted a passing tug which took the vessel and the canal boat to a safe berth. Of an award of $750, the tug received $50 and the three men divided $700. [The Mary Freeland, 62 F 943, DC ED NY 1894.]

A moored tug was pressed into service quickly with a "pick-up" crew. The successful group of volunteers included, among others, a newspaper editor who acted as a deckhand, an engineer from another vessel, and a fire department chief engineer. All were rewarded as meritorious salvors of a vessel in distress. [The Josephus, 116 F 124, DC RI 1902.]

In 1947 the body of a drowned fisherman was found floating in Great South Bay, Long Island, New York by a man in a small boat. The body was towed ashore and the police notified. On the body was found currency in the amount of $2,133. The finder of the body claimed the money as a salvage award. The court allowed the claim, holding that money found on a floating body was no different from money found on a wreck. [Broere v Two Thousand One Hundred Thirty-Three Dollars, 72 F Supp 115, DC ED NY 1947; 78 F Supp 635, DC ED NY 1948.]

252

Knowing Salvage Law

The members of the seafaring profession, in general, are courageous and honest people accustomed to facing danger with disarming matter-of-factness. A boat or persons in distress will get from them unstinting aid and ready assistance. But among the professional seafarers are a small coterie of avaricious men who seek to take advantage of the helpless or unwary. They assume all too readily that if one can afford to own a pleasure boat, then he must be rolling in wealth and be fair game for a big picking. It is therefore well for the boatowner to know the ins and outs of salvage law so that he may not become a naive and sophomoric victim of this ilk.

*

8

crimes on the high seas

Maritime Crimes

There are no policemen, no courts, and no prisons on the high seas. If a crime is committed on an American flag vessel or in the territorial waters of the United States, then the long arm of Uncle Sam can reach out and take the miscreant into custody. In short, should a crime take place aboard an American recreational boat outside the jurisdiction of any particular state of the United States, then by statute, the federal authorities and the federal courts have the right to arrest and try the wrongdoer.

When crimes have been committed upon the high seas or any other waters within the admiralty and maritime jurisdiction of the United States and out of the jurisdiction of any particular state, or on any Government-owned vessel or a vessel owned by an American citizen or corporation, the trial must be held in a United States District Court in the district where the offender is apprehended, or into which he may first be brought. [Constitution of the United States, Art 3,

255

§ 2 and the Sixth Amendment; Judicial Code § 41; 18 United States Code § 7; 28 United States Code § 102.]

Should you be unfortunate enough to have a crime committed on your boat while it is on the high seas or in the territorial waters of a foreign country, then, as quickly as possible, put in to an American port if at all feasible. Report the criminal act to the local police authorities and to the United States attorney at once, or, if not available, to a United States marshal. If you put in to a foreign port, report the crime to the local police authorities immediately. Be sure to see a United States consul and make a report to him.

Crimes occurring on waters within a state boundary and under state jurisdiction will be treated by that particular state's criminal laws just as are crimes which take place on land. The jurisdiction of criminal acts which take place on rivers or bodies of waters which divide states is governed by the location where the offense occurred. The boundary line which marks the territorial waters of the state is usually fixed by the statutes of the respective states.

By way of illustration—let us assume that an inland lake separates a portion of Ohio and Illinois. The Ohio borderline as well as the Illinois borderline will, by agreement of the states, run through the lake. This borderline is shown on any appropriate chart or map of the lake. A boat sets out from the Ohio side to cross over to the Illinois shore. Should a crime take place while the vessel is in Ohio's waters, then Ohio would have jurisdiction of the matter. Similarly, Illinois would take jurisdiction of any crime occurring on the Illinois side of the lake.

Federal Jurisdiction of Maritime Crimes

The federal jurisdiction of maritime crimes has been set forth by an act of Congress. This statute refers to this jurisdiction as the "special maritime and territorial jurisdiction of the United States." [18 United States Code § 7.] This term includes the following:

(1) The high seas, any other waters within the admiralty and maritime jurisdiction of the United States and out of the jurisdiction of any particular state, and any vessel belonging in whole or in part to the United States or any citizen thereof, etc., when such vessel is within the admiralty and maritime jurisdiction of the United States and out of the jurisdiction of any particular state.

(2) Vessels registered, licensed, or enrolled under the laws of the United States and on a voyage upon the waters of any of the Great Lakes or any of the waters connecting them, or upon the St. Lawrence River where the same constitutes the international boundary line.

(3) Lands reserved or acquired for the use of the United States and under the exclusive or concurrent jurisdiction thereof, or any place purchased or otherwise acquired by the United States by the consent of the legislature of the state in which the same shall be, for the erection of a fort, magazine, arsenal, dockyard, or any other needful building.

(4) Any island, rock, or key containing deposits of guano may, at the discretion of the President, be considered as appertaining to the United States.

In a territorial sense the term "United States" includes all places and waters, continental or insular, subject to the jurisdiction of the United States, except the Canal Zone. [18 United States Code § 5.]

Seduction

Any master, officer, seaman, or other person employed on board of any American vessel who, during

257

the voyage, under promise of marriage, by threats, by the exercise of authority, by solicitation, or by the presentation of gifts, seduces and has illicit sexual intercourse with a female passenger, is liable to a fine of $1,000 or imprisonment of not more than one year, or both. Subsequent marriage of the parties may be pleaded as a defense. No conviction can be obtained solely on the testimony of the female seduced. There must be other evidence in addition to her testimony. [18 United States Code § 2198.]

There can be no prosecution, trial, or punishment for such seduction unless the indictment is found or the information filed within one year after the vessel on which the offense was committed arrives at its port of destination. [18 United States Code § 3286.]

Any fine imposed as a consequence of such a conviction may, upon the direction of the court, be paid for the use of the female seduced or for her child, if she has one. [18 United States Code § 3614.]

It should be noted that these statutes pertain to a member of the crew (or other employee) of a vessel and a female passenger. Therefore, the statutes have never been applied, and are not likely to be, in connection with recreational small boats.

Seduction is a statutory crime in most states of the United States. A statutory crime is one established as such by an act of a legislative body. At one time seduction was punishable under the common law. Under the common law a crime was recognized as such by the accumulated court decisions on the subject. Seduction has been defined as "the act of inducing a woman to consent to unlawful sexual intercourse by enticements which overcome her scruples," [Ryan v Oswald, 134 Neb 265, 278 NW 508, 1938] and also as "any act, solicitation, or statement by a man which overcomes

258

the unwillingness of a woman and causes her to yield her virtue." [Bradshaw v Jones, 103 Tenn 331, 52 SW 1072, 1899.]

The surrender of chastity must have been brought about by persuasion, which may be in the form of a promise of marriage, flattery, or deception. The seducer must be a male and the person seduced a female. The victim must have been an unmarried female of a previously chaste character. Most state statutes provide that the actual marriage of the parties prior to the final judgment against the man is a bar to conviction of seduction. In some states the statutes provide that a bona fide offer of marriage is a complete defense.

Rape

"Rape is the carnal knowledge of any woman above the age of consent against her will, and of a female child under the age of consent with or against her will; its essence is the felonious and violent penetration of the person of the female." [Commonwealth v Mc-Can, 277 Mass 199, 203, 178 NE 633, 78 ALR 1208, 1931.]

Another definition of this crime is as follows: "Rape is an act of sexual intercourse accomplished forcibly, and without the consent of the female. If it be with her consent, though some coercion is used to procure consent, and the intercourse is illegal, the crime is 'adultery' or 'fornication' as the case may be." [Whidby v State, 121 Ga 588, 49 SE 811, 1905.]

When a statute pertains to carnal knowledge of a female child below a stated age (the age of consent), the consent of the child is not a defense. Unlawful sexual intercourse with a girl under the age of consent is a crime whether she consents or not. [Perkins: Criminal Law, p. 119, 1957.]

The Mutiny Statute

The authority to punish for the crime of mutiny is found in a federal statute. [18 United States Code § 2193.] This statute reads as follows:

"Whoever, being of the crew of a vessel of the United States, on the high seas, or on any other waters within the admiralty and maritime jurisdiction of the United States, unlawfully and with force, or by fraud, or intimidation, usurps the command of such vessel from the master or other lawful officer in command thereof, or deprives him of authority and command on board, or resists or prevents him in the free and lawful exercise thereof, or transfers such authority and command to another not lawfully entitled thereto, is guilty of a revolt and mutiny, and shall be fined not more than $2,000 or imprisoned not more than ten years, or both."

The statute applies to all members of the crew below the rank of master, that is, officers and crewmen. Fletcher Christian, the mate of H.M.S. Bounty, was just as much a mutineer as the common sailors on that vessel who participated in the usurpation of the authority of Captain Bligh.

The Act of Mutiny

Mutiny of a ship's crew consists of the following elements: (a) resistance to the free and lawful exercise of the master's authority; (b) deposing the master from his command; (c) transfer of the master's power to a third power by the party accused.

The mere passive disobedience on the part of a single member of the crew, unaccompanied by force, intimidation, or fraud upon the master or other officer in command is not the act of mutiny. But if the con-

262

duct and intention of the individual is to resist the
master actively, or to stir up and excite his shipmates
into joining him in his act of disobedience and resistance, then he, as well as all who join or conspire with
him, is subject to the punishment of this statute,
whether or not their conduct resulted in a successful
revolt against the master. [United States v Huff, 13
F 630, CC Tenn 1882.]

A classic example of a mutiny at sea is presented
in the case of United States v Haskell. [F Cas No
15321, CC Pa 1823.] Captain Garland had retired for
the night, leaving the mate in charge while the vessel
was on the high seas. The captain heard scuffling going
on above him. Hurrying on deck, he found that the
mate had been assaulted and was in a dying condition.
While stooping over the mate, Captain Garland was
attacked by a seaman named Smith, who stabbed him
twice in the neck with a knife. The captain fought
with Smith, succeeded in seizing the knife, and threw
it overboard. He then called to the crew to help him
in subduing Smith, but his commands were ignored.
Smith stated that he had command of the ship and gave
orders to two of the seamen, Haskell and Francois, to
go forward and take in the sails. The captain then
ordered Haskell, who was at the helm, not to obey
Smith and to keep the vessel on her course, but his
commands were again ignored. Seeing that the crew
was against him, Captain Garland went below deck.
There Peter, a young sailor, brought him his gun, and
thus fortified, the captain returned to the deck. He
fought again with Smith and during this encounter
he shot the mutineer and threw him overboard. The
vessel was brought into port and Haskell and Francois
were indicted for mutiny.

It was claimed by the defendants that they acted

263

Displaying a false light, or extinguishing a light, in order to wreck a ship is punishable by imprisonment for not less than 10 years and by a maximum term of life imprisonment. [18 United States Code § 1658.] During the Middle Ages it was a common practice to confiscate the cargoes of shipwrecked vessels under the guise of its becoming the property of the lord of the territory where the wreck took place. To increase the numbers of such wrecked vessels beyond the normal toll of the sea, false lights would be displayed so that on dark and stormy nights ships would be inadvertently steered upon the rocky coast. As recently as the eighteenth century, the inhabitants of Cornwall and Wales were accused of robbing and sometimes murdering shipwrecked seamen.

Destruction of Vessels

An owner who wilfully and corruptly destroys a vessel for the purpose of collecting insurance may be imprisoned for life or for any term of years. If a person other than an owner perpetrates this act, he may be imprisoned for not more than 10 years. [18 United States Code § 2273.] The wilful destruction includes "scuttling," that is, boring holes in a vessel or opening her sea cocks for the purpose of sinking her.

Breaking or entering any vessel with the intent to commit a felony, or for the purpose of maliciously cutting, splitting, or destroying any cordage, cable, buoys, buoy rope, anchors, or moorings, etc., is prohibited, and a prison sentence of 5 years, or a fine of not more than $1,000, or both, is provided by a federal statute. [18 United States Code § 2276.]

Setting fire to or placing bombs or explosives in a vessel with the intent to injure or endanger the safety of the vessel, her cargo, or the persons on board, whether the injury or danger is intended to take place within the jurisdiction of the United States or after the vessel has left a United States port, is a crime punishable by imprisonment for not more than 20 years or a fine of not more than $10,000, or both. [18 United States Code § 2275.]

Robbery at Sea

Robbery is the taking by force, violence, or intimidation, from the person or persons of another, any property or money or any other thing of value.

When it occurs aboard a boat within the special maritime jurisdiction of the United States, it can be punished by imprisonment for not more than 15 years. [18 United States Code § 2111.]

Arson

The crime of arson, when committed within the special maritime jurisdiction of the United States, is punishable by a fine of not more than $1,000, or imprisonment for not more than 5 years, or both.

The maritime aspect of arson has been defined as the wilful and malicious setting fire to, or burning, or attempting to set fire to or burn, any vessel or any appliance used for navigation or shipping. [18 United States Code § 81.]

Murder

Murder is the unlawful killing of a human being with malice aforethought. Every murder perpetrated by poison, lying in wait, or any other kind of wilful, deliberate, malicious, and premeditated killing, or committed in the perpetration of, or attempt to perpetrate, any arson, rape, burglary, or robbery, or perpetrated from a premeditated design unlawfully and maliciously to effect the death of any human being

271

other than the person who is killed, is murder in the first degree. Any other murder is murder in the second degree.

For the crime of murder in the first degree committed within the special maritime jurisdiction of the United States, the penalty upon conviction is death, unless the jury qualifies its verdict by adding to that verdict, "without capital punishment." In such an event, the convicted person can be sentenced to life imprisonment.

Conviction for the crime of murder in the second degree committed within the special maritime jurisdiction of the United States is punishable by imprisonment for any term of years or for life. [18 United States Code § 1111.]

Criminal Jurisdiction Between Nations

Should your boat (which flies the American flag) go into a foreign port, and should a serious crime take place aboard the boat, which country would have jurisdiction to try the culprit? The logical answer would be that the country where the crime was committed would have jurisdiction of the matter. But in international law the question has not been disposed of that easily.

Jurisdiction can be claimed by the sovereign country whose flag the ship is flying. Jurisdiction is also concurrent, and the country where the crime occurred may act unless it chooses to yield the prisoner to the country of the vessel's flag.

In one instance a Belgian seaman killed a man on a Belgian vessel while it was lying in New Jersey waters. He was arrested by the New Jersey police. The Belgian consul sought to have him released on a writ of habeas corpus, presumably for trial in Belgium. Re-

272

fusal to release him was upheld by the United States Supreme Court, which said:

"If crimes are committed on board of a character to disturb the peace and tranquility of the country to which the vessel has been brought, the offenders have never, by comity or usage, been entitled to any exemption from the operation of the local laws for their punishment, if the local tribunals see fit to assert their authority." [Wildenhus' Case, 120 US 1, 30 L ed 565, 7 S Ct 385.]

*

9

boatyard damages

On Boats and Bailments

While boatyards and marinas are not nearly as numerous as drugstores or gasoline filling stations, nonetheless they dot the shoreline along the coasts, bays, and rivers. In 1961, according to one authoritative estimate, there were 4,000 boatyards and marinas in existence in the United States. The number, it need hardly be stressed, is growing steadily.

It is more than likely that there will be several occasions when your boat will be in a yard for repairs, storage, or maintenance work. It is important for you to know your rights and obligations with respect to the boatyard operator, and perhaps of greater importance, his obligations to you in the event of damage to your boat.

When your boat is taken to a boatyard or to a marina for repairs or for storage and it is accepted for that purpose, the situation thus created is known in law as a bailment. This means that the person who receives the boat has the obligation of using ordinary care

275

of the property while it is in his custody and of accounting for any damage or destruction thereto.

The word bailment is derived from the French word "bailler," which means "to deliver." A simple definition of a bailment is as follows: "Bailment is a delivery of something of a personal nature by one party to another to be held according to the purpose or object of the delivery, and to be returned or delivered over when that purpose is accomplished." [Hardin v Grant, 54 SW2d 189, 190, Tex Civ App, 1932.]

The person who receives the property is called the "bailee." When you deliver your boat to the custody of the boatyard you become the "bailor" and the boatyard operator is the "bailee."

In everyday life the bailment situation is created many times and in numerous forms. A common example is that of taking your blue suit to the local tailor for cleaning and pressing. When you delivered that suit a bailment was created and the tailor became a bailee. The legal consequence of delivering your boat to the boatyard operator parallels the delivery of your suit to the tailor.

Differing Bailment Situations

Not all bailments are alike. The situations involved in leaving personal property in the care of another individual differ and with that difference there are also varying standards of responsibility. In general, the greater the benefit to the bailee, the greater his responsibility and liability.

The most usual form of bailment is the one which mutually benefits both parties. When you place your boat in a yard for repairs, or take your blue suit to the tailor, it is a bailment for the mutual benefit of both parties. The yard operator or the tailor (bailees)

276

receive the profit involved, and your property benefits from their services. A bailment for hire, also called a reciprocal bailment, is one for mutual benefit. An example of this is the hiring of an automobile. The hirer of the automobile (the bailee) benefits from the use of it; the owner (the bailor) also benefits because he receives the financial proceeds involved in the transaction.

The responsibility of the bailee for the property entrusted to him in a mutual benefit bailment, in the absence of a special agreement, is as follows: the bailee is held to the exercise of ordinary care in relation to the property and is responsible only for ordinary negligence. The matter of duty of care will be considered more fully in subsequent sections.

Another type of bailment is the one intended for the sole benefit of the bailor, that is, of the owner of the property. It is a gratuitous bailment. The mechanic who agreed to repair an automobile without charge was a bailee for the sole benefit of the owner and without reward. Leaving your baggage with someone to care for it in your absence without any recompense is a further example of a gratuitous bailment and one for the sole benefit of the bailor. Although the bailee has the duty to exercise some care, he is held merely to the duty of exercising slight care with regard to the property entrusted to him. He would be liable to the owner only for gross negligence, bad faith, a wilful act, or fraud.

Finally, there is the bailment for the sole benefit of the bailee. Should you lend your boat to a friend, without charge, with the understanding that it be returned to you, it would be a bailment for the sole benefit of the bailee (your friend). It is generally a bailment for an indefinite period which ends when

277

you decide that you wish to have your property returned to you. Here, the bailee is bound to exercise great care or extraordinary diligence with regard to the property and is responsible for slight neglect of it. While he is required to return the property in as good condition as when he received it, it has been held that he is not responsible for reasonable wear and tear or for its loss or damage without blame or neglect attributable to him. [See: Cowan v Sutherland, 6 Misc 2d 71, 117 NYS2d 365, S Ct NY 1952.]

Boatyard's Duty of Care

When a boat is placed in a boatyard or at a dock for repairs or for storage a bailment results for the mutual benefit of the owner of the boat and the operator of the boatyard or dock. Unless otherwise stipulated, the yard or dock operator in his capacity as bailee owes the duty to exercise ordinary and reasonable care in the protection of the boat. [Stegemann v Miami Beach Boat Slips, Inc. 213 F2d 561, 1954 AMC 1372, CA5th 1954.]

Condition of Property

If the blue suit which you left at the tailor's shop had a frayed area which weakened the fabric, you could not expect the tailor to pay for the damage to the garment should the material tear in the course of ordinary and customary handling. Similarly, if you deliver your boat to the yard with an inherent or latent defective condition (which condition is not the subject of repairs) and the boat is damaged as a consequence of that condition, the repairman will not be held to be liable.

In 1952, a yacht, then 58 years old, was brought to a boatyard for repairs. Her structural framework was badly rotted. The yacht's owner was advised of this condition. It appeared that the timbers had deteriorated so badly that they could no longer hold tight the fastenings of the planking and as a result the seams had sprung. The consequence was that after the stipulated repairs had been completed and the boat was restored in the water, she began to fill. It was held by the court that the repairman was not liable for the leaking condition of the yacht. It was the inherently rotted condition of the framework rather than the failure of the repairman to perform properly the work he was hired to do which was responsible for the ultimate condition of the boat. [Bromfield Manufacturing Co., Inc. v Yacht Brown, Smith and Jones, 117 F Supp 630, 1954 AMC 350, DC Mass 1954.]

Bailee Is Not an Insurer

When personal property is left with a bailee, he does not, by receiving the property, assume the obligations of an insurer. [Niagara Fire Insurance Company v Dog River Boat Service, Inc., 187 F Supp 528, 1961 AMC 1299, DC Ala 1960.] The position of an insurer has an important and particular connotation in law. An insurer is one who agrees to become responsible for the goods in his care "no matter what." In short, an insurer must either return the property to you in a reasonably fit condition or make monetary restitution.

The bailee's position, however, is quite different. He too is expected to return your property to you in a reasonably fit condition, but if he does not, he is given the opportunity to show that his failure to do so was not due to his negligence. [See: Lackritz v Petersen, 31 F Supp 415, 1940 AMC 257, DC SD NY 1940.]

279

When you call for your blue suit at the tailor shop and the tailor cannot produce it, do not assume that he must reimburse you. He may show that the suit was either damaged, destroyed, or stolen, through no fault on his part. If he does so you have no recourse and you must, however reluctantly, accept the loss. That is the law!

Burden of Proof

When you have left your personal property with a bailee and he has failed to return it to you, or has failed to return it in a condition reasonably comparable to what it was when left with him, then you have the burden of proving that he failed in his duty of caring properly for your property.

Initially, your burden of proof is not a difficult task. All you need to show is that you delivered the property to the bailee in good condition and that it was returned in a damaged condition or not returned at all. Upon doing this you have established a presumption of negligence on the part of the bailee. [Gelb v Minneford Yacht Yard, Inc., 108 F Supp 211, 1952 AMC 1955, DC SD NY 1952.]

While the bailee does not have the legal burden of proving how the damage occurred, nevertheless he must come forward with an explanation.

The bailee can show either (1) how the accident happened and that it could not have been prevented by the exercise of due diligence on his part, or (2) if the cause of the damage is not shown, that he had nevertheless not been guilty of any negligence. [Yacht Almar, 1955 AMC 1830, DC Md 1955.]

The United States Supreme Court has stated the bailee's obligation as follows:

"Since the bailee in general is in a better position than the bailor to know the cause of the loss and to show that it was one not involving the bailee's liability, the law lays on him the duty to come forward with the information available to him." [Commercial Molasses Corp. v New York Tank Barge Corp., 314 US 104, 86 L ed 89, 62 S Ct 156, 1941 AMC 1697, 1941.]

If the bailee fails to convince the judge or the jury of his absence of fault, then they are free to fall back on the inference of negligence created by the failure of the bailee either to deliver the property or to deliver it in an undamaged condition.

Boatyard Liability

In the preceding section, I stated that the bailee was required either to exercise due diligence or to demonstrate freedom from negligence in order to avoid liability. In the following examples we will see two actual cases where boatyards have been held liable to the boat owner for destruction or damage to the boats left in their care.

The yacht Rambler III had been purchased for $15,000. Several months later she was brought to a boatyard in the New York area for winter storage. The yard accepted the boat, temporarily moored her to a buoy, and agreed to "bring it in" to the yacht basin on the following day. Actually she was left moored at the buoy for a week. The boatyard people were engaged in constructing a new building and apparently were concentrating their attention on that. A storm came up at night which tore the yacht loose from its moorings and sent it drifting downstream in the Hudson River. The Rambler III was so badly damaged that she virtually became a total loss. Storm warnings had been issued.

281

The boatyard claimed a new mooring rope had been used and that the storm was an act of God. The trial judge found that the mooring line which had been used was in a worn and badly damaged condition and was not a new one. The president of the boatyard corporation had testified: "I don't keep myself posted on the weather reports; it's not my duty to do so," and "I am running a boatyard and not a weather bureau." After observing that the yacht was in the care of the boatyard, a compensated bailee, the court said:

> "They took no interest in the vessels except for a casual 'look around' about midnight and did nothing for them. The defendant let things go as they were and it must take the consequences of its complete disregard of weather conditions and weather warnings. The defendant has failed by far to show that an Act of God was responsible for the damage." [Yacht Rambler III, 1956 AMC 2368, S Ct NY 1956.]

The damage to the Rambler III was so severe that her owner decided that the cost of repair would be more than the vessel's worth. The Rambler III was sold in her damaged condition for $3,200. Judgment was given to the boat owner in the amount of $11,800, the amount of the judgment representing the difference between the original value of the yacht and the distressed sale price.

A boat had been brought to a west coast boat repair-yard for necessary repairs. She was then placed in a floating drydock. The drydock was moored to a pier by means of lines. A fire broke out during the night. The yard's night watchman concentrated his efforts on an attempt to save the buildings. In doing so he failed to cast off the lines from the drydock which would have allowed it and the boat carried by it to drift free of the conflagration. As a consequence the fire from the buildings spread to the drydock and the boat, badly damaging them. It was held that the boatyard, through its control of the drydock, also controlled the mobility of the boat. Because of the watchman's failure to take proper steps to save the boat by the freeing of the drydock, the boatyard was liable to the boat owner for the loss. [Lake Union Dry Dock & Machine Works v United States, 79 F2d 802, 1936 AMC 250, CCA9th 1935, reh den 81 F2d 230.]

When the Boatyard Is Excused

In this section are presented several court cases which show those instances where boatyards have not been held financially responsible for the loss or damage of property in their care. These cases illustrate the principles discussed in prior sections of this chapter.

A yacht in a Maryland boatyard was undergoing repair work which entailed the installation of hull plates. A fire broke out in the boat's linen locker. The repairmen had been doing electric welding work on the outside of the yacht and below the linen locker porthole. The yard called a number of witnesses to demonstrate that the fire was not caused by the welding work and furthermore that the boatyard had exercised ordinary diligence and care in doing this particular type of work. The court held that the yacht owner had failed to show that the fire was due to the failure of the boatyard to use ordinary care in performing its repairs. When the boatowner failed to show this breach of obligation, the case was lost. [The Dupont, 14 F Supp 193, 1936 AMC 738, DC Md 1936.]

The yacht Resolute, carrying a 137-foot mast, was brought into a yard for repairs. During the night the weather changed. A strong wind blew up and the mast

283

broke about 10 or 12 feet above the deck and toppled over, damaging the deck. The cost of replacing the mast amounted to $400. Merely because the mast broke and damaged the yacht, said the trial judge, does not of itself indicate negligence on the part of the boatyard. It is not enough to say that the damage would not have occurred if the yacht had been moored at another location or if that mast had been removed by the yard workers before the big blow took place. The yacht owner had to show that at the time of the accident the failure of the repairmen to take proper precautions was unreasonable. Failing to show such lack of prudent conduct under the particular circumstances involved in the case, the yard was held to be free of liability. [Federal Insurance Co. v Herreshoff Mfg. Co. 6 F Supp 827, 1934 AMC 413, DC RI 1934.]

A yard on the Anclote River at Tarpon Springs, Florida, agreed to do repair and conversion work on a sponge boat. One of the boatyard employees who lived on the grounds retired at about 10:30 p.m. one night after having found everything in the yard in good order. Later that night there was an explosion followed by fire. The sponge boat was totally destroyed by fire. The owner contended that the boatyard was negligent in failing to have an adequate road which would have permitted ingress by the fire department equipment, in failing to provide fire hydrants and hoses, and in failing to provide a watchman. The court held that these conditions were open, obvious, and well known to the boatowner. By placing his boat in the yard he assumed any risks which went with it. The boatyard was not negligent and consequently not liable for the destroyed boat. [Motor Vessel J. Stalin, 1954 AMC 1383, DC Fla 1954.]

A 44-foot cabin cruiser equipped with two 150

horsepower Packard engines and Maxim silencers was left at a yacht basin for winter wet storage. Before the owner left for Florida he visited the boat. He found that there was an accumulation of water in the hatches. He gave the keys to the boatyard and asked that the water be pumped out and this was done. A month later the boat sank at its moorings. The boat-owner contended that the shipyard was negligent in not inspecting the boat from time to time to see if there was an undue amount of water in the boat and, if so, to pump it out. The court found that what had caused the boat to sink was the withdrawal, by the owner, of the plugs from the Maxim silencers, and his failure to fit wooden plugs into the exhaust pipes. There was no custom, practice, or special promise, found the court, for the boatyard to open hatches and determine the quantity of water in the bilges when there was no outward evidence of excessive water accumulation. The loss had to be borne by the boatowner. The boat-yard had conceded that it was its duty to do every-thing reasonably possible to prevent the sinking when her visible appearance indicated that pumping was necessary. [Yacht Almar, 1955 AMC 1830, DC Md 1955.]

In 1956, Hurricane Flossy caused the destruction of a small houseboat. The houseboat had been left at a boat repair yard at Kreb's Lake, near Pascagoula, Mississippi. The boatyard owner was charged with being negligent in failing to exercise ordinary prudence in securing the houseboat to ride out the hurricane. The proof was that the yard had used a ¾-inch rope on each end of the craft, and rubber tire fenders between the boat and dock. There was enough slack so that the boat could rise and fall 4 feet without jamming. Other boats at the yard were secured in the same manner. Private boatowners tied their boats in the same way. The yard owner, a man with 44 years of experience, testified that he took all necessary precautions. It was held that when the yard owner came forward with proof of due care, the burden of going forward with proof of negligence was on the houseboat owner. When he failed to meet this burden, the boatyard owner was held to be free from fault in the destruction of the houseboat. [Buntin v Fletchas, 257 F2d 512, 1958 AMC 2416, CA5th 1958.]

Repair Bill Disputes

When your boat is brought for repairs to a boatyard it is a good idea to get a written estimate of the cost. While it may not necessarily be the same in total amount to the final bill, it should nevertheless give you a fairly good idea of what the repair job will cost.

The pitfalls encountered by a boatowner who agreed to repair work on a "time plus material" basis is illustrated in the case of Martin v The Amiga Mia. [80 F Supp 42, 1948 AMC 647, DC SD NY 1948.]

An 80-foot former Coast Guard patrol boat was to be converted into a private yacht. The owner's naval architect estimated that the cost of this work would be about $10,000. It was informally agreed that the yard would do the job on a time and material basis. Two weeks later the owner received a bill for $1,347.54 including labor charges at $2.85 per hour. Subsequently the yard submitted successive bills which totaled $16,320.40 of which $12,539.03 was for labor (4,399 5/8 hours) and $2,923.78 for materials. The work still was not completed and it was estimated that it would cost $4,500 more. By this time the owner had had enough. The owner's proctor (admiralty lawyer) brought a possessory libel in a federal court as a means of obtaining a quick determination. A possessory libel is an action to determine who rightfully should have the possession of a boat. It was found that the boatyard had greatly overcharged the customer. The work performed called for no more than a total of 2141 hours. It was also found that the owner had been charged for repairs of damages for which the yard was responsible. This item was disallowed. Of a total bill of $16,320.40, the court allowed the repair yard $9,695.34.

In another case where the propriety of the charges was in dispute, the judge was impelled to the following observation: "The record shows that much of the trouble was a direct result of crude, inaccurate, undependable books and records of the shipyard." [Yacht Mary Jane v Broward Marine, Inc., 313 F2d 516, CA5th 1963.]

Sometimes a boatyard dispute will show both parties—the boatowner and the repairman—in an unfavorable light. The boatowner is far from guileless, consenting to the proposal of further repair work or initiating such proposals and then balking at the bill which he is expected to pay. On the other hand, the yard may be one ill equipped in the facilities and skill for the work to be performed, thus delaying the time of completion and adding to the cost of the job. Such a situation was present in the case of the man who bought a surplus government boat and wanted it restored to its original condition. The boatyard gave a written estimate of $3,748. This estimate was later changed to a cost-of-materials plus labor agreement. To the increased costs the owner raised no objection. "It was a case," said the court, "of a man able to afford it wishing to gratify a whim." The yard lacked power tools and consequently much of the work had to be done by hand. After the owner had made several payments aggregating $10,000, he was assured that the job would be completed by December. In February the work was far from completed. The boat was still in a torn-up shape. Furthermore the boatyard had damaged the craft. It appeared to the owner that the repair work would prove endless in cost and in time of completion. By this time the bill had totaled almost $20,000. The boatowner had the craft moved to another yard where the work was completed for about $5,000. At the rate at which the first yard was progressing the work would have cost, in all, $29,000, which the court observed was "a figure out of all reason." Had it not been for the yard's inefficiency, lack of skill and of proper facilities and equipment, the entire job, the court further said, could have been completed for the $20,000. The boatowner was told to pay the bill, less $5,000 spent at the other yard and $2,000 deducted for damages to his boat. [Calmes v Hyman, 113 F Supp 240, DC La 1953.]

Quality of the Work

It is a well-known principle of law that in all undertakings of work and labor there is an implied warranty (unless a specific agreement against such a warranty exists) that the work will be done in a reasonably skilled and workmanlike manner. When one holds himself out as specially qualified to do work of a particular type he impliedly agrees that the materials furnished by him will be suitable for the purpose and that the finished job will be reasonably fit for its intended use. [Economy Fuse & Mfg. Co. v Raymond Concrete Pile Co., 111 F2d 875, CCA4th 1940.]

The test of the quality of a boatyard's repair work is not that it should meet with the approval of the most critical or fastidious individual, but that the work be done in a properly workmanlike fashion and in a reasonably competent and skilled manner.

288

The principles regarding an implied warranty to do
a repair job or a service in a reasonably skilled and
workmanlike way were discussed in a case where a
recreational cruiser was brought into a boatyard for
painting and for minor repair work. The bottom and
sides of the cruiser were to be painted with a marine
paint furnished by the boatowner. The boat was removed from the water and placed in the yard's repair
shelter. She was sanded down to the bare wood on
the bottom of the hull, and sanded to a rough surface
on the sides. Two coats of copper-based paint were
applied to the bottom and two coats of the marine paint
were applied to the sides. Soon after the paint had
been applied and before the boat was placed in the
water, the new paint on the sides of the hull blistered
and peeled in several places. The paint applied to the
boat's bottom did not blister. The boatowner claimed
that the blistering was the result of applying the paint
to the hull at a time when it was wet or damp. The
boatyard denied this and asserted that the blistering
was due to some deficiency in the paint.

There was evidence presented that the boat had been
painted in an open-front shelter during the rainy
season. The shelter opened onto a river. One witness
stated that he saw the cruiser with a wet hull, and
when he again saw it about a week later it was painted.
There was other testimony that the paint used had been
applied extensively on other marine equipment without
similar results.

The court held that the painting of the side of the
hull had not been done in a workmanlike manner. If
the work performed by the boatyard was so poorly
done, said the court, as to be of no benefit to the owner
of the cruiser, then the repairman would not be entitled
to recover for the work done. In this case, however,

289

the boatowner operated the cruiser in the condition in which he had received it. The sides of the hull were not repainted except for touching up the blistered areas. Two years later the owner had the hull re-sanded and repainted. From this the court deduced that the work had not been so poorly executed as to be of no benefit to the boatowner. The boatyard was permitted to recover the reasonable value of the work performed. [Dog River Boat Service, Inc. v The Francis D., 1961 AMC 1286, DC Ala 1961.]

After a boat has been repaired and satisfactorily passes the usual tests, any future claim of poor workmanship must be proved by the boatowner. A tanker had been repaired at a Pacific Coast repair yard. After the repairs had been completed the work was tested and met with the approval of the owner. Eleven days later and 2,000 miles from the repair yard the tanker suffered an engine failure. It was held that the burden of proof was on the shipowner to show that the malperformance of the repair work was the proximate cause of the engine breakdown. When he failed to do so the suit against the repairman was dismissed. [Compania Naviera Limitada v Black, 183 F2d 388, 1950 AMC 1319, CA9th 1950.]

In conclusion, it is an incorrect assumption to believe that a boatyard is automatically responsible and liable for damage to a boat in its care. If the boat has been placed in a boatyard for work or services to be performed on it, the boatyard is held to the duty of ordinary or reasonable care and is responsible for ordinary negligence. The failure of the boatyard to care properly for the property must be proved. It is the boatowner who has the burden of proving such negligence.

Repair bill disputes can be largely avoided if you obtain an estimate of the cost of repairs before the work is begun. If there are additional items included as the work progresses be sure that you have an accurate idea of how much these items will cost.

●

parties on a cruise along the Atlantic seaboard. Negotiations were begun through the mail and the terms agreed upon. In due time the Girl Scout leaders received a contract. Not being versed in maritime legal matters, they asked two lawyers, each of whom had a daughter in the troop, to review the contract and advise them on its acceptability.

The fathers were very able lawyers. One was an executive of a large insurance company, the other was house counsel for a nationally known corporation. However, the wording of the charter party—for such it was—appeared strange and unfamiliar to them. Believing that they were somewhat out of their depth they sought out a maritime lawyer who lived in their midst. And so on a Sunday afternoon I sat in my living room examining the contract while my two lawyer-neighbors looked on expectantly.

A quick perusal showed that the contract was a bareboat type of charter, also known as a demise charter. The boatowner's contract had provided that the control of the vessel was to be turned over to the Girl Scout Council for the 2-week period and the captain and the crew were to be under their orders. "Gentlemen," I said to the two fathers, "do you realize that under this form of charter agreement the local Girl Scout Council becomes the virtual owner of this auxiliary schooner with all of the legal liabilities and responsibilities which ownership entails? If the Girl Scout Council enters into this arrangement they must be advised that in doing so they should be prepared to assume responsibility if a member of the crew becomes sick or injured, or should the schooner become involved in a collision."

Whether through inadvertence or by intention the Girl Scouts had been sent a completely unacceptable bareboat charter instead of a time charter. Faced with the legal responsibility involved, the Girl Scout leaders decided to drop the project. There is a decided difference between a bareboat charter and a time charter, as will be pointed out in this chapter.

Charter Defined

A charter is a contract. It is a specific and express contract by which the owner lets a vessel or some particular part of it to another person for a specified time or use. [Jones & Laughlin Steel Corporation v Vang, 73 F2d 88, CCA3d 1934, cert dismd 294 US 735, 79 L ed 1263, 55 S Ct 406.]

The contract form used in a chartering arrangement is called a "charter party." It has received its name from a legal instrument in medieval times. The contract was written in duplicate on a single sheet and then torn from top to bottom with jagged or indented edges, so that when placed together the torn edges fitted in the manner of a jigsaw puzzle. One part was retained by the shipowner and the other was given to the charterer. Since it was unlikely that any two sheets torn in this fashion would be identical, there was little possibility of another agreement being substituted in its place. In ancient Latin the torn paper was called a "carta partita" or divided card. It was later changed through usage to "charter party." From the indented edges has come the word "indenture," meaning a deed or an agreement.

Chartered Boats

A charter can be entered into either by means of a written contract or by an oral agreement. Most arrangements for the chartering of a small boat, scow, or barge, are consummated by a verbal understanding. A written agreement is usually preferable, for it is

295

ferred to as a license. The court, in deciding that the United States had the right to seek limitation of liability, stated that the mere fact that the word "charterer" was not used was not of paramount importance. What was important was the fact that by obtaining exclusive possession and management of the boat from the title owner, the government became the owner pro hac vice, and was therefore able to limit liability. [Austerberry v United States, 169 F2d 583, 1948 AMC 1682, CCA6th 1948.]

The bareboat charterer owes an obligation to the boatowner of paying the agreed hire and, at the expiration of the period of the charter, of returning the boat in as good condition as it was received, ordinary wear and tear excepted.

The legal liabilities ordinarily placed upon the title owner in the management and operation of the ship or boat devolves upon the bareboat charterer. The charterer becomes liable for the vessel's fault in the event of collision [The Barnstable, 181 US 464, 45 L ed 954, 21 S Ct 684, 1901]; and for personal injuries to shore workers, such as longshoremen and repairmen [Cannella v United States, 179 F2d 491, 1950 AMC 858, CA2d 1950]; and, under the Jones Act, for personal injuries to the seamen, since he has become the employer of the crew [see: Cromwell v Slaney, 65 F2d 940, 1933 AMC 1514, CCA1st 1933].

The usual form of demise charter contains a so-called "salvage clause." Generally, the title owner and the bareboat charterer agree to share in any salvage award to which the vessel may be entitled by virtue of any salvage service rendered by her. If the charter party is silent on the subject of salvage, then, as a rule, the bareboat charterer receives all of the ship's share of the salvage money, provided that the charter makes

298

him responsible in the event that the chartered ship is damaged. [Johnson Lighterage Co. No. 24, 248 F 74, CCA3d 1918.]

Time Charter

In this type of charter arrangement the vessel is chartered or "leased" to the time charterer with the control being retained by the owner through the master who is selected and paid by the owner. The owner pays all of the operating expenses of the vessel and the time charterer merely has the use of the vessel for the charter money which he pays.

Translated to recreational boats, it would be similar to the following situation. You agree to the use of a motorboat for a period of 2 weeks. The boatowner or his representative operates the boat and pays for all supplies, fuel, subsistence, wages, docking fees, etc. Generally, you have the right to issue orders regarding the waters over which the boat will travel.

In commercial time charters, provision is sometimes made for the sharing of any salvage moneys between the vessel owner and the time charterer. [The Kanawha, 254 F 762, CCA2d 1918.]

Since, in a time charter arrangement, the control of the ship remains with the owner, any liability under the Jones Act for personal injuries to the crew or for maintenance and cure is that of the owner and not the time charterer. [Bergan v International Freighting Corp., Inc., 254 F2d 231, 1958 AMC 1303, CA2d 1958.]

Voyage Charter

Recreational boatowners are not likely to use a voyage charter. However, since it is an accepted form of charter, it is herewith included. The voyage charter form is used where the charterer wishes to engage the

299

ship to carry a full cargo on a single voyage. As with
the time charter, the control and navigation of the
vessel remains with the owner. The legal status of
the charterer with particular reference to his duties
and liabilities is the same as in the time charter.

Seaworthiness

Every charter—whether bareboat, time, or voyage
—has read into it by the general maritime law a warranty of seaworthiness, unless the contrary is stipulated in clear and unequivocal language. The test
of seaworthiness is that the vessel or boat be reasonably fit for the intended service. This concept finds
its counterpart in the language of most charter parties
which describe the ship being offered as "tight, staunch,
strong and in every way fitted for the service."

The warranty of seaworthiness may be waived where
the defect is evident upon inspection and the charterer
has had an opportunity to inspect.

If the vessel is unseaworthy and the unseaworthiness
is so substantial as to defeat or frustrate the purpose
of the charter, then the charterer can repudiate the
contract and refuse to accept the vessel. If, however,
he does accept her and puts the vessel to use, he must
pay the agreed hire. [The Tento, 1950 AMC 947,
CA2d 1950.]

11

maritime liens

What Is a Maritime Lien?

In the opening chapter of this book, reference was made to buying a boat and to the probability of the existence of outstanding maritime liens. This is common in the maritime field and is unlike the usual liens found ashore.

A maritime lien has been defined as "a privileged claim in a vessel in respect to some service rendered to it in the nature to facilitate its use in navigation, or an injury caused by the vessel in navigable waters, to be carried into effect by legal process in the admiralty court." [The Westmoor, 27 F2d 886, 887, DC Or 1928.]

When a vessel or pleasure boat receives services or materials, such as repairs, fuel, boat supplies, food items, wages of seamen, etc., on credit, the person who provides the supplies or services obtains a lien on the boat or vessel.

The maritime lien is in substance and effect a right in the boat itself. The lien commences as soon as the supplies or the services have been furnished. Since it is a right in the property involved it is said that its "origin lies in the personification of the ship itself." [Todd Shipyards Corp. v The City of Athens, 83 F Supp 67, 1949 AMC 572, DC Md 1949 affd 177 F2d 961, 1950 AMC 282, CA4 1949.] In short, the person who holds the lien becomes entitled to an interest in the boat (called a "jus in re") and can look to the boat for the payment of the debt rather than to the personal liability of the owner. In effect, the maritime law treats the boat as a separate entity. It is, figuratively speaking, the giving of the boat as security for a debt or claim.

Characteristics of a Lien

The outstanding characteristic of a maritime lien is that possession of the boat is not necessary in order for the lien to be a good one. [The China, 7 Wall 53, 68, 19 L ed 67, 1869.] This means that if your boat is repaired on credit and the credit has been extended to the boat rather than to you as owner, the maritime lien is valid even after the boat has left the repair yard. The repairman's maritime lien does not have to be filed. Because the maritime lien is not required to be filed, it has been called a "secret lien."

The maritime lien is not wiped out because another lien has been created against the boat or the boat has been sold. Although the boat has been sold to a purchaser who has bought in good faith without any notice of the existence of the lien, the maritime lien has not lost its vitality. Until the lien has been acted upon it is regarded, in spite of its secret nature, as being good "against the world."

The lien can be "executed" (similar to a "foreclosure") only by an admiralty court (a United States District Court judge sitting in the admiralty part) in a suit "in rem." This means that the repairman—to use the example previously given—can "execute" or "foreclose" his lien by bringing a suit against the boat (rather than against the owner) in the federal court. The suit against the property involved is a suit "in rem."

The maritime lien may come into being either as a consequence of a maritime contract or from a tort, such as the result of a collision or a personal injury claim (except a Jones Act seaman's action).

The maritime lien is not affected by the bankruptcy of the boatowner. It is applicable to the property itself and it is not dependent upon the solvency of the individual.

A maritime lien can be extinguished by the payment of the claim which underlies it. If you pay your bill at the boat repair yard, that ends the repairman's lien against the boat. The lien can be lost if the lienholder waits too long before seeking to enforce it, particularly where the boat has been sold to an innocent purchaser. Holding a lien too long makes the lien "stale" and it is said to have been lost through "laches," that is, an inexcusable delay. The subject of "stale claims" is discussed more fully further on in this chapter. Finally, a lien can be extinguished when another lienholder having higher priority has brought an in rem suit against the boat and the boat has been sold by court order.

A boat may have more than one maritime lien. Within the same class of liens (the "class" will be explained later in this chapter), the lien which came into being last has priority. Therefore, unlike shoreside liens, the maritime lien operates in inverse order; last in time is first in right; or, in other words, the most recent lien is first in line.

Federal Lien Statutes

By statute, any person who furnishes repairs, supplies, towage, the use of a drydock or marine railway, or other necessaries to any ship or boat upon the order of the owner or of any person who is authorized by the owner, receives a maritime lien on it. This lien can be enforced by a suit against the ship or boat. The lienor does not have to allege or prove that credit was given to the ship or boat. [46 United States Code § 971.] This statute was intended to remove the pre-existing distinction between giving credit to the owner and giving credit to the ship or boat.

In spite of the wording of the statute, the furnisher of supplies or services who deals directly with the boat-owner would be well advised if he made it clear (as in billing the boat rather than the owner) that he claims his lien and that he is not extending credit only to the owner.

With respect to the authority to incur the lien, the statute includes the managing owner of the ship or boat, the ship's husband (the agent who manages her and arranges for repairs, etc.), the master, and any person to whom the management of the ship or boat has been entrusted at the port where the services or supplies have been furnished. A thief, an unauthorized person, or one unlawfully in possession or in charge of the ship or boat does not have the authority to create a maritime lien. [46 United States Code § 972.]

There are certain circumstances under which the person who furnishes the services or supplies will not get a lien, namely, where he knew, or by the exercise of reasonable diligence could have ascertained, that by the terms of a charter party, or an agreement for the sale of the ship or boat, or for any other reason, the person ordering the repairs, supplies, or other necessaries did not have the authority to bind the ship or boat. [46 United States Code § 973.]

304

The prior maritime laws regarding undue delay in enforcing the lien (laches), the ranking of the lien, the right to proceed against a ship for advances given, and the right to sue the owner personally, are not affected by these statutes.   [46 United States Code § 974.]

Finally, the federal statute declares that it supersedes all state statutes conferring liens on ships and boats for repairs, supplies, towage, the use of a dry dock or marine railway, and other necessaries.   [46 United States Code § 975.]

Necessaries

The statute considered in the previous section makes it clear that repairs, supplies, towage, and the use of a dry dock or a marine railway are items for which a maritime lien can be obtained. It is less certain regarding those services which could rightfully come within the category of "other necessaries."

The many court cases on this subject do not always agree on what items constitute necessaries.   In the case of the ship "Tradewind" [Atlantic Steamer Supply Co. v The Tradewind, 153 F Supp 354, 1957 AMC 2196, DC Md 1957], it was said that "necessaries are considered" to be "more in the nature of supplies than services," and yet this belief has been belied by cases which held otherwise.

In The Artemis [53 F2d 672, 1932 AMC 195, DC SD NY 1931], a claim for the winter storage of a yacht, for the crew's uniforms, and even the taxi fare for delivering provisions to the yacht, were all held entitled to be covered by a maritime lien.

In determining what supplies are necessaries, regard is taken of the type of boat and the use to which it is put. A 60-foot yacht was brought to Miami during a winter season to be sold or chartered. The captain was in charge of the boat. He had been instructed by the owner not to "run up any bills other than strict emergency expenses" without the owner's authorization. The captain placed orders for foodstuffs, including liquor. The supplier sought to impose the lien upon the yacht. The court ruled that knowledge of special instructions from the owner to the master could not be imputed to the supplier. As to the liquor, the judge said: "Both the character and the quantity of the provisions furnished in the instant case are within the usual requirements of a pleasure yacht spending the winter months at a fashionable resort like Miami, Florida. I find that the provisions including the liquors were necessaries for the pleasure yacht Bavois." [Walker-Skageth Food Stores, Inc. v The Bavois, 43 F Supp 109, 1942 AMC 211, DC SD NY 1942.]

It may be too that the judge believed that if the liquor was used to entertain prospective buyers, charterers, and guests (rather than for a freeloading captain), its presence was consonant with the boat's type and the purpose for which it was at Miami.

The tendency today is to give the words "other necessaries" a broad reading rather than a narrow interpretation. Cigarettes supplied to a shrimp fishing boat (in addition to meats and groceries) were regarded as necessaries [Allen v The M/V Contessa, 1961 AMC 2190, DC Texas 1961] and so was the fumigation of a ship [The American, 1931 AMC 197, DC Mass 1930].

Maritime Transactions

In order to obtain a maritime lien it is necessary that the transaction on which the lien is based be maritime in nature and that the admiralty court have jurisdiction of the matter.

"It is essential, in order to maintain an admiralty

lien on a vessel for supplies or advances, that she be at the time engaged in a maritime venture." [J. C. Penney–Gwinn Corp. v McArdle, 27 F2d 324, CA5 1928, cert den 278 US 632, 73 L ed 550, 49 S Ct 31, reh den 278 US 570, 73 L ed 512, 49 S Ct 92.]

A money loan to a boatowner would not entitle the lender to a maritime lien. It is regarded as a personal obligation of the owner rather than a transaction which enures to the benefit of the boat. Attorneys' fees to a boatowner have been placed in this category. [United States v The Laconia, 81 F Supp 661, DC Va 1948.]

There is no lien, in the federal maritime law, in favor of an insurance company for unpaid premiums, although state law may provide for such a lien. [Grow v Steel Gas Screw Loraine K, 310 F2d 547, 1963 AMC 2044, CA6 1962.] The general agent of a shipowner is not given a lien for services rendered, on the theory that he acts not as a stranger relying on the security of the ship, but as an agent of the owner to whom he looks for payment. [Savas v Maria Trading Corporation, 285 F2d 336, 1961 AMC 260, CA4 1960.]

Claims regarded as "maritime," and for which a maritime lien arises, are: seamen's wages (but not the wage of the master, who is regarded as the personal representative of the owner), salvage services, repairs, supplies, collision damages, personal injury claims (except a seaman's Jones Act claim), contribution in general average, towage, wharfage, pilotage, etc. A number of other maritime transactions peculiar to cargo need not be mentioned here.

A contract to build a ship or to supply materials for her construction is not a maritime contract. Work on a boat in construction or on a boat which has not yet been launched does not give rise to a maritime lien. No admiralty court has jurisdiction of such a boat or of any claims of supplies or services to it. Even after the new boat has been placed in the water, but before she has been placed in operation, no maritime lien can come into existence. [Boat La Sambra v Lewis, 321 F2d 29, CA9 1963.]

The Boat in Custody

When the holder of a maritime lien decides to collect the debt owed to him he must first be certain where the boat is located. Having located the boat, he then commences his lawsuit against the property by filing a libel (this is similar to the "complaint" in a civil court action) against the boat involved, in a United States District Court within whose geographical jurisdiction the property is located. The clerk of the court then issues a legal document called a "monition" which is addressed to "all persons interested" to appear on a day certain and show cause why the property should not be condemned and sold to satisfy the demand of the libelant, the lienholder.

The monition is then given to the United States marshal, an officer of the Federal District Court, to attach the property and to hold it in safety until the court makes the appropriate order regarding its disposition. The taking of the boat into custody by the United States marshal is known as an "arrest" or "seizure" of the property.

The United States marshal, who is obliged to keep the seized property in a safe and secure manner in order to prevent damage or deterioration, may incur expenses necessary to carry this out, such as wharfage fees, salaries to watchmen, etc. The custodial expenses are often paid first out of the proceeds of the sale of the boat. [The Valiant Power, 1961 AMC 226, DC Va 1960.] If the matter is settled before the property is sold, these expenses are generally paid by the boat-owner.

As a general rule no new maritime liens can be created while the boat is in custodia legis (in the custody of the law). "Events subsequent to the seizure do not give rise to liens against a vessel in custodia legis." [Collie v Fergusson, 281 US 52, 55, 74 L ed 696, 50 S Ct 189, 1930 AMC 408, 1930.] Neither the captain nor the owner of the boat can create liens against the boat while it is under arrest and in the custody of the court unless the arrest was illegal or irregular. [New York Dock Co. v The Poznan, 274 US 117, 71 L ed 955, 47 S Ct 482, 1927 AMC 723, 1927.]

The unpaid wages of a seaman, as a rule, are protected by a maritime lien of high priority. But a maritime lien is not allowed to a seaman for wages accruing after the ship has been taken into legal custody. [Putnam v Lower, 236 F2d 561, 1956 AMC 2059, CA9 1956; Irving Trust Company v The Golden Sail, 197 F Supp 777, 1962 AMC 2676, DC Ore 1961.] This is equally true of the "hired hand" of a pleasure craft who remains aboard after the boat has been seized.

Priority of Liens

The question of priority arises when there is more than one lien on the boat. In such case which lien will receive preference? This problem will be of paramount importance to the holders of liens, particularly when it becomes apparent that the estimated sale price of the seized boat will not be sufficient to pay the expenses and all of the liens. To the boatowner, of course, this question will undoubtedly be an academic one, especially when it becomes clear that there will be no money left over for him after the boat has been sold.

The order of priority among liens is also referred to in admiralty law as "marshaling the liens" and "ranking the liens." The order of priority has not been fixed by statute law, but rather by various court decisions over the years. It has been said that other than that wage and salvage liens have the highest rank and that damage claims generally outrank contract claims, there is no certainty regarding the order of priority among classes. [Gilmore and Black: The Law of Admiralty, p. 514, 1957.]

The word "class" in connection with maritime liens means the placing in a certain group of liens of equal rank.

I rank maritime liens in the following order:

1. Legal costs, tonnage and light dues, taxes.

2. Salvage. The salvage lien is given a high rank on the theory that "by saving the ship all is saved."

3. Seamen's wages (but not the master's) and wages of longshoremen directly employed by the owner or master and not through an independent contractor. The seamen's wage liens are regarded as "sacred liens."

4. Collision liens; contributions and general average sacrifices; liability for bodily injury and for wrongful death.

5. Preferred ship mortgage registered in the home port.

6. Repairs, supplies, towage, wharfage, pilotage, stevedoring, and other necessaries.

7. Bottomry bonds in inverse order of application.

All liens of the classes above outlined outrank all liens of an inferior class regardless of when in point of time the lien has been imposed.

All liens of the same class which arose during the same year are treated equally. All share in the proceeds of the sale of the property.

"Stale Claims"

The lienholder who waits too long may find that his lien is subordinated to other liens which came into being at a later date ("last in time is first in right"). Under these circumstances the first lien will lose its precedence but the lienholder will not lose the lien itself. However, if he delays too long in enforcing his lien he runs the danger of having his claim become "stale," thus losing his lien entirely. Such delay is called "laches." Laches, in its simplest definition, has been said to be "an inexcusable delay in the assertion of a right."

When has a lien become "stale"? What is an inexcusable delay? It can be explained in this way: Laws which set a definite time when rights can be enforced before they are lost are called statutes of limitation. Statutes of limitation set a precise period of time within which the right can be enforced, such as 6 months, 1 year, 2 years, 6 years, etc. If you wait beyond the applicable period before acting, your right of action is said to be "time-barred," and the right is lost.

Admiralty courts are not governed in maritime lien cases by any statute of limitations. The delay which will result in a lien being declared lost will depend on the equitable circumstances in each particular case. While state statutes of limitation are not binding upon an admiralty court, they can be considered in determining whether the delay in a particular case constitutes laches.

When the boat is still owned by the person who incurred the debt which is the subject of the lien, the delay in bringing suit can extend until the time when the claim becomes time-barred. But a lapse of even a comparatively short period of time will result in the lien being lost when it is sought to be enforced against a purchaser who bought the boat in good faith and without notice of the lien.

A delay of 21 months after the claim became due was held to be fatal so far as a purchaser in good faith was concerned, where a marine supplier had furnished material and supplies to the boat Nola Dare, amounting to $715.24 during the period from March 15, 1950, to October 6, 1950, and the Nola Dare was sold on June 21, 1951, to a purchaser in good faith without knowledge of any outstanding lien and without any reason to believe that such lien existed. Before buying the Nola Dare, he had made diligent effort to discover whether the boat was subject to any maritime lien by inquiring of the seller, and by making inquiries at the Customs House at Wilmington, North Carolina, where the boat was documented.

Not until July 14, 1952, did the supplier bring suit against the Nola Dare for the 1950 debt. This was 13 months after the boat had been sold and 21 months after the debt had been incurred. The court found that the material and supplies had in fact been furnished to the Nola Dare and that undoubtedly the supplier had a lien unless it was lost by his failure to assert it. The failure to enforce his lien in time was precisely what led the court to hold that there was "laches" which barred recovery. The North Carolina lien statute provided that a suit on the lien for labor and materials must be brought within 6 months. While the state law did not bind the court in applying the 6-month limit, it was proper to consider that law in deciding whether or not laches was involved in the current case. The

attitude of the court was summed up in the following
words:

> "It would be inequitable to require the present
> owner to pay this claim, of which he had no notice
> when he bought the *Nola Dare*, in view of the
> delay by libellant (the supplier) in taking steps
> to enforce his lien against the vessel." [Davis v
> The Nola Dare, 1958 AMC 951, DC NC 1957. The
> case of Phelps and Berry v Motor Boat Cecelia
> Ann, 199 F2d 627, 1952 AMC 1968, CA4 1952
> is virtually identical on the facts with the Nola
> Dare case.]

Bank Loans

Because of the secret nature of maritime liens, loan
institutions, banks, and other lenders of money may
find that their security in the boat can be seriously
impaired. It is quite possible that at the time of the
loan one or more maritime liens may be in existence
with no written recordation to disclose that fact. Furthermore, since actual written notice of the seizure of
a boat when a lienholder commences legal proceedings
against the property need not be given to interested
parties, the moneylender can find that the property has
been sold before he is even aware that a sale is pending.

Two recent cases show how differently this problem
has been met in the courts. In California, the Security
First National Bank held a $17,500 mortgage on the
boat Relaxin. A boatyard had done certain repair
work amounting to $1,072.44 and held a maritime lien.
The boatyard brought an action in rem in a Federal
District Court. The boat was seized by the United
States marshal and in due time notice was published
by the marshal that the Relaxin would be sold at public
auction at a certain date and time. The lawyer for
the boatyard, having learned of the bank's mortgage,
notified the bank's branch manager that a sale had been

ordered. At the time neither he nor the bank manager knew of the date of sale. The Relaxin was sold at public auction to a purchaser for $3,000. The bank sued to have the sale set aside claiming that it had not received notice of the proceedings and that the sale price was grossly unfair.

Because of the role of time financing in the purchase and sale of small craft in California, that state had recognized the holder of a registered chattel mortgage as the "legal owner" of a boat and the person giving the mortgage as the "certificate-of-number" owner. The dilemma that the court was faced with was the undoubted fact that the state statute regarding the position of the mortgage holder must accommodate to the supremacy of the federal law and the exclusive right of the federal court to enforce a maritime lien by a proceeding against the property. Leaning on the declared policy of the Federal Motorboat Act of 1958 to encourage uniformity of boating laws, rules, and regulations among the states, the court stated: "To permit destruction of the mortgagee's security interest without actual notice of the sale, this Court would be condoning inequity as well as undermining the financial structure of the local maritime industry. Both reason and policy dictate a contrary result." The court ruled that actual notice of the auction date and time should have been given to the bank, and set aside the sale upon condition that Hardcastle, the innocent purchaser, be reimbursed by the bank for his expenses in caring for the boat since his purchase of it. Undoubtedly the purchase price was also returned. [New v Yacht Relaxin, 1963 AMC 152, DC Cal 1962.]

Local Admiralty Rule 125 of the United States District Court, Southern District of California, issued on April 8, 1964, now calls for actual notice to be given to the boatowner, and legal owner if any.

It is said that "hard cases make bad law." According to accepted maritime law principles, a mortgagee such as the bank in the California sale is not entitled to actual and specific notice of the sale of the seized boat, for it is considered that the seizure by the marshal is in itself notice to all interested parties of the existence of the suit and the consequences which may follow.

About 3 months after the California case was decided a somewhat similar case was tried in Brooklyn, New York. The Marine Midland Trust Company of Rockland County moved to have set aside the sale of the boat Ral to one Valentine. Ral Industries, Inc., had purchased the craft from a boat dealer. The conditional sales contract was assigned to the bank, which filed it in the office of the clerk of Nassau County. Two boat repairmen filed suits in rem against the Ral. No notice of the seizure of the boat was served upon the bank. The boat was sold at public auction to Valentine. The bank first became aware of the sale when it commenced an action to attach the boat. The bank then tried to have the U.S. marshal's sale nullified. In deciding against the bank, the federal district judge ruled that a properly filed conditional bill of sale did not take precedence over a maritime lien. To the bank's contention that the sale was invalid because it did not receive notice, the court pointed out that the marshal's public notice of sale was all that was required. Valentine, the purchaser at the auction, was permitted to keep the boat. [Tivoli Radio & Marine Co., Inc. v The Ral, 215 F Supp 643, 1963 AMC 1602, DC ED NY 1963.]

Charter Restrictions

The owner of a vessel, particularly when it has been bareboat chartered and is under the control and navigation of the charterer, will wish to protect his property against encumbrances. To do so, the owner will have a clause in the charter party which expressly prohibits the charterer from creating liens.

The furnisher of repairs, supplies, and necessaries, by statute, will not have a lien when he "knew, or by exercise of reasonable diligence could have ascertained, that because of the terms of a charter party, agreement for sale of the vessel, or for any other reason, the person ordering the repairs, supplies, or other necessaries was without authority to bind the vessel."

It is clear, therefore, that the furnisher of supplies or services cannot obtain a lien when he knows that a charter is in existence which prohibits the charterer from creating a lien. If he does make a reasonably diligent inquiry and is unable to discover the existence of a charter then his lien will not be impaired. [The Kongo, 155 F2d 492, 1946 AMC 1200, CA6 1946.] What constitutes reasonable diligence is a question which may differ in each case depending upon the particular circumstances. [Dann v The Dredge Sandpiper, 222 F Supp 838, DC Del 1963.]

The inquiries regarding the existence of a charter which the furnisher of repairs, supplies, and necessaries can make are as follows: inquire of the person who is doing the ordering; inquire of the owner; look at the Custom House records; look at the ship's papers; inquire of the predecessor in the title of the ship.

With respect to pleasure boats the certificate of number should show the name of the purported owner. If the individual who is ordering the supplies or services is different from the registered name, further investigation should be made concerning his authority to make the boat responsible for the debt.

316

Federal Preferred Ship Mortgage

A mortgage on a ship is not regarded as a maritime contract and the admiralty court does not have jurisdiction of a suit based upon a mortgage. Therefore, in any foreclosure proceeding a ship can be sold subject to maritime liens thus reducing the security value of a mortgage or extinguishing it entirely. After World War I, when Congress decided to sell the wartime fleet of ships to private shipping lines, the Ship Mortgage Act [46 United States Code §§ 911 et seq.] was passed in order to make private investment in shipping attractive. The mortgage issued under the terms of this act has a preferred status and ranks among the maritime liens.

The preferred ship mortgage has application only to documented vessels of the United States, i.e., boats of five or more net tons. Since less than one-half of one percent of all pleasure boats are documented (either licensed or enrolled by the Collector of Customs at the boat's home port) the use of the preferred ship mortgage as an instrument of pleasure boat financing is extremely limited.

*

12

collision and the
rules of the road

Introduction

"The purpose of the Rules, [of the Road] is to prevent collision." [Societa Anomina Navigazone Alta Italia v Oil Transport Company, 232 F2d 422, 1956 AMC 1073, CA5th 1956.]

This succinct statement explains in capsular form why we have rules and regulations governing nautical conduct on the high seas and navigable inland waters. Since there are no traffic policemen on the navigable waters, a system of laws or rules had to be adopted so that effective control can be exercised by masters and boat operators. The system provides for a well-understood series of signals designed to advise the navigators of the kind of boat, type of operation involved, the intention with respect to direction and maneuver, and the obligation and privileges which each boat has in a specific situation.

Because the high seas are international waters, any set of rules, to be effective, had to be formulated by various nations whose vessels operated on these waters. At a conference of the maritime nations of the world held at Washington, D.C. in 1889, the rules which are now known as the International Rules of the Road were accepted. They superseded rules adopted as early as 1863 and which were recognized by certain seafaring nations.

The United States, as well as the other nations participating in the 1889 conference, adopted the International Rules of the Road. They are now a part of our statutory law, having been enacted by Congress.

Rule 30 of the International Rules permits local rules to be made governing harbors, rivers, lakes, or other inland waters. The International Rules of the Road do not apply inshore of the lines of demarcation (shown on the appropriate charts) between the inland waters of the United States and the high seas. The Inland Rules of the Road are, of course, applicable within this area.

The Inland Rules of the Road have been established by various acts of Congress. They cover the rules for the navigation of rivers, harbors, and inland waters of the United States, not including the Great Lakes and certain Western rivers.

Great Lakes Rules apply on the Great Lakes and their connecting and tributary waters as far east as Montreal.

The Western River Rules apply on the waters of the Mississippi River between its source and the Huey P. Long Bridge (near New Orleans) and all of the tributaries emptying thereinto and their tributaries, and that part of the Atchafalaya River above its junction with the Plaquemine-Morgan City alternate waterway, and the Red River of the North.

In addition to the statutory Rules of the Road, there are the "pilot rules," which consist of the regulations promulgated by the United States Coast Guard amplifying and interpreting the rules applicable to the local waters of the United States.

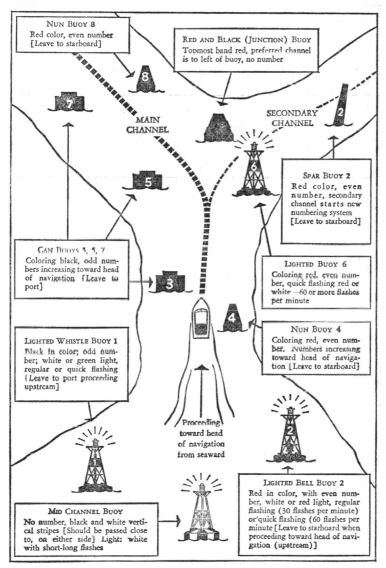

NUN BUOY 8
Red color, even number [Leave to starboard]

RED AND BLACK (JUNCTION) BUOY
Topmost band red, preferred channel is to left of buoy, no number

MAIN CHANNEL

SECONDARY CHANNEL

SPAR BUOY 2
Red color, even number, secondary channel starts new numbering system [Leave to starboard]

GAN BUOYS 3, 5, 7
Coloring black, odd numbers increasing toward head of navigation [Leave to port]

LIGHTED BUOY 6
Coloring red, even number, quick flashing red or white—60 or more flashes per minute

LIGHTED WHISTLE BUOY 1
Black in color; odd number; white or green light, regular or quick flashing [Leave to port proceeding upstream]

NUN BUOY 4
Coloring red, even number. Numbers increasing toward head of navigation [Leave to starboard]

Proceeding toward head of navigation from seaward

MID CHANNEL BUOY
No number, black and white vertical stripes [Should be passed close to, on either side] Light: white with short-long flashes

LIGHTED BELL BUOY 2
Red in color, with even number, white or red light, regular flashing (30 flashes per minute) or quick flashing (60 flashes per minute [Leave to starboard when proceeding toward head of navigation (upstream)]

Types of Buoys Used by Coast Guard

WATERWAY MARKER SYSTEM (CALIFORNIA)

[unless otherwise indicated shaded areas are orange]

BOATS KEEP OUT

EXPLANATIONS MAY BE PLACED OUTSIDE THE CROSSED DIAMOND SHAPE SUCH AS DAM, RAPIDS, SWIM AREA

DANGER

THE NATURE OF DANGER MAY BE INDICATED BY WORDS INSIDE THE DIAMOND SHAPE SUCH AS SHOAL, REEF, WRECK, DAM

CONTROLLED AREA

TYPE OF CONTROL IS INDICATED WITHIN THE CIRCLE SUCH AS 5mph, NO ANCHORING

INFORMATION

FOR DISPLAYING OFFICIAL INFORMATION SUCH AS DIRECTIONS, DISTANCES, LOCATIONS

MARKER ON PILING

MARKER ON SPECIAL PURPOSE BUOY

FLAG IS RED STRIPE WHITE

THE DIVERS FLAG

WHITE BUOY WITH BLUE STRIPE

A MOORING BUOY

COAST GUARD CHANNEL MARKERS
ADOPTED FOR USE ON ALL STATE WATERS

MARKS LEFT SIDE OF CHANNEL

MARKS CENTER OF CHANNEL

WHEN RETURNING FROM MAIN WATER BODY OR PROCEEDING UPSTREAM

MARKS RIGHT SIDE OF CHANNEL

RED CHANNEL MARKER WITH WHITE LETTERS

Local Aids to Navigation

All of these Rules are contained in three pamphlets designated and numbered as follows: "Rules of the Road, International-Inland" (CG–169); "Rules of the Road, Great Lakes" (CG–172); "Rules of the Road, Western Rivers" (CG–184). They are issued by the United States Government Printing Office,

Washington, D. C., and can be obtained free from any United States Coast Guard Marine Inspection Office in the major seaports.

The International Rules of the Road have been revised pursuant to regulations formulated at the Fourth International Conference on Safety of Life at Sea, held in London, May 17 to June 17, 1960. The United States is a signatory to this convention. The revised rules will become effective on September 1, 1965. All references in this chapter to the International Rules are to the revised rules.

Obeying the Rules

It is imperative for the boat operator to realize and understand that the rules of the road must be obeyed. The rules are mandatory and are not optional. A departure from the rules will be justified only in an emergency, that is, to avoid immediate danger. Rule 27 of the International Rules, known as the General Prudential Rule, states that in obeying and construing the rules of the road, due regard shall be had to all dangers of navigation and collision, and to any special circumstances which may render a departure from the rules necessary in order to avoid immediate danger.

When the rules of the road are properly applied, it should be physically impossible for collisions to take place. That they do happen indicates either unfamiliarity with the rules, negligence, or both. I am sure that no recreational boat operator would wish to find himself described in terms similar to those used by a Federal District Court judge when he referred to inept small-boat handlers in the Gulf of Mexico. He said that "these rig tenders and crew boats, more often than not, are operated by illiterate persons who are unaware even that Rules of the Road exist." [Dill

323

v Plaquemine Towing Corporation, 167 F Supp 866, 1959 AMC 491, DC La 1958.]

It should be remembered that the rules of the road apply to all vessels on navigable waters irrespective of size and speed. Unless the rule itself provides for an exception, it is equally applicable to naval vessels, freighters, ferries, and passenger liners.

When action is called for by the rules of the road, it must be performed in time. The rules are intended to prevent the risk of collision as well as the collision itself.

Lights

Most boatsmen who are beginners in the navigation of pleasure boats will pursue their activities during the daylight hours. It is then that objects about us are familiar and easy to identify. The coastline, jetties, bridges, buoys, and the sizes and types of various boats as well as their direction are easily comprehended. At night, however, all of these well-understood landmarks and familiar shapes disappear. What we do see are dots of light of various colors. The ability to "read" the lights correctly distinguishes the experienced or knowledgeable boat operator from the inept and unsafe helmsman.

It has been said that the purpose of lights is not only to show the presence of a vessel and boat, but also to disclose the type of craft and her course.

Unlike automobiles, boats do not operate on man-made paths. Other boats approach from many angles. It is necessary therefore to determine, from the lights which the other craft carries, its angle of approach and its relative movement. By observing the lights and by ascertaining the other boat's course, each navigator should be able to determine, by the situation presented,

324

who has the right of way, the responsibilities of each, and the procedure for taking proper action.

It is also imperative that no light be shown unless it is displayed in strict compliance with the rules of the road. Obstructed lights, those improperly displayed, malfunctioning lights, or no lights at all will, when there is a collision, place the boatowner in the difficult position of proving that the improper light not only did not cause the accident, but could not have caused it.

Every vessel must show the required lights after sunset, whether she is underway, at anchor, made fast to the shore, or aground. "Underway" has been defined by Rule 1(c)(v) of the International Rules, and by

INFORMATION SOURCES ON LIGHTS
FOR MOTORBOATS

LIGHT	WATERS SAILED	
	International	Inland
Forward, or Masthead	International Rule 7	Motorboat Act, Sec. 3 (46 U.S.C. 526b)
After, or Range	No requirement for motorboats under the International Rules	Do.
Side, or Combination	International Rule 7	Do.
Stern, or Overtaken	International Rule 10.	Inland Rules, Art. 10
Anchor	International Rule 11	Inland Rules, Art. 11

LIGHT	WATERS SAILED	
	Great Lakes	Western Rivers
Forward, or Masthead	Motorboat Act, Sec. 3 (46 U.S.C. 526b)	Motorboat Act, Sec. 3 (46 U.S.C 526b)
After, or Range	Do.	Do.
Side, or Combination	Do.	Do.
Stern, or Overtaken	No requirement in Great Lakes Rules	Western Rivers Rule No. 10
Anchor	Great Lakes Rule 9	Western Rivers Rule No. 13

325

Article 1 of the Inland Rules as a vessel not at anchor, made fast to the shore or aground. A drifting vessel would therefore be underway.

The words "steam vessels," used in the Inland Rules, include any vessel or boat propelled by machinery.

The use of lights is prescribed by the Motorboat Act of 1940 for boats operating only in United States waters. When boats are operated on the high seas the lights, as set out in the International Rules, must be carried and shown. Boat operators who frequent international and inland waters follow the International Rules, since the lights requirements are such that they can be used in both waters.

Lights: Motorboat Act of 1940

Motorboats (inboard and outboard) under 26 feet in length must carry the red and green combination light forward and lower than the white light aft, showing green to starboard and red to port, so fixed as to throw the light from right ahead to 2 points abaft the beam on their respective sides. The red and green combination light forward must be visible at 1 mile. In addition, the boat must carry a bright white light aft to show all around the horizon. The white light aft is known as a 32-point light. A point represents $11\frac{1}{4}$ degrees, and therefore 32 points equals 360 degrees.

Motorboats (without sail) from 26 to 65 feet in length, operating in the navigable waters of the United States, must carry and exhibit the following lights:

(a) A bright white light in the forepart of the vessel as near the stern as practicable, so constructed as to show an unbroken light over an arc of the horizon of 20 points of the compass, so fixed as to throw the light 10 points on each side of the vessel, namely, from right ahead to 2 points abaft the beam on either side.

(b) A bright white light aft to show all around the horizon and higher than the white light forward.

326

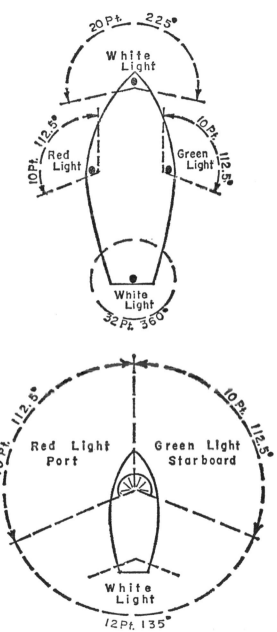

Diagrammatic Representations of Various Lights   **327**

(c) On the starboard side, a green light so constructed as to show an unbroken light over an arc of the horizon of 10 points of the compass, so fixed as to throw the light from right ahead to 2 points abaft the beam on the starboard side. The same requirements apply to the red light on the portside. The lights must be fitted with inboard screens of sufficient height and so set as to prevent the lights from being seen across the bow.

Motorboats *under 26 feet* in length when propelled by sail alone carry the combined red-green bowlight but not the white light aft. Motorboats from *26 to 65 feet* in length when propelled by sail alone carry the colored side lights suitably screened, but neither of the white lights. Boats in the two categories described in this paragraph must also carry ready at hand a lantern or a flashlight showing a white light which should be exhibited in sufficient time to avert collision.

The lantern or flashlight is called a "flareup." It is used on the Great Lakes instead of the stern light. A "flareup" can be flashed temporarily when in the area of other vessels and should be easily accessible for immediate use.

The white lights mentioned above must be visible at a distance of at least 2 miles. The colored lights must be visible at a distance of at least 1 mile. By "visible" is meant capable of being seen on a dark night with clear atmosphere.

Lights: International Rules of the Road

Motorboats operating in both international waters and inland waters must be able to exhibit the lights required by the Motorboat Act of 1940 and also meet the requirements of the International Rules.

Rule 7 of the International Rules provides that power-driven vessels of less than 65 feet in length, vessels under oars or sails of less than 40 feet in length, and rowing boats are exempted from the lights requirement of Rule 2. If these vessels do not carry the lights required by Rule 2, then power-driven vessels of less than 40 feet in length are not required to carry the white light 9 feet above the gunwale, but it should be carried 3 feet above the sidelights or the combined lantern. Power-driven vessels of less than 65 feet in length are required to carry forward at a height above the gunwale of not less than 9 feet, a white light so constructed as to show an unbroken light over an arc of the horizon of 225 degrees (20 points of the compass) and of such a character as to be visible at a distance of at least 3 miles, and green and red sidelights so constructed as to show an unbroken light over an arc of the horizon of 112½ degrees (10 points of the compass) and of such a character as to be visible at a distance of at least one mile, or a combined lantern carried not less than 3 feet below the white light and showing a green light and a red light from right ahead to 22½ degrees (2 points abaft the beam on their respective sides.

Rule 10(a) states that "a vessel when underway shall carry at her stern a white light, so constructed that it shall show an unbroken light over an arc of the horizon of 135 degrees (12 points of the compass), so fixed as to show the light 67½ degrees (6 points) from right aft on each side of the vessel, and of such character as to be visible at a distance of at least 2 miles.

Rule 10(b) provides that in a small vessel, if it is not possible because of bad weather "or other sufficient cause" for the stern white light to be fixed, "an electric torch or a lighted lantern shall be kept at hand ready for use and shall, on the approach of an overtaking vessel, be shown in sufficient time to prevent collision."

329

The display of anchor lights for vessels under 150 feet is described in Rule 11(a). A white light must be burned in the forward part of vessels at anchor. The anchor light must be visible for at least 2 miles. A second white light may be carried. If so, it should be visible at a distance of at least 2 miles and so placed as to be as far as possible visible all round the horizon.

Vessels of over 150 feet at anchor carry in the forepart, at a height of not less than 20 feet above the hull, a white 30-point light, and at the stern, not less than 15 feet lower, a similar light. These lights must be visible for at least 3 miles and so placed as to be as far as possible visible all round the horizon.

Lights for small vessels in bad weather are provided for in Rule 6(a). This rule states as follows: "When it is not possible on account of bad weather or other sufficient cause to fix the green and red side lights, these lights shall be kept at hand lighted and ready for immediate use, and shall, on the approach of or to other vessels, be exhibited on their respective sides in sufficient time to prevent collision, in such manner as to make them most visible, and so that the green light shall not be seen on the port side nor the red light on the starboard side, nor, if practicable, more than $22\frac{1}{2}$ degrees (2 points) abaft the beam on their respective sides."

Rule 6(b) states: "To make the use of these portable lights more certain and easy, the lanterns containing them shall each be painted outside with the colour of the lights they respectively contain, and shall be provided with proper screens."

Sail vessels of less than 40 feet in length (unless they are small rowing boats), carry the red and green lantern if they do not have the side lights. The lantern must be visible for a distance of at least 1 mile and so fixed that the green light is not seen on the portside, nor the red light on the starboard side. When it is not possible to fix this light, it should be kept ready for immediate use and should be exhibited in sufficient time to prevent collision, the green light not to be seen on the portside nor the red light on the starboard side. This phase is covered in Rule 7 (d).

Rule 7 (f) provides that "small rowing boats whether under oars or sail, shall be required to have ready at hand only an electric torch or a lighted lantern showing a white light which shall be exhibited in sufficient time to prevent collision."

Lights: Inland Rules of the Road

The running lights of vessels propelled by machinery are covered in part by Article 2 of the Inland Rules. Under Article 2 (a) such vessel when under way must carry on or in front of the foremast a bright white light to show an unbroken light over an arc of the horizon of 20 points of the compass. If the vessel does not have a foremast, then the light should be placed in the forepart of the vessel. The light is to be "so fixed as to throw the light ten points on each side of the vessel, namely, from right ahead to two points abaft the beam on either side, and of such character as to be visible at a distance of at least five miles."

Seagoing steam vessels when underway can carry an additional white light, according to Article 2 (e). The two lights "shall be so placed in line with the keel that one shall be at least fifteen feet higher than the other, and in such a position with reference to each other that the lower light shall be forward of the upper one. The vertical distance between these lights shall be less than the horizontal distance."

The aft light is a white light carried at an elevation of at least 15 feet above the light at the head of the

331

vessel. Article 2 (f). This requirement does not apply to seagoing vessels and ferryboats. "The headlights shall be so constructed as to show an unbroken light through twenty points of the compass, namely, from right ahead to two points abaft the beam on either side of the vessel, and the after lights so as to show all around the horizon."

Side Lights. The side green and red requirements are identical with the requirements contained in Rule 2 (iv), (v), and (vi) of the International Rules of the Road.

Lights for small vessels in bad weather are provided for in Article 6 of the Inland Rules. This rule is identical with Rule 6 of the International Rules, previously considered.

Rowboats, whether under oars or sail, must have at hand a lantern showing a white light which should be temporarily exhibited in sufficient time to prevent collision. Article 7.

Rafts or other nondescript craft navigated by hand power, horsepower, or by the current of the river, must carry one or more white lights placed in the manner prescribed by the Commandant of the Coast Guard. Article 9. The appropriate rules are set forth in § 80.32 of the Pilot Rules for Inland Waters, contained in the same pamphlet which sets out the International and the Inland Rules, viz., CG–169.

Anchor Lights. The anchor light for a vessel under 150 feet in length should be placed forward where it can best be seen, but at a height of not more than 20 feet above the hull. The light is "a white light in a lantern so constructed as to show a clear, uniform, and unbroken light visible all around the horizon at a distance of at least 1 mile." Article 11. Larger vessels

332

carry, in addition, a similar light at or near the stern at a height of not less than 15 feet lower than the forward light.

In order to attract attention, all vessels may carry additionally a flareup light.   Article 12.

The lights requirements for motorboats are contained in the Motorboat Act of 1940 and are not stated in the Inland Rules of the Road.

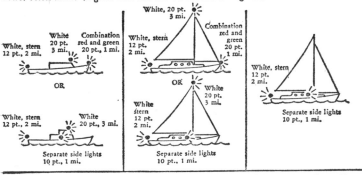

MOTORBOATS: INBOARDS, OUTBOARDS, AND AUXILIARIES

Under Power alone	Auxiliaries under Sail and Power	Auxiliaries under Sail alone

INLAND RULES.—These lights may be shown only on Inland Waters, Western Rivers, and Great Lakes.

Under 26 Feet

White, aft all around 32 pt., 2 mi. — Combination red and green 20 pt., 1 mi. | White, aft all around 32 pt. 2 mi. — Combination red and green 20 pt. 1 mi. | White stern 12 pt. 2 mi. — Combination red and green 20 pt. 1 mi.

26 feet or over, but not more than 65 feet

White, aft all around 32 pt. 2 mi. — White 20 pt., 2 mi. — Separate side lights 10 pt., 1 mi. | White, aft all around 32 pt. 2 mi. — White forward 20 pt. 2 mi. — Separate side lights 10 pt., 1 mi. | White, stern 12 pt. 2 mi. — Separate side lights 10 pt., 1 mi.

INTERNATIONAL RULES.—Lights under International Rules may be shown on Inland Waters, Western Rivers, and Great Lakes, and are required on the high seas.

Power vessel under 40 gross tons and sail vessels under 20 gross tons

White, stern 12 pt., 2 mi. — White 20 pt. 3 mi. — Combination red and green 20 pt., 1 mi.

OR

White, stern 12 pt., 2 mi. — White 20 pt., 3 mi. — Separate side lights 10 pt., 1 mi.

White, 20 pt. 3 mi. — White, stern 12 pt. 2 mi. — Combination red and green 20 pt. 1 mi.

OR

White stern 12 pt. 2 mi. — White 20 pt. 3 mi. — Separate side lights 10 pt., 1 mi.

White, stern 12 pt. 2 mi. — Separate side lights 10 pt., 1 mi.

Recreational Boating Guide, CG-340, U. S. Coast Guard

Lights Required on Pleasure Boats Underway During Night

The rules regarding lights for vessels on the Great Lakes and the Western Rivers are not separately considered here. They are set out in Coast Guard pamphlets CG–172 and CG–184, respectively.

Lights Must Be Displayed

The only safe course regarding lights is to follow the rules closely during the sunset and sunrise hours. While failure to display lights in the manner called for in the regulations will not necessarily relieve a vessel from responsibility for a collision, the failure to show any light at all is virtually tantamount to finding the rundown boat at fault. The reason for a boat's failure to show her lights is usually due to neglect. It may be that the lights are not maintained in proper condition or, if they are, the boat operator has failed to turn them on in time. Either situation is inexcusable.

A 16-foot aluminum outboard motorboat was moving in the waters of Lake Erie one night. Her owner and three guests were in the boat. The outboard was low in the water with a freeboard of 10 to 15 inches. It had no light of any kind. The outboard was struck by the Kay Dee II, a 34-foot cabin cruiser. The cruiser was properly lighted and navigated by Mrs. Dunn, an experienced pilot familiar with those waters. The operator of the outboard motorboat was held to be solely at fault for failing to show a light and for not having a lookout present. The court held that Mrs. Dunn was not negligent in failing to see the low-lying, unlighted outboard motorboat in time to avoid the collision. [Petition of Dunn, 1957 AMC 577, DC Ohio.]

A ferryboat ran into the 57-foot motorboat Carlton. The Carlton was running without lights. The master of the ferry did not see the Carlton until it was too late. It was held that the failure to display lights was the cause of the collision, for which the Carlton was solely liable. [Evans v Ferry Miss Constance, 1937 AMC 1422, DC Md 1937.]

The Fourth Marie, a 47-foot cruiser, ran down a 14-foot outboard motorboat in the Detroit River at night. The Fourth Marie had on board the owner and his wife, two other couples, and an employee who was acting as pilot. The cruiser was operating on automatic pilot at the time of the running down. The lights on the outboard were working perfectly. It was a hazy night. The Fourth Marie appeared out of the darkness and was not seen by the three men in the outboard motorboat until she was 150 feet away. The Fourth Marie was operating without her portside light burning. The Fourth Marie was held to be negligent in failing to have the port light in working order. "The failure to carry proper lights," said the court, "required by statutory rules of navigation, is one of the most recklessly unlawful faults a vessel can commit, and merits the severest condemnation." [H. & H. Wheel Service, Inc. v Cornet, 219 F2d 904, 1955 AMC 1017, CA6th 1955.]

It is a general rule that where a moving boat collides with an anchored boat, the burden of proof is on the moving vessel to explain the collision. An anchored outboard motorboat was on Lake Norfolk, Kansas. There were three occupants in the outboard boat, facing toward the bow and engaged in fishing off the portside. The boat had a single source of light emanating from a Coleman lantern, 10 to 12 inches high, equipped with a canopy and reflector to divert the light downward. It had been placed on an oar lying horizontal with the middle seat and was based below the gunwale with the glass part of the lantern above it. The light was being used to attract fish and as a warning signal. An inboard motorboat traveling at 25 miles per hour came to the area where the outboard was anchored. The speeding boat's operator and his wife did not see the anchored boat until they were hard upon it. The occupants of the anchored boat did not see or hear the moving boat until seconds before the collision. The speeding boat struck the anchored boat amidship, turning it over and throwing the occupants into the water, causing them to suffer personal injuries.

While the burden is on the moving vessel to explain the collision, nevertheless, when it is apparent that the cause of the collision was lack of lights on the anchored vessel, then the anchored vessel has the burden of showing that it did have proper lights at, and immediately prior to, the time of the collision. It was held by the court that the operator of the speeding boat was negligent in the operation of his boat, and because the anchored light was improperly placed, contrary to Article 11 of the Inland Rules, the occupants of the outboard motorboat were contributorily negligent. The owner of the outboard boat received reduced damages of $1,500 for his personal injury; his wife, who apparently was severely injured, received $20,000; and the third occupant, a man, received $400. [Rogers v Saeger, 247 F2d 758, 1958 AMC 71, CA10th 1957.]

The Five Risk Situations

There are five situations encountered when vessels and boats meet which are of prime importance to pleasure boat owners and operators. The rules pertaining to these situations should be thoroughly known and understood if collisions are to be avoided. They are:

First Situation—Meeting Head-On

When powerboats (including auxiliaries propelled

by sail and power) meet head on, or nearly so, the procedure is for both boats to steer to starboard passing on the right, that is, on the portside of each other, each having previously given one blast of the whistle.

The boat operator can identify the head-on situation by daylight as well as by night. During the daytime the silhouette of the other boat is symmetrical, in that the stack, mast, and wheelhouse are in line, or nearly so, and line up with the stem. Sighting over your own stem, you can see that the other boat continues in line with the keel of your boat.

At night the red and green lights of the other boat will be visible to you. The white range lights will line up one above the other.

Rule 18(a) of the International Rules of the Road and Article 18, Rule 1 of the Inland Rules, do not apply, by day, to cases where the red light of one vessel is opposed to the red light of the other; or where the green light of one vessel is opposed to the green light of the other; or where a red light without a green light or a green light without a red light is seen ahead; or where both green and red lights are seen anywhere but ahead.

The Great Lakes rule for the head-on situation is the same as the Inland Rules. On Western Rivers, the boat going downstream has the right of way over the ascending boat. The descending boat may elect to pass the upstream boat on whichever side she considers safe.

Here is the diagram of the head-on situation:

Recreational Boating Guide, CG-340, U. S. Coast Guard

The Inland Rules, Article 18, Rule 1, also provide that "if the courses of the vessels are so far on the

337

starboard of each other as not to be considered as meeting head and head, either vessel shall immediately give two short and distinct blasts of her whistle, which the other vessel shall answer promptly by two similar blasts of her whistle, and they shall pass on the starboard side of each other."

Rule 18(a) of the International Rules of the Road does not apply where both the green and red lights are seen anywhere but ahead. Properly screened side lights should not show more than half a point from dead ahead. When one of the vessels shows either her red light or both the red and the green side lights more than half a point on the starboard bow of the other vessel, it is a crossing situation rather than a head-and-head meeting situation.

A Head-and-Head Collision

Two tugs collided in the East River, because each captain, in violation of Article 18, Rules 1 and 3 of the Inland Rules, was determined to keep on his course "come what may." At night the tug Pottsville with a barge in tow was going south, keeping a short distance off the Brooklyn piers. The tug Wilma S., also with a barge in tow, was going north. The captain of the Wilma S. blew a single blast on his whistle to indicate a port-to-port passage and repeated the signal 30 seconds later when he received no answer. Again receiving no answer, he swung the Wilma S. to starboard, but was too late and too slow to avoid the collision. The Pottsville's captain claimed that the two tugs had about 100 feet of water between them and he saw no reason why a starboard-to-starboard passage could not be effected. The collision occurred when the barges struck each other.

338

The court held that both tugs were mutually at fault. The Wilma S. was negligent for failing to sound the danger signals when her previous single blasts were ignored and while the Pottsville was bearing down on her. The Pottsville was equally at fault in failing to answer the signal of the Wilma S.; in failing to signal his intention of pursuing a starboard-to-starboard passage; and for failing to reduce speed and sound a danger signal if the Wilma S.'s proposal for a port-to-port passage was thought to be inappropriate.

Of Rule 1 of Article 18 of the Inland Rules the court said: "It is not in any sense optional, nor does the rule permit any deviation from its express requirements. Its terms are precise and mandatory. The controlling factor is the position of the ships. If they are meeting end on, or nearly so, there must be a port-to-port passage. Only if they are meeting so far on each other's starboard as not to be within the statutory definition may the starboard-to-starboard passage be effectuated. In either case, however, a signal is required by the Inland Rules. The drafters of those rules realized that navigation on an inland waterway was such that the respective ships must communicate with each other so that there might be no doubt in the mind of either of them of the path to be taken." [Sargent Line Corporation v Tug Pottsville, 212 F Supp 360, 1963 AMC 2592, DC SD NY 1963.]

Second Situation: Parallel Courses, Port to Port

In this situation the red light only will be visible to each, the screens preventing the green lights from being seen. Both vessels are obviously to the port of each other and may so pass after both vessels have sounded one blast to signify that they are keeping to the right.

The second situation diagram is as follows:

Recreational Boating Guide, CG–340, U. S. Coast Guard

On the Western Rivers each vessel will pass the other on the side determined by the descending power-driven vessel.

Third Situation: Parallel Courses, Starboard to Starboard

In this situation the green light only will be visible to each, the screens preventing the red light from being seen.   Both vessels are therefore passing to starboard of each other, which is proper in this situation, after both vessels have sounded two blasts to signify that they are keeping to the left.

The diagram for this situation is as follows:

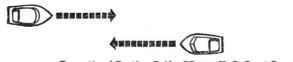

Recreational Boating Guide, CG–340, U. S. Coast Guard

On the Western Rivers each vessel will pass the other on the side determined by the descending power-driven vessel.

Fourth Situation: Overtaking

A vessel coming up with another vessel (that is, overtaking her) from some point more than the angle of $22\frac{1}{2}$ degrees (two points) abaft her beam may pass either on the starboard or portside of the vessel ahead. The overtaking situation is covered by Rule 24 of the International Rules of the Road and by Article 24 of the Inland Rules of the Road.   The rules are virtually identical.

Since two points abaft the beam mark the limit of visibility of side lights, the overtaking rule has easy application at night. During the day it may be difficult for the overtaking vessel to determine the exact angle of the approach and this factor is taken into consideration by the International and Inland Rules. The rules tell the vessel astern that in case of uncertainty she is to assume that she is an overtaking vessel and keep out of the way.

Under the Pilot Rules for Inland Waters (§ 80.6), if the overtaking vessel wishes to pass to the right or starboard hand of the vessel ahead she must give one short blast of her whistle. If the vessel ahead answers with one blast, then the overtaking vessel can direct her course to starboard. If the overtaking vessel desires to pass on the left or port side of the vessel ahead, she must give two short blasts of her whistle. If the vessel ahead answers with two short blasts, then the overtaking vessel can direct her course to port. But if the vessel ahead does not think it is safe for the vessel astern to pass at that point, the vessel ahead must immediately signify the same by giving several (not less than four) short and rapid blasts of her whistle. Under *no* circumstances must the vessel astern attempt to pass the vessel ahead until such time as they reach a point where it can be done safely. At that point the vessel ahead should signify her willingness by blowing the proper signals. The Great Lakes Rules call for "not less than five" short and rapid blasts.

In an overtaking situation it is the obligation of the passing vessel to keep clear of the vessel ahead. It is the overtaken vessel's duty to maintain her course and speed.

There are two features of every overtaking situa-

341

tion. They are: (a) the overtaking vessel must proceed in the same general direction as the vessel forward, and (b) the overtaking vessel must be moving at a greater speed.

After the overtaking vessel has gone ahead of the other vessel, the overtaking rule continues to apply until all danger of collision is over. The overtaking vessel may not cross the bow of the overtaken vessel until she has gone so far forward that she could cross that bow without collision.

The diagramatic study of the Overtaking Situation is as follows:

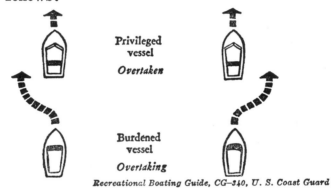

Privileged
vessel

Overtaken

Burdened
vessel

Overtaking

Recreational Boating Guide, CG–340, U. S. Coast Guard

Overtaking Faults

The absolute mandate that the overtaking vessel must keep clear of the overtaken craft is illustrated in the following two cases. The tug S.&H. No. 2 with a barge in tow was going up the East River, New York. She was being followed by the tug Lackawanna which was slightly to her port. The pilot of the S.&H. No. 2 was not aware that the Lackawanna was behind him. When about 700 feet off shore, the S.&H. No. 2 turned left, intending to enter a pier slip. The Lackawanna collided with the tow of the S.&H. No. 2. The Lackawanna was held to be solely at fault. She was the overtaking vessel, said the court, and was bound to keep out of the way of the S.&H. No. 2 and her tow. The pilot of the S.&H. No. 2 was not obliged to look behind for overtaking vessels. Neither was he under a duty to take steps to avoid a collision by the Lackawanna unless, after seeing the latter, it became apparent that without precautions on the part of the S.&H. No. 2 a collision could not be avoided. [Steamtug S.&H. No. 2, Inc. v Steamtug Lackawanna, 119 F2d 666, 1941 AMC 957, CA2d 1947, cert den 314 US 660, 86 L ed 529, 62 S Ct 115.]

One night in Boston Harbor the tanker Ventura was leaving port. She was shaping her course through Broad Channel going at 13 or 14 knots, full speed. When between 250 and 400 yards behind the trawler Lynn, the Ventura sounded two blasts of her whistle. She received no answering signal from the Lynn. Nevertheless the Ventura undertook to pass the Lynn on her portside. The stern of the Ventura struck the portside of the Lynn, capsizing her. Fifteen of the Lynn's crew of seventeen men were lost. For failing to keep out of the way of the overtaken Lynn, the Ventura was held solely at fault. The failure of the Lynn to sound a danger signal did not cause the collision. Had the Lynn done so, the signal would not have told those on the Ventura anything they did not already know.

"Nor was the captain of the Lynn," said the court, "under any duty to keep the Ventura under observation. He was not in narrow waters at a busy time. He was in an open sound, his lights were burning brightly and no other vessels were in the vicinity to screen his vessel from view or distract the attention of the pilots of overtaking vessels or to interfere with the navigation of any such vessel. Under these circumstances he was fully justified in assuming that any overtaking vessel, large or small, would obey the mandate of Article 24 of the Inland Rules and keep out of the way." [The Texas Company v R. O'Brien & Co., Inc., 225 F2d 280, 1955 AMC 1968, CA1st 1955.]

Fifth Situation: Crossing Courses

In this situation two vessels approach each other at right angles or obliquely (other than in overtaking), so that there is the likelihood of collision. The vessel which is on the right, or starboard side of the other vessel, has the right of way. She is known as the "privileged" vessel. The privileged vessel must maintain her course and speed. The other vessel, which is on the portside of the privileged vessel, is known as the "burdened" vessel. The burdened vessel has the duty of keeping clear of the privileged vessel by passing astern of her, and if it is necessary to do so, to slacken speed, stop, or reverse.

The Crossing Situation is covered by Rules 19, 20, 21, 22, and 23 of the International Rules of the Road; by Articles 19, 20, 21, 22, and 23 of the Inland Rules of the Road; by Rules 18, 20, 21, and 23 of the Great Lakes Rules; and by Rules 19, 21, 23, and 24 of the Western Rivers Rules.

Article 19 of the International Rules is often called the "starboard hand rule." There are some who do not care for the appellations "privileged" and "burdened" vessels, contending that since both vessels have definite legal obligations the terms "holding-on" vessel and "giving-way" vessel would be more appropriate.

Compass bearings or relative bearings taken on the other boat as it is proceeding on course will reveal whether there is danger of collision. If the angle remains the same with neither boat making any change of course then the risk of collision is present. During nighttime boating, under these circumstances, the red or port light of the boat on the right will be constantly in view.

There is an important difference between the International and the Inland Rules regarding signals given in the crossing situations. In Rule 28(a) of the International Rules, a vessel "taking any course authorized or required by these Rules shall indicate that course" by one short blast meaning "I am altering my course to starboard." Two short blasts mean "I am altering my course to port." Three short blasts mean "My engines are going astern." A white light visible all round the horizon at a distance of at least 5 miles can be used to work simultaneously with the whistle signals. Similar provisions are not contained in the Inland Rules.

Under the Pilot Rules for Inland Waters (§ 80.03) one short blast by the privileged vessel means "I intend to hold course and speed." The burdened vessel is required to answer with one blast when meeting at a distance within half a mile of each other.

Under International Rules the privileged vessel, although required to hold her speed and course as long as there is time for the burdened vessel to give way, must, when collision appears inevitable, take definite and positive action to avert the collision. The action to be taken depends on the circumstances. It may be to stop and reverse or to take the proper helm action, usually right rudder. At a time of impending collision, under the Pilot Rules for Inland Waters, the privileged vessel and the burdened vessel must sound the danger signal—several short and rapid blasts, not less than **four.**

The privileged vessel cannot ignore completely the dangers which may arise on her portside. While the privileged vessel is required to maintain her course and speed, it does not give her a right of way into a collision. The rule is not to be followed blindly without due regard to common sense. Articles 27 and 29 of the Inland Rules of the Road expressly provide that in obeying the rules, due regard should be had for all dangers of navigation and collision which render a departure from the rules necessary in order to avoid immediate danger, and that nothing in the rules exonerates any vessel for the neglect of any precaution which may be required by the special circumstances of the case.

The duty to persist in her course and speed is not absolute when a crisis has arisen and collision appears to be imminent. If the navigator believes that under these circumstances his best maneuver is to remain on his course and maintain his speed, the courts have at times upheld him, although collision was not thereby avoided and his judgment was proved to be faulty. The privileged vessel, however, while maintaining her course and speed constantly, must observe the burdened vessel so as to notice if the latter fails in her duty. [Curtis Bay Towing Company v Sadowski, 247 F2d 422, 1957 AMC 1847, CA4th 1957.]

The diagram of the Crossing Situation is as follows:

DANGER ZONE
10 points
112½°

Burdened vessel
. . . *give way*

Privileged vessel
. . . *hold course and speed*

Recreational Boating Guide, CG-340, U. S. Coast Guard

A Crossing Mishap

The crossing situation is replete with the hazard of collision. The Rules enjoin the privileged vessel to hold her course and speed and the burdened vessel to keep out of the way of the former. The pilot of the privileged vessel, observing the burdened ship on his port hand, is oftentimes tensed and concerned while wondering if the burdened vessel will obey the rule and stay out of his way.

This was the situation when the ferryboat Dongan Hills crashed into the tanker Tynefield. The collision occurred in Upper New York Bay on February 8, 1958, at about 8 p.m. on a clear night with excellent visibility. The Tynefield was moving across the Bay, making $2\frac{1}{2}$ to 5 knots, and heading east before going up the Hudson River to Kingston, New York. The Dongan Hills was on its run from South Ferry, Manhattan to Staten Island, southwest, at 13 knots. The Tynefield, the privileged vessel, was maintaining her course and speed while her pilot observed the Dongan Hills about a mile away. The ferryboat kept on at full speed ahead until she was 600 to 700 feet away from the tanker and then the Dongan Hills gave a series of danger blasts, went full astern but could not avoid hitting the Tynefield. Previously, the Tynefield had indicated her intention to maintain her course and speed by one long blast of her whistle. Receiving no response, a second blast was sounded. When a collision seemed imminent, the danger signal consisting of a series of short blasts was sounded, the engines put full astern and the rudder hard right.

The court held that the ferry Dongan Hills was solely at fault, for it was the ferry's duty to change her course and speed, if necessary, to avoid the collision. The Dongan Hills could have and should have

347

veered to starboard and passed astern of the tanker. It was not reckless for the Tynefield to rely on her privilege of maintaining her course and speed, for she was obliged to do so under Inland Rule Article 19 and Pilot Rule 80.7(a). The court also made a passing reference to two navigational truths: (a) that "the entire purpose of any navigational rule is to create as much certainty as possible so that each vessel can conduct itself accordingly"; and (b) that a ferryboat does not have any special "prescriptive rights" to a fairway but must obey the rules just as other vessels are required to do. [Northern Petroleum Tank Steamship Co., Ltd. v The City of New York, 282 F2d 120, 1961 AMC 409, CA2d 1960.]

Narrow Channel Rule

Power-driven vessels, that is, those vessels operated by machinery, when proceeding along the course of a channel, must, when it is safe and practicable, keep to the side of the fairway or mid-channel which lies on the starboard side of those vessels. Rule 25(a), International Rules; Article 25, Inland Rules.

When a power-driven vessel is nearing a bend in a channel in an area where an approaching power-driven vessel cannot be seen, the first vessel, when within one-half mile of the bend, must sound a signal. The signal is one prolonged blast of her whistle. Any approaching power-driven vessel within hearing around the bend must answer this signal by a similar prolonged blast. Irrespective of whether the approaching vessel is heard, the bend should be rounded with alertness and caution. Rule 25(b), International Rules.

In a narrow channel a power-driven vessel of less than 65 feet in length shall not hamper the safe passage of a vessel which can navigate only inside such channel. Rule 25(c), International Rules. This rule is designed to prevent small vessels from hampering the safe passage in narrow channels of larger vessels which cannot maneuver easily.

The Inland Rule, Article 18 (Rule V) is the same as Rule 25(b) of the International Rules, with this addition: if the one long blast of the whistle by the vessel within half a mile of the bend or curve in the channel is answered by the approaching vessel, then the usual signals for meeting and passing must be given. If the first long blast of the whistle by the vessel within half a mile of the bend or curve in the channel is not answered, then that vessel may consider the channel to be clear and may govern herself accordingly.

The Narrow Channel Rule is a particularly important one, because of its application to the passing of vessels in narrow and dangerous waters. It is therefore especially necessary for each vessel to believe that the other will act in accordance with and in obedience to the rule.

The fact that the channel curves or bends does not alter or affect the application of the rule.

The Narrow Channel Rule applies in foggy weather; indeed, at times of bad weather it is all the more imperative for vessels to keep to the proper side of the channel.

Sailboats

A powerboat must keep out of the way of a sailboat except when she is overtaking the powerboat. The sailboat has the right of way and must maintain her course and speed, at least until there is a risk of collision. In short, a sailing vessel cannot blindly or blandly rest on her privilege and sail into a collision.

Rule 20(a) of the International Rules and Article 20 of the Inland Rules provide that when a powerboat and a sailboat are proceeding in such directions as to involve risk of collision, the powerboat shall keep out of the way of the sailboat.

This rule does not give to a sailing vessel the right to hamper, in a narrow channel, the safe passage of a power-driven vessel which can navigate only inside such channel. Rule 20(b), International Rules.

Nor is this rule applicable when the sailboat is overtaking the powerboat or when the sailboat meets with boats fishing with nets, lines, or trawls. Fishing boats, however, are not given the right to obstruct a fairway.

Regarding the right of way between sailboats, the Rules of the Road are explicit. Article 17, Inland Rules.

The right of way depends upon how they are sailing with relation to the wind.

(a) A sailboat which is running free, or before the wind, must keep out of the way of a sailboat which is close-hauled (pointing as nearly against the wind as she can go).

(b) The sailboat which is close-hauled on the port tack must keep out of the way of a sailboat which is close-hauled on the starboard tack.

(c) When both sailboats are running free, with the wind on different sides, the vessel which has the wind on the portside must keep out of the way of the other.

(d) When both sailboats are running free (before the wind) with the wind on the same side, the sailboat which is to windward must keep out of the way of the sailboat which is to the leeward, that is, the downwind boat (to the leeward of the other) has the right of way.

(e) The sailboat which has the wind aft must keep out of the way of the other sailboat.

There are no whistle signals exchanged between sailboats or between powerboats and sailboats.

The new Rule 17 of the International Rules of the Road which goes into effect on September 1, 1965, has been written so as to give recognition to the fact that most sailing vessels today are fore and aft rigged. The rule provides that when each has the wind on a different side, the vessel which has the wind on the port side shall keep out of the way of the other and, when both have the wind on the same side, the vessel which is to windward shall keep out of the way of the vessel which is to leeward. Such rule reads as follows:

"(a) When two sailing vessels are approaching one another, so as to involve risk of collision, one of them shall keep out of the way of the other as follows:

(i) When each has the wind on a different side, the vessel which has the wind on the port side shall keep out of the way of the other.

(ii) When both have the wind on the same side, the vessel which is to windward shall keep out of the way of the vessel which is to leeward.

(b) For the purposes of this Rule the windward side shall be deemed to be the side opposite to that on which the mainsail is carried or, in the case of a square-rigged vessel, the side opposite to that on which the largest fore-and-aft sail is carried."

Fog

There are few conditions of nature which present the hazards in navigation that fog does. When fog is thick and close, the boat operator must proceed with extreme caution in view of the uncertainty of position and the possibility of collision.

Fog, in essence, is a cloud at a low level. Both result from the cooling of the atmosphere to a temperature below its dew point, that is, to the temperature at which air becomes saturated and the moisture in it starts to condense.

The two main types of fog are those caused by radiation and by advection. Radiation fog is created by heat being emitted from the earth's surface, which flows into space and then is cooled down, to—or slightly below—its dewpoint. Radiation fog is principally a land phenomenon. The fog, however, will often drift over inland waters or out to sea.

Advectional fog is the type most often encountered by navigators. It is caused by horizontal movement where warm moist air near saturation is cooled when drawn across a colder water surface. Fog of this type at sea may persist all day. Generally, however, fog is produced during the early morning hours and dissipates or "burns off" as the sun moves high. Fog is frequently formed at a seacoast flanked by a cold or cool current over which pass onshore winds. Such coastlines are found at Cape Cod, the southeast coast of Newfoundland, and the central California coast from Point Conception northward.

Patchy fog can be particularly dangerous. Collisions have occurred—the Andrea Doria–Stockholm disaster of 1956 is a notable one—at the edge of a fog bank when one vessel is in the fog and the other is in the clear. Fog can be so low-lying that from a high vantage point such as a crow's nest other vessels can be seen, although they are completely hidden at the deck level.

Speed in Fog

The Rules of the Road are explicit with regard to careful navigation in adverse weather. Rule 16(a) of the International Rules of the Road and Article 16 of the Inland Rules of the Road enjoin every vessel in fog, mist, falling snow, heavy rainstorms, or in similar conditions of restricted visibility to "go at moderate speed, having careful regard to the existing circumstances and conditions."

As to what constitutes "moderate speed" in fog must depend upon the circumstances. When in fog the speed of a vessel must be reduced. If the fog is very dense, and the vessel is in waters where other ships are to be expected, then her speed should not exceed bare steerageway. [The Martello, 153 US 64, 38 L ed 64, 14 S Ct 723, 1894.]

It has been said that a test of moderate speed is the ability to stop the vessel dead in the water within one-half the distance of visibility. [The Silverpalm, 94 F2d 754, CA9th 1937, cert den 304 US 576, 82 L ed 1539, 58 S Ct 1046.]

Another test is that your vessel must be able to stop before colliding with another vessel which has been sighted, provided the other vessel is going at a moderate speed. [The Umbria, 166 US 404, 41 L ed 1053, 17 S Ct 610, 1897.]

The ability to come to a stop within half of the visible distance applies particularly where vessels are sighting each other head and head. When approaching an anchored vessel in fog, your boat must be able to stop before reaching that anchored vessel. With regard to crossing vessels the vessel furthest from the point of intersection should be able to stop before the intersection point is reached.

In general, when the weather is so thick that there is serious danger in navigating, a boat should not leave her pier. This general rule does not apply to ferryboats or to fireboats responding to alarms, but they must navigate with all possible precaution.

When moving does not involve danger, a vessel can proceed at moderate speed. But, particularly in congested waters, if the fog is so thick that it constitutes a dangerous condition for navigation, a boat should drop anchor or tie up.

Going beyond moderate speed in fog is a statutory violation. A boat violating this statute has the burden of proving that her speed did not and could not have contributed to the collision. [The Pennsylvania, 86 US 125, 22 L ed 148, 1874.]

When a power-driven vessel hears a fog signal apparently forward of her beam, coming from a vessel whose position has not been ascertained, she must, "so far as the circumstances of the case admit, stop her engines, and then navigate with caution until danger of collision is over." Rule 16(b), International Rules; Article 16, Inland Rules.

A new rule, Rule 16(c), International Rules, has been introduced for the benefit of radar-equipped vessels. A ship so equipped when detecting another vessel on her radar scope, forward of her beam, without hearing her fog signal or sighting the other ship, can give her a wide berth and avoid a close quarters situation. Such rule reads as follows:

"A power-driven vessel which detects the presence of another vessel forward of her beam before hearing her fog signal or sighting her visually may take early and substantial action to avoid a close quarters situation but, if this cannot be avoided, she shall, so far as the circumstances of the case admit, stop her engines in proper time to avoid collision and then navigate with caution until danger of collision is over."

354

Fog Whistles

Recreational boats of less than 16 feet (Class A) are not required to be equipped with a whistle or bell under the Motorboat Act of 1940. Boats of Classes 1, 2, and 3 must have an appropriate and efficient whistle, and boats in Classes 2 and 3 must be equipped with a proper bell. Irrespective of the minimal requirements under the Motorboat Act of 1940, the Rules of the Road require all boats to make an "efficient sound signal."

In addition to the requirement of moderate speed in fog and other conditions of adverse weather, the Rules of the Road set out specific instructions regarding the type of equipment used and the sound signals given.

Rule 15(a) of the International Rules of the Road and Article 15 of the Inland Rules state that a power-driven vessel must be equipped with a whistle, an efficient foghorn, and an efficient bell. By the Inland Rules of the Road, power vessels can use either a whistle or a siren. Sailing vessels of 40 feet or more in length must be provided with an efficient foghorn and an efficient bell.

The sound signals are to be given by power-driven vessels, under the International Rules, on the whistle; under the Inland Rules, on the whistle or siren.

Sailing vessels, under both Rules, sound their fog signals on the foghorn.

Vessels being towed signal on the whistle or foghorn, under the International Rules of the Road. Such towed vessels, under the Rules of the Road, give their fog signals only on the foghorn.

Under the International Rules of the Road (Rule 15i), when a power-driven vessel is making way through the water in fog and under other adverse

355

conditions, she must sound her whistle by giving a prolonged blast at intervals of not more than 2 minutes. The requirement under the Inland Rules (Article 15a) is for such a vessel to give a prolonged blast on her whistle or siren at intervals of not more than one minute. The same time intervals apply to sailing vessels.

Rule 15(c)(ii) of the International Rules of the Road requires that a power-driven vessel under way, but stopped and making no way through the water, sound, at intervals of not more than 2 minutes, two prolonged blasts, with an interval of about one second between the blasts. There is no similar rule under the Inland Rules of the Road.

The sound signals to be given by sailing vessels under way are the same under Rule 15(c)(iii) of the International Rules and Article 15(c) of the Inland Rules. The signals must be sounded at intervals of not more than one minute. When the sailing vessel is on the starboard tack one blast is sounded; when on the port tack, two blasts in succession; and when the wind is abaft the beam, then three blasts in succession.

At anchor, the bell is rung rapidly for about 5 seconds during intervals of not more than one minute. Rule 15(c)(iv), International Rules, Article 15(d) Inland Rules. Large vessels at anchor, that is, over 350 feet, sound the bell in the forepart of the ship and in addition, in the ship's after part, ring a gong of a tone or sound different from the bell. A vessel at anchor can in addition sound three blasts in succession: one short, one prolonged, and one short blast, to warn other ships of her position. A vessel aground gives the same rapid ringing of the bell as does a vessel at anchor, and in addition the grounded ship gives "three separate and distinct strokes on the bell immediately before and after such rapid ringing of the bell."

The last three requirements are under the International Rules of the Road.

All boats of less than 40 feet in length are not obliged, by Rule 15(c)(ix) of the International Rules, to give these fog signals, but if they do not, they must "make some other efficient sound signal at intervals of not more than one minute."

Article 15(f) of the Inland Rules states that "all rafts or other water craft, not herein provided for, navigating by hand power, horsepower, or by the current of the river, shall sound a blast of the foghorn, or equivalent signal, at intervals of not more than one minute."

The fog signal of fishing boats is to sound at intervals of not more than one minute, three blasts in succession, namely, one prolonged blast followed by two short blasts. Rule 15(c)(viii), International Rules.

Great Lakes and Western Rivers

The Great Lakes Rules of the Road make provision for fog signals in Rule 14. Power-driven vessels must have an efficient whistle which can be heard in ordinary weather for a distance of at least 2 miles. Sailing vessels must have an efficient foghorn and a bell. The Great Lakes rules call for sounding at intervals of not more than one minute; but instead of a single prolonged blast, there must be three distinct blasts of the whistle.

Vessels in tow must strike the bell four times, at intervals of one minute. The striking is done as follows: twice in quick succession, followed by a pause, and again striking twice. A vessel with a raft in tow sounds a screeching or Modoc whistle for from 3 to 5 seconds at intervals of not more than one minute. Sailing vessels under way sound the signal

357

at intervals of not more than one minute as follows:
if on the starboard tack with wind forward of abeam,
by one blast of her foghorn; if on the port tack with
wind forward of the beam, by two blasts of her foghorn; if she has the wind abaft the beam on either
side, by three blasts of her foghorn.

A vessel at anchor or aground under the Great Lakes
Rules, in or near a channel or fairway, signals during
fog at intervals of not more than 2 minutes by ringing
her bell rapidly for from 3 to 5 seconds and, in addition, at intervals of not more than 3 minutes by sounding on the whistle or horn a signal of two short blasts
in quick succession. Vessels on the Great Lakes of
less than 10 tons (which include most pleasure boats),
are not required to sound the fog signals outlined above,
but if they do not, then they must make some other
efficient sound signal at intervals of not more than one
minute.

The Western Rivers Rules of the Road have distinctive directions regarding sound signals in weather
characterized by fog, mist, falling snow, heavy rainstorms, or other conditions of restricted visibility.
These signals are used both by day and by night. A
power-driven vessel under way must sound its whistle
at intervals of not more than one minute, three distinct blasts, the first two blasts being approximately
of equal length and the last blast "to be longer."
When such a vessel is towing another, the whistle is
blown three times of approximately equal length during intervals of not more than one minute.

A power-driven vessel on the Western Rivers with
or without a tow while lying to, that is, holding her
position near or against the bank by using her engines,
or while temporarily moored to the bank, must sound
her fog signal upon the approach of another vessel.

358

If the vessel moored or lying to is at the right bank, then two taps of the bell are given. These signals are to be sounded at intervals of not more than one minute and are to continue until the approach vessel has passed. Right and left bank means facing downstream or with the flow of the current. A vessel at anchor during foggy and other adverse conditions must ring her bell rapidly for about 5 seconds at intervals of not more than one minute.

Liability Is Based on Fault

The mere fact that ships have collided does not necessarily mean that one of the owners must stand the loss. Liability is based on fault, that is, the negligence of either or of both vessels.

When neither vessel is at fault, each vessel must stand its own loss, and neither vessel is held liable.

No liability is decreed in cases of "inevitable accident" and "inscrutable fault." "Inevitable accident" implies that no one has been at fault but that the accident has nevertheless occurred. When winter ice in a river broke up after an ice jam, tearing loose a moored ship and sending her drifting downriver where she struck several vessels, it was considered to be an "inevitable accident." [The Anna C. Minch, 271 F 192, CCA2d 1921.]

"Inscrutable fault" is a legal conclusion where fault is known to exist but the court is unable, from the conflict of testimony or for other reasons, to locate it. In one case the court said: "Fault may exist, but we are unable to discover it; it is inscrutable. Where the evidence is so conflicting that it is impossible to determine to what direct and specific acts the collision is attributable, it is a case of damage arising from a cause that is inscrutable." [The Jumna, 149 F 171, CCA2d 1906.]

If the cause of the collision is placed upon one of the vessels, it is said to be a case of "sole fault." That vessel must pay for the damages of the other ship and bear her own loss as well.

When both vessels are held to be at fault—"both-to-blame"—the damages are divided.

Divided Damages

The policy of equalizing or dividing the damages between the owners of vessels when both are at fault is peculiar to the admiralty law. It does not have its counterpart in the common law on land.

The manner in which the damages are divided by the admiralty court results in the losses of both vessels being equal. For example, Abbott's cruiser collided with Baker's outboard boat. Both boats were at fault. The consequence of the collision was that Abbott's cruiser was damaged to the extent of $2,000 and the damage to Baker's outboard amounted to $500. Baker will have to pay one-half of the difference between his damage and Abbott's damage, or $750. Thus, the losses of both parties would be equalized at $1,250. Another way of calculating the damage would be if each of the owners paid one-half of the damages of the other. So that Baker would pay one-half or $1,000 to Abbott and Abbott would pay one-half of Baker's damage or $250. Each owner would end up with a net loss of $1,250.

In the "both-to-blame" or "mutual fault" situation, the degree of fault does not affect the amount of damages paid. Although in the illustration given Abbott may have been 70 percent at fault to Baker's 30 percent, the damages are divided equally. Under American Law the effect of the fault is not proportioned.

The admiralty doctrine of "major-minor fault" has the tendency of softening this rather harsh rule. In applying the "major-minor fault" doctrine, the courts will sometimes excuse the minor fault of one of the boats in view of the gross fault of the other, holding in effect that the minor fault could not be said to be a contributing cause of the collision. When the courts take this view, the boat which indulged in the gross fault is held solely to blame.

*

GLOSSARY OF NAUTICAL AND LEGAL TERMS

Abaft abeam. Any point between the beam (the widest part of the boat) and the stern.

Abandonment. In salvage law, the giving up or leaving of marine property without hope or expectation of recovery. In marine insurance, the act of the assured in notifying the insurance carrier that owing to damage to the insured's property he elects to take the insurance money in place of the damaged property which he turns over to the insurer.

Absolute total loss. A boat so completely destroyed that she has no residual value.

Act of God. A disaster resulting from natural causes such as lightning, earthquakes, violent storm, unprecedented floods, etc. The disaster must be due to the natural causes without human intervention.

Admiralty court. The admiralty side of the United States District Courts.

Aft. Toward the after or stern part of the boat. The word is also used to designate the area behind the boat.

Aground. Resting on the ground or bottom (other than in a dry dock, marine railway or when brought on shore).

Amidship. Generally, midway between the bow and the stern. The point of intersection of two lines, one drawn from stem to stern, the other across the beam (the widest part) is the actual midships.

Anchor. A device, usually of iron, so shaped as to grip the bottom and hold the boat in a desired location against wind and sea, by means of the attached rope or cable.

Anchorage. An area or place where boats may anchor.

Anchor aweigh. When the anchor is free from the bottom.

Arrest. The act, in maritime law, of taking maritime property into custody by the United States marshal. It is also known as the "seizure of property".

Astern. Toward the stern. Abaft (behind) another object or the boat.

Automatic pilot. A method of steering a vessel or boat by automatic means, thus displacing the human element. The automatic pilot applies to the rudder a deflection proportional to the deviation of the ship from the prescribed course. Commonly called the "Iron Mike".

Avast. An order to stop. To cease doing any activity.

Bailee. The person, not the owner, to whom the property has been entrusted with an understanding with respect to its return.

Bailment. The delivery of personal property by one person to another to be held in trust for a specific purpose. There is a contract accompanying it, either express or implied, that the property will be returned or duly accounted for when that specific purpose has been accomplished.

Bailor. The maker of the bailment; the person who delivers or entrusts the property.

Bareboat charter or demise charter. The entire vessel or boat is "leased". The owner relinquishes possession, command and navigation of the vessel or boat to the charterer who assumes, in legal contemplation, the responsibilities of the owner.

Bare steerageway. The lowest speed of forward movement consistent with the maintenance of headway; having headway enough so that the boat will respond to her rudder.

364

Barratry. An act to the ship committed by the master, officers or crewmen of that ship for some unlawful or fraudulent purpose, contrary to their duty to the owner, and to the latter's injury.

Belay. To twist a rope around a cleat or belaying pin in a figure 8 without tying it in a knot.

Bend. In nautical language to fasten anything, particularly by rope, is to bend. A knot by which one rope or line is made fast to another rope or line. In sailing, it is to lie over under press of canvas; to make fast to its proper yard, gaff or stay.

Bilge. The deepest part of the hull about the keelson where water collects.

Bill of sale. A written document by which one person transfers his title, right to or interest in personal property to another.

Both-to-blame. In ship collision cases the loss is equally divided among the vessels at fault. Also known as the divided damages rule.

Bottomry bond. A contract for the loan of money for the use or repair of the vessel. The loan is at an extraordinary rate of interest, it being stipulated that if the ship is lost during the time specified in the contract by any of the perils therein listed the lender loses his money.

Bow. The forward part of the boat. Also, the sides of the fore-part of the boat, as, the port bow and the starboard bow.

Bowsprit. A main spar of a boat projecting forward from the stem and taking the forestays and bobstays.

Breast line. A mooring line used to secure a boat to a wharf or pier. It leads directly to a cleat abreast the boat.

Buoy. Floating aids to navigation moored to a certain location and employed to mark the navigable limits of channels, shoals, sunken dangers, etc.

Burdened vessel. The vessel which has the duty to keep out of the way of the other one in accordance with the Rules of the Road.

Capsize. The complete turning over of a boat.

Caveat emptor. Let the buyer beware. A maxim of the common law that the buyer purchases at his peril.

Charter. A contract by which a ship or boat owner leases her, or some particular part of her, to another person for a specified time or use.

Charter party. The nautical term for a contract of charter.

Chattel mortgage. A mortgage given on personal property.

Cleat. A fitting of metal or wood with two horns around which a line is secured.

Close hauled. The trim of a boat's sail when she is sailing as close to the wind as she can go. Sailing with the sails drawn close to the side of the boat.

Cockpit. A small well in the boat.

Comparative negligence. A doctrine of law whereby the negligence contributed by one of the parties is measured by degrees. For example, in maritime law if the injured party in a personal injury action was contributorily negligent to the extent of 30%, damages awarded in his favor will be first reduced by 30%.

Compass bearing. A compass direction expressed as a compass course, that is, in degrees and fractions of a degree.

Compass point. One of the 32 divisions of the compass card. Each point extends over an arc of $11\frac{1}{4}°$.

Concourse of claims. In a limitation of liability proceeding in a Federal District Court an injunction is issued stopping all lawsuits except the one in the admiralty court. Thereafter, all claims must be presented in the admiralty court.

366

Conditional bill of sale. An agreement whereby title of personal property remains in the seller until the purchase price has been paid.

Constructive total loss. It is also called "technical total loss". The vessel has been so injured that the cost of repairing the part or remnant remaining, plus the cost of recovering her, exceeds the insured value less her scrap value.

Contract salvage. That type of salvage service entered into between the salvors and the owners of the imperiled property, or by their respective representatives, pursuant to an agreement written or oral, fixing the amount of compensation to be paid whether successful or unsuccessful in the enterprise.

Contributory negligence. Negligence on the part of the plaintiff so as to make the accident the result of his mutual or concurring fault.

Crossing situation. When two boats approach each other at right angles or obliquely, it is a crossing situation. The boat on the right, or starboard side of the other, has the right of way. She is said to be "privileged" and must maintain her course and speed. The other boat is deemed to be the burdened one and has the duty of keeping clear of the privileged boat.

Dead ahead. Directly ahead.

Dead reckoning. The method by which the position of a ship at any moment is found by applying the courses steered and distances run to the last well-determined position. The reckoning is made independent of sights or bearing.

Deck. What a floor is to a building a deck is to a ship.

Derelict. Property on navigable waters which is abandoned and deserted by those who were in charge of it, without hope on their part of recovering it and without the intention of returning to it.

Dinghy. A small boat carried or towed by a larger boat.

367

Divided damages. See, "both-to-blame".

Drift. Being carried by a current or stream; the force of the current. In a boat there is the implication of not being under control.

Exoneration from liability. A finding that the owner of a boat is not liable for the damage or injury; therefore, it is not necessary to pass on the question of limiting liability.

Express warranty. A promise or statement made by the seller intended, or having the tendency, to induce the purchaser to buy. A statement which a party undertakes will be a part of the contract.

Fairway. The open channel; the waters inside of the channel buoys.

"F. C. & S." clause. In a marine insurance policy, the letters stand for "free of capture and seizure". Under this clause the policy is warranted to be free of any claim for loss or damage due to warlike acts such as capture, restraint, arrest, seizure, detainment, civil war, revolution, rebellion, insurrection, acts of piracy and damage caused by atomic bombs.

Flame arrestor. Any device which is suitable for the stopping of the spread of flame into enclosed spaces containing explosive vapors.

Flare-up. A lantern or flashlight. Used on vessels operating on the Great Lakes as a stern light.

Flotsam. Goods which float from a ship which has been sunk or otherwise imperiled.

Foremast. Generally, the mast nearest the bow.

Fornication. Unlawful sexual intercourse (with mutual consent) between two unmarried persons or between a married person and an unmarried one. In the latter instance the married person can be guilty of adultery and the unmarried person of fornication.

Founder. To fill and sink; the boat is sunk due to an excessive intake of water with resultant loss of buoyancy.

Freeboard. That part of the boat's side which is above or "free" of the water.

General Maritime Law. That body of law stemming from the ancient sea codes and including admiralty court decisions but excluding those decisions based upon modern statutes.

Genoa jib. A triangular headsail setting on the fore topmast by hanks and used in reaching. It was first used on an American yacht when racing in Genoa. Commonly called a "jenny".

Gratuitous bailment. A bailment without compensation or benefit to the one to whom the property has been entrusted.

Gunwale. In a boat it is the rail or the top piece.

Halyard. A rope used to raise or lower sails, spars (pieces of timber) or yards (long spars).

Haul up. To pull up.

Head on. The bow is directly toward or in a straight line with an object, the wind or the sea.

Helm. The steering apparatus of the boat; the tiller; the wheel.

Hull. The body of the boat, exclusive of the masts, housing, etc.

Implied warranty. It arises by operation of law and exists without the intention of the seller to create it.

Inchmaree clause. A written clause in a marine insurance policy whereby the underwriter assumes the liability for any loss or damage to a boat or vessel caused by explosion, breakage of shafts, or by a latent defect in the machinery or hull.

369

Inevitable accident. The implication is that no one has been at fault but that the accident has nevertheless occurred. Each damaged party must stand its own loss.

Inscrutable fault. Fault is known to exist but the admiralty court is unable, from the conflict of testimony or for other reasons, to locate it.

Insurable interest. In order to prevent a contract of insurance from being a mere wager policy, the person seeking the policy must have a real and substantial interest in the property insured.

Invitee. Also called a "business guest". One who comes on property by the express or implied invitation of the owner. The owner's duty is to use reasonable care for his safety.

Jetty. A breakwater constructed usually in order to protect a harbor entrance or river mouth. It serves the purpose of narrowing a channel and controlling the current.

Jones Act. A statute enacted by Congress which gives a seaman the right to sue his employer for personal injuries. In the event of death, the seaman's personal representative can bring suit.

Jury rudder. A makeshift or improvised contrivance to enable a boat to be steered when her rudder has been damaged or carried away.

Knot. A measure of speed equal to one nautical mile per hour. It is not a measure of distance.

Knowledge. In limitation of liability matters, means personal cognizance which the owner of a boat has prior to the casualty or the condition which brought about the accident.

Laches. An inequity founded upon an undue delay in asserting a right and prejudice thereby caused to the party against whom the claim is made.

Lay up. To tie up a boat; to allow her to remain idle.

Lee. The side of a boat opposite to that upon which the wind is blowing.

Leeward. Toward the lee, that is, on the side turned away from the wind.

Libel. The initial pleading in a suit in the admiralty court corresponding to the "complaint" in civil law.

Libelant or libellant. The complaining party in a suit in an admiralty court corresponding to the "plaintiff" in an action in the civil courts.

Licensee. A person whose presence on property is not invited but is tolerated. The owner's duty is to warn him of a dangerous condition within the owner's knowledge and which is not open and apparent.

Lien in rem. A lien against the property.

Lienor. One who holds a lien.

Limitation of liability. The owner, or chartered owner, of a vessel or boat which operates on navigable waters is permitted, when she causes damage, to limit his liability to the damaged value of his craft provided that the incident was not caused with his privity or knowledge.

Luff (to). To bring the boat into the wind by putting the helm down. It is done to slow the boat's headway or to help in setting or dousing the sails.

Mainsail. The sail spread by the main gaff and the boom.

Maintenance and cure. A right given by the general maritime law to seamen, ill or injured in the service of the ship without wilful misbehavior on his part, wages to the end of the voyage and subsistence, lodging and care to the point where the maximum cure attainable has been reached.

Major-minor fault. The court will excuse the minor fault of one of the boats in a collision in view of the gross fault of the other.

Marina. A dock or basin providing moorings and services for small boats.

Maritime lien. A claim in a vessel for services rendered or supplies furnished to her or for an injury caused by her in navigable waters. Possession of the vessel is not necessary in order for the lien to be a good one.

Marshalling the liens. Also called "ranking the liens". The order of priority among maritime liens.

Mayday. The radio telephone signal for help. It is usually transmitted on 2182 kilocycles.

Mizzenmast. The aftermost mast of many types of boats. The third mast forward where there are more than two masts.

Monition. A process in the admiralty court calling for the appearance and answer of the party being sued. It is similar to a summons in a civil case.

Mutiny. A rebellion of the crew against the authority of the master in the command, navigation or control of the ship.

Mutual benefit bailment. A bailment which is of benefit to both the deliverer and the receiver of the property.

Mutual fault. In collision cases, both vessels have been found at fault.

Narrow channel rule. Under the International and Inland Rules of the Road, a power-driven vessel when proceeding in a channel must, when it is safe and practicable, keep to the side of the channel which lies on the starboard side of the boat.

Navigable waters. In American maritime law bodies of water which are navigable in fact and which permit interstate or international transportation, are navigable waters in law and subject to admiralty jurisdiction.

"No cure, no pay". An agreement to salvage property in distress on navigable waters with the understanding that the compensation to be paid will depend upon a successful outcome.

Overtaking situation. When a boat comes upon or overhauls another boat from some point more than the angle of 22½ degrees (two points) abaft either beam it is an overtaking situation and the boat astern may pass either on the starboard or port side of the boat ahead.

Parallel courses. When two boats are either passing each other or sailing in the same direction on courses which are parallel, that is, which will bring them port-to-port or starboard-to-starboard.

Perils of the sea. Those perils which are peculiar to the sea, which are of an extraordinary nature or arise from irresistible force or overwhelming power and which cannot be guarded against by the ordinary exertions of human skill and prudence.

Piracy. Robbery committed on the high seas. Acts of piracy may also include homicide, burning of property or enslavement of persons.

Port. The left side of the boat looking forward. At one time it was called larboard. Also, a harbor.

Possessory libel. A suit brought in the admiralty court to determine who rightfully should have possession of marine property.

Preferred ship mortgage. By an act of Congress a mortgage issued under the terms of the Ship Mortgage Act has been given a preferred status and rank among maritime liens.

Privateer. One who plunders on the seas under governmental authority.

Privileged vessel. That one of two vessels which, under the Rules of the Road, ordinarily has the right or duty to hold her course and speed.

Privity. In limitation of liability matters, it is some fault or neglect in which the owner of a boat personally participates and which fault or neglect caused or contributed to the loss or injury.

373

Proctor. An officer of the admiralty court corresponding to an attorney at law. Today, it connotes an attorney admitted to practice in the United States District Courts.

Proximate cause. That cause of an injury which, in a natural and continuous sequence, unbroken by any efficient intervening cause, produces the injury, and without which the injury would not have occurred.

Pure salvage. A voluntary service rendered to distressed property on navigable waters when compensation is dependent upon success and where no prior agreement or arrangement had been made.

Rape. Carnal knowledge of any woman above the age of consent against her will, and of a female child under the age of consent with or against her will; its essence is the felonious and violent penetration of the person of the female.

Relative bearing. A direction relative to the line of the boat's keel. It is expressed in points or degrees from the boat's head, beam or stern, as: 3 points on the starboard bow; or, 2 points on the port quarter.

Rudder. An appurtenance hung from the stern post of a vessel or boat and by which it is steered.

Running down clause. The collision clause in a marine policy.

Running free. Sailing with the sheets eased and the wind well abaft the beam.

Running lights. The various required lights carried when a boat is under way.

Salvage. A marine service voluntarily performed by one under no legal obligation to do so of maritime property in peril on navigable waters.

Salvage award. Also referred to as a "salvage reward". The compensation allowed to meritorious salvors who rescue or aid marine property in distress on navigable waters.

Scuttling. Cutting holes or making openings in the hull of a vessel below the water line, or opening her seacocks, for the purpose of sinking her.

Seduction. The act of inducing a woman to consent to unlawful sexual intercourse by enticements which overcome her scruples.

Ship's husband. The agent who manages the ship and arranges for her repairs, supplies, victuals, berthings, etc.

Shoals or shoal water. An area of shallow water; a shallow place.

Side lights. Lights carried on each side of a boat, so screened as to show from ahead to two points abaft the beam. There is a screen projected ahead on the inner side to prevent the light from being seen across the bow. The red light is on the port or left side; the green light is on the starboard or right side.

Sole benefit bailment. It is a bailment (depending on the circumstances) intended to solely benefit one of the parties, i.e., the bailor or the bailee.

Stability. The tendency of a vessel to remain upright or the ability to right itself from a roll; the force which keeps a boat upright.

Stack. The pipe from which the combustion gases are led to the open air; the funnel.

Stale lien. A lien held for so long a period of time that it will no longer be enforced by the maritime law.

Starboard. The right side of the boat looking forward.

Stem. The upright timber or steel bar of the bow.

Square-rigged. A general term given to that procedure where sails are hung athwartship. It is in contradistinction to sails hung in the same line as the keel and which are called "fore-and-aft".

Stern. The after part of the boat; the rear.

Stiff. The quality of stability possessed by a boat whereby she returns quickly to an upright position.

Stranding. The act of a boat going aground.

Sue and labor clause. A clause in a marine insurance policy which authorizes the insured to incur expenses in the interest of safeguarding the insured property.

Tack. To change from one direction to another in relation to the wind. This is done by bringing the boat's head to the wind and letting the wind fill her sails on the other side. The object is to make progress against the wind.

Tender. Lacking in stability; slow rolling.

Time charter. The vessel or boat is "leased" to the charterer with control of her being retained by the owner.

Transom. The flat planking across the stern of a boat.

Trawl. A large conical fishing net.

Trespasser. One who enters upon the property of another without invitation, express or implied, or against the wishes of the owner. The owner owes him no duty of care and can be liable only for wilfully harming him.

Trim. The position of the boat in the water with regard to the horizontal; the way in which a boat floats in the water. In sailing, to draw in a sheet.

Underway. A boat not at anchor, made fast to the shore, or aground.

Unseaworthiness. A vessel or boat which is not reasonably fit for its intended use.

Vanishing stability. That point in a deep roll where the force of gravity acting downward and the force of the boat's buoyancy acting upward are in alignment. If the boat goes beyond this point, she will capsize.

Voyage charter. It is somewhat similar to a time charter. The charter is restricted to a single voyage.

Wake. The track which a boat leaves behind her on the surface of the water.

Ward of the admiralty courts. A seaman is regarded in maritime law as a feckless and improvident individual whose legal rights must be protected by the courts, much like an infant or an incompetent person.

Windward. The direction from which the wind is blowing; the weather side.

•

INDEX

References are to page numbers

379

INDEX

References are to page numbers

DATE DUE

MY 19 '7	AG 6 '76	
	MR 9 '78	
MY 26 '71		
JY 18 '72 5:15	JUL 9 1978	
JY 20 '72	DEC 5 1978	
JY 21 '72		
MR 7 '73	FEB 2 5 1980	
MY 9 '73	MAR 1 7 1980	
MY 30 '73	MAY 2 0 '85	
NO 5 '73	MAR 3 '86	
NO 19 '73	MAR 6 '89	
MR 6 '74	NOV 2 7 '89	
MY 29 '74	AUG 2 0 '90	
AG 8 '74	APR 1 5 '91	
OC 30 '74	APR 0 5 2002	
NO 30 '74		
MR 6 '76		
MY 27 '76		
		PRINTED IN U.S.A.